A beginner's guide to futures trading for success

Futures
made simple

Kel Butcher

Wrightbooks

First published in 2013 by Wrightbooks
an imprint of John Wiley & Sons Australia, Ltd
42 McDougall St, Milton Qld 4064

Office also in Melbourne

Typeset in 11.5/13.4 pt Berkeley

© Trading Wisdom Pty Ltd 2013

The moral rights of the author have been asserted

National Library of Australia Cataloguing-in-Publication data:

Author:	Butcher, Kel.
Title:	Futures made simple : a beginner's guide to futures trading for success / Kel Butcher
ISBN:	978-0-7303-7683-5 (pbk.)
Notes:	Includes index.
Subjects:	Futures.
Dewey Number:	332.45

Cover design and images by Peter Reardon, pipelinedesign.com.au

10 9 8 7 6 5 4 3 2

Disclaimer
The material in this publication is of the nature of general comment only, and does not represent professional advice. It is not intended to provide specific guidance for particular circumstances and it should not be relied on as the basis for any decision to take action or not take action on any matter which it covers. Readers should obtain professional advice where appropriate, before making any such decision. To the maximum extent permitted by law, the author and publisher disclaim all responsibility and liability to any person, arising directly or indirectly from any person taking or not taking action based on the information in this publication.

Contents

The future is no more uncertain than the present.

Walt Whitman

*Standard education brings standard results ... self-education
brings outstanding results.*

Jim Rohn

About the author

Kel Butcher is a private trader, entrepreneur and investor with more than 20 years' experience in financial markets, trading shares, futures, options, warrants, CFDs and forex. As well as trading his own funds, Kel is consultant to a managed fund, a boutique trading company and a share-trading software developer. He is a regular contributor to *YourTradingEdge* magazine and is the author of three other books: *Forex Made Simple: a beginner's guide to foreign exchange success*, *A Step-by-Step Guide to Buying and Selling Shares Online* and *20 Most Common Trading Mistakes and How You Can Avoid Them*. He also featured in *The Wiley Trading Guide* and *Give Your Trading the Edge*.

Passionate about money management, risk management and position-sizing techniques, Kel acts as a mentor and coach to fellow traders. He can be contacted by email at kel@tradingwisdom.com.au.

When he's not trading, Kel enjoys snowboarding, mountain-bike riding and surfing. He lives on the NSW Central Coast with his wife Cate and his two sons Jesse and Ollie.

Acknowledgements

My thanks as always go to the staff at Wrightbooks for all their help and support in getting this book from concept to print. I would also like to thank Glen Larson and staff at Genesis Financial Technologies for the use of the Trade Navigator software program and for most of the charts reproduced throughout the book; my futures broker Jason Achijian for his advice, knowledge and input; and the guys at Beyond Charts for the use of Beyond Charts Plus software and for the ASX share price charts used in this book. Thanks also to Larry Williams for his foreword and for sharing information over the years. I am always honoured by the opportunity to write a book and could not do it without the support of my wife Cate and my boys Jesse and Ollie, who tolerate the long periods of time I am locked away, immersed in piles of paper, typing furiously to meet yet another deadline. I also appreciate the input and shared experiences of the hundreds of traders and other market participants with whom I have spoken and corresponded over many years.

Foreword

I first met Kel at one of my Million Dollar Challenge workshops in Sydney, Australia in 2002. Since then he has become a successful trader, author and educator in his own right. He has developed his own unique trading style and techniques, many derived from the information and mentoring I have been able to provide him over the years.

Launching into any new business venture or activity in life involves a learning process—one that begins with building a solid foundation onto which the rest of the business structure is then built. So it is in the world of trading. To become an 'overnight' success requires years of hard work and dedication built on a solid foundation. Too often these days, people are drawn to the markets with the promises of huge riches and overnight success for less than a few hours work each day. I'll vouch for the fact that this isn't the case. Those that achieve success begin with a solid base and spend considerable time developing and refining their trading skills.

This introductory guide is just such a foundation. It provides almost all the information any trader, either new to the markets or just new to the futures markets, will need to get started on the journey to successful futures trading. It is a comprehensive resource that covers everything from the drivers of the price of corn, and the machinations of the bond markets, to the ever-important topic of money management, and a mass of information in between.

This is the book I wish I had written—it presents a concise history of this business and an understanding of how it continues on a day-to-day basis. This is a must-read starting point for all futures traders.

Larry Williams

Commodity trader and author

August, 2012

Preface

Sydney, Australia, 18 May 2022.

As private futures trader Margaret Anderson sits down at her home office desk to begin her daily trading routine, she pauses to reflect on the price movements the market has experienced over the past few years. Triggered by increased demand for raw materials from China and for food to feed a growing world population, prices have been in a steady upward trend, providing a wealth of opportunities to participate in a great generational bull market. With persistent drought in the Southern Hemisphere, prices for corn, wheat, soybeans and other agricultural commodities have risen sharply. Base metal prices have also continued to climb, driven by production demand and the ever-present fear of inflation. Margaret notes the steady decline in the price for crude oil and other energy commodities following the development of alternative energy sources that allow today's cars to run on hydrogen derived from water, and houses and businesses to meet all their energy requirements from a combination of wind and solar energy sources. Equities and equity indexes continue to amble along, stuck in a five-year trading range that has had a devastating impact on trend traders, while short-term traders have been able to profit from trading the 'swings' from high to low in this trading range ...

Or maybe not. Here's an alternative scenario: the severe global recession that took hold in 2012 and continues in 2022 has reduced the global economy to a shadow of its former self. Demand for consumer products has been wiped out by massively high interest rates, soaring unemployment, and a general feeling of doom and gloom. As a result, demand for base metals and other manufacturing raw materials has plummeted, sending prices down the slippery slope of a bear market. Oil prices have skyrocketed as demand continues to outstrip supply, and alternative energy sources such as wind and solar have proven too difficult and costly to harness on a commercial scale. The use of genetically modified crops has increased global food production of staples such as corn and wheat, so the prices for these commodities has fallen substantially. Equity markets have been in a long-term downtrend for years, providing rich opportunities to trade the short side of the market but giving little joy to the buy-and-hold investors, who have seen their portfolios decimated. The one shining light has been gold: still seen as the only true store of value on the planet, it has risen to over $4000 per ounce ...

Both of these scenarios are completely fictitious, *or maybe not* ...

Margaret and others like her who have learned to trade the futures markets are presented with a constantly changing array of market conditions and trading opportunities. Futures are formalised agreements to buy or sell a commodity or financial instrument at a specified future date. Trading futures contracts allows us to participate in price moves in any direction—up, down or even sideways—in a range of commodities including grains, metals, energy products, meats, 'softs', equity indexes and interest rate products. As futures traders, we can speculate on price moves over short or long time frames in any of these and other markets. We can also use futures contracts to 'hedge' production and manufacturing outputs, to 'lock in' prices for the purchase of raw material inputs or manufacturing outputs, and even to trade the 'spread' between different prices in the same or different contracts in different months or delivery periods.

The futures markets offer the active trader ever-changing opportunities across a wide variety of markets and trading instruments. We explore this wonderful and profitable world in this book, which is divided into three parts. Part I addresses the fundamentals of futures trading—its history, principles and practice. We begin, in chapter 1, with a brief survey of the history and evolution of futures exchanges, from their ancient origins to the sophisticated electronic markets of today. Chapter 2 looks more closely at what futures contracts are and introduces the role of the clearing house, the price discovery process and some basic concepts in trading. In chapter 3 we examine hedging and speculating activities and discover who is drawn to each mode of trading. Chapter 4 delves into the mechanics of trading, unpacking essential concepts such as short selling and stop orders, and offering basic advice on choosing and dealing with a broker. Perhaps most importantly, chapter 5 discusses the risks and rewards associated with the futures markets, and the importance of risk- and money-management.

Parts II and III introduce and systematically review the major futures contracts, including a description of each contract along with its main users, contract specifications and trading characteristics. Part II (chapters 6 to 10) is devoted to the natural commodities contracts, including the most actively traded grains, food and fibre, energy and metal resources commodities. Part III examines financial markets futures, reviewing some of the main interest rate futures (chapter 11) and equity index futures (chapter 12).

Futures Made Simple will provide those interested in breaking into this exciting trading area with a solid understanding of what futures contracts are and how they are traded. Futures trading is a truly global trading arena that has no boundaries or borders. From your home office in Brisbane or Bombay or anywhere else on the planet, you can trade Chicago wheat futures, German Bunds (interest rates), the Japanese Nikkei Index, Australian wool futures and a host of other futures contracts.

Let's roll the dice!

Part I

Trading futures — principles and practice

To operate in the present and prepare for the future it is necessary to understand the past. So before we delve into its mechanics we will take a look at the history of futures trading—how it began, and how it has developed and evolved over time into the futures markets as we know them today. In part I we will also discover how futures work, identify the various market participants and their reasons for trading futures contracts, explore the fundamentals of order types and order placement, and introduce the critically important subject of money management.

chapter 1

The history and evolution of futures exchanges

The origins of the use of agreements to deliver a specific commodity at some future time for an agreed price date back to ancient Greek and Roman marketplaces. As well as centres of political and cultural life, the Agora in Athens and the Forum in Rome were commercial centres where commodities brought from distant lands were exchanged for currency or precious metals such as gold and silver. The traders, merchants, producers and buyers of the ancient world faced many of the same demands as today's traders, merchants, producers and consumers, notably the need to manage price and delivery risk, and the need for timely and transparent market and price information. Although there is no comparison with the timeliness of today's electronically accessed information, these traders of yesteryear established and accessed information and prices through the informal networks they created. The first formalised futures exchange, however, is generally recognised as the Dojima Rice Exchange in Osaka, Japan, in the early 1700s.

Forward contracts

For many centuries commodity markets have thrived wherever producers and consumers have traded goods in exchange for cash. At some stage agreements began to be made between the counterparties to deliver a commodity at a designated time in the *future* at a price agreed on in the present. Payment would be made on receipt of the agreed quantity of the commodity at the specified quality. These agreements, which came to be known as forward contracts, meant the producer, usually a farmer, could plant his crop knowing he was guaranteed a return for his time and investment, and the buyer was assured of receiving the contracted commodity from the producer.

Initially these forward contracts were frequently not honoured by one or other party if market conditions—namely, price—had changed significantly from when the contract was first negotiated. If the price had risen dramatically because of adverse climatic conditions, for example, the seller might back out of the agreement claiming an inability to deliver the contracted quantity or quality due to the effects of drought or flood, even though they might not have suffered any ill effects on their own production, but were now able to sell at a higher price to another buyer. Similarly, in years of overproduction, when prices fell, the buyer might back out because crop prices were now much cheaper on the open market. Other problems with these early forward contracts included lack of liquidity, quality issues, the practical difficulties of buyers and sellers locating each other and then negotiating a contract, the individual nature of each forward contract and the lack of any formal way of ensuring these contracts were honoured.

Tip

Forward contracts are not traded on a formalised exchange, but are customised on an individual needs basis and are privately negotiated.

4

Forward contracts can expose both parties to several risks, including credit risk if either party defaults on the deal or has insufficient funds to honour the agreement; negotiation risk if either party is operating in bad faith; and the risk that future events such as adverse weather, political or economic events could prevent one or both sides from fulfilling their obligations. Clearly a more formalised and secure commercial arrangement was needed.

The development of futures exchanges

In the 1840s Chicago emerged as the market centre for grain farmers in the United States. Each year at harvest time producers would arrive to sell their grain. In abundant years there would be too few buyers, prices would be low, and with no way of storing the excess production much of it would be dumped. In the winter, prices would rise as supply fell. Privately negotiated forward contracts were arranged between buyers and sellers. In 1848 a group of grain merchants banded together to form an organised grain exchange where buyers and sellers could meet and conduct business at a central location. The Chicago Board of Trade (CBOT) was formed, and the first official forward contract was written on 13 March 1851.

In 1865 the CBOT introduced standardised futures contracts for corn, wheat and oats. These contracts specified the quantity and quality of the commodity being traded and the delivery date, but not the price. They were also interchangeable or 'fungible', which meant they could be exchanged between buyers and sellers many times before the specified delivery date as prices fluctuated. With a formal exchange now in place, the ability to access product year-round became a priority and storage silos were built to handle the excess that occurred each year at harvest time. This storage also helped to smooth out the wild fluctuations in price that had occurred previously.

In 1898, inspired by what had occurred in the grain markets, a group of merchants formed the Chicago Butter and Egg Board to allow the buying and selling of futures contracts on other agricultural products, including eggs, butter, hides, onions and potatoes. In 1919 its name was changed to the Chicago Mercantile Exchange (CME). Over the years more contracts were added, starting with frozen pork bellies in 1961, followed by financial and currency futures in the 1970s, interest rate products in 1981, and equity index futures and options in the 1980s. These included the first cash-settled futures contract for Eurodollar futures in 1992 and the first equity index futures contract for the S&P 500 Index.

The growth of financial futures coincided with the breakdown in the late 1970s of the Bretton Woods exchange rate mechanism, under which global currency exchange rates were effectively pegged to the value of the US dollar, which itself was fixed to the value of gold via the gold standard. Once these pegs were removed a free market developed for the discovery of exchange rate values and to allow hedgers and speculators to participate in this price discovery process. Free-floating exchange rates exposed manufacturers and consumers to currency fluctuations, and the futures markets provided a valuable mechanism for hedging. Speculators were drawn to these contracts as volumes and liquidity increased. Financial futures provided for exposure to interest rate products for both hedging and speculative purposes.

In the 1850s forward contracts for cotton were also being traded in New York. In 1870 organised trading of standardised futures contracts began on the New York Cotton Exchange, with rules and procedures formalising the process announced in 1872. That year also saw the formation in New York of the Butter and Cheese Exchange (later the New York Mercantile Exchange, or NYMEX), which was acquired by CME Group in 2008. In 1882 formalised futures trading began on the New Orleans Cotton Exchange.

During the 19th century, metal commodities and coffee were being traded in England on an informal, ad hoc basis on the grandly titled 'Royal Exchange'. More often than not, these 'trades' were conducted in one of many coffee houses where traders sat at fixed points around a circle drawn in chalk on the floor, giving rise to the term *ring trading*, the English traders' equivalent to *floor trading* or *pit trading* in the US. In 1877 a group of English merchants formed the London Metals and Mining Company trading in tin, copper and pig iron. The name was later changed to the London Metals Exchange, which remains a leading futures exchange for a range of metals contracts today.

Following the removal of currency controls and the CME's successful launch of currency futures on its sibling exchange the International Monetary Market (IMM), in 1982 the London International Financial Futures Exchange (LIFFE) was formed. In 1996 LIFFE merged with the London Commodity Exchange and in 2002 it was acquired by the Euronext exchange group (itself created by the merger of the Amsterdam Stock Exchange, Brussels Stock Exchange and Paris Bourse). In 2007 Euronext merged with the New York Stock Exchange to form NYSE Euronext, which incorporates LIFFE, although the latter continues to operate under its own governance.

Controversy

The history of futures trading has not been without controversy, and to this day there are those who argue that it is little more than glorified gambling. Mostly these attacks come from the ignorant and uneducated, those who simply don't understand or, loudest of all, those who have either tried and failed or have never attempted any form of trading but who condemn it from some perceived higher moral ground. In this, little has changed over the 150-plus years that trading futures has been a legal and legitimate form of both hedging to protect profits and speculating to create profit. As today, many in the 1800s and early 1900s were both fascinated and appalled by the notion of trading futures. There has been endless litigation and public debate surrounding its legitimacy. The distinction between outright gambling and speculating in futures contracts was (and still is) lost on a large proportion of the general public. While gambling is essentially a game of chance in which 'lady luck' plays a significant role in the outcome and the odds are stacked against the 'punter', futures trading, like all other trading endeavours, requires education, a detailed plan, and strict trading and money management rules. Drawing on an understanding of these concepts and a solid grasp of probability, trading of any type is a legitimate business venture.

Through the 19th century there were many attempts to restrict or prohibit futures trading in the United States. To give a few examples, in 1812 short selling became illegal in New York (this legislation was repealed in 1858); in 1841 failing to cover short sales within five days was deemed a misdemeanour under Pennsylvania law (repealed in 1862); in 1879 California's constitution invalidated futures contracts (repealed in 1908); and in 1882 Ohio and Illinois tried unsuccessfully to restrict cash settlements of futures contracts.

As well as the persistent legal assaults on futures trading activities, two other challenges in the late 1800s seriously threatened the fledgling futures markets. The first was the anti-option movement, which sought to outlaw trading in both futures and options. This campaign culminated in the passage through both houses of the US Congress of two anti-option bills. Had either bill passed into law it would have spelt the end of futures trading in the US, but both eventually failed on the basis of legal technicalities.

The second challenge was the controversy surrounding 'bucket shops'. These were essentially groups of punters who met in premises outside the recognised exchanges and 'bet' on the direction of price movements. Although they relied on price data from the exchange, they did not trade on the official exchange. The 'bucket shop' era was a colourful chapter in futures history that came to an end in 1915 following a ruling by the US Supreme Court that exchanges, and in particular the CBOT, could restrict the dissemination of price information to a third party.

Hand signals

Like many other professional bodies, stock and futures traders developed their own specialised modes of communication. Originally all futures contracts were traded by open outcry in the trading 'pit', where brokers had evolved a unique system of hand gestures to facilitate trade execution. These hand signals are still used in trading pits today. Some simple examples are shown in figure 1.1.

Figure 1.1: simple hand signals used in pit trading

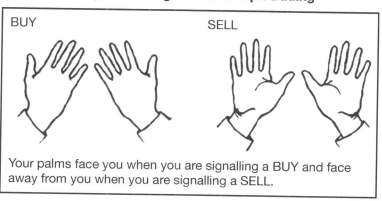

Your palms face you when you are signalling a BUY and face away from you when you are signalling a SELL.

(continued)

Figure 1.1: simple hand signals used in pit trading *(cont'd)*

QUANTITY

To indicate quantity—the number of contracts being bid or offered—touch your face:

- To signal quantities one through nine, touch your chin.
- To show quantities in multiples of 10, touch your forehead.
- To show quantities in multiples of 100, make a fist and touch your forehead.

ONE   TEN   SEVEN

Source: CME Group Inc.

Electronic markets

As internet use expanded in the early 1990s exchanges began introducing electronic trading on some futures contracts in off-exchange hours, and the transition from floor-based trading to electronic trading via computer terminals began to gather momentum. In 1992 the CME launched the CME Globex electronic trading platform. Since then electronic trading has expanded to include side-by-side electronic trading, in which markets are traded simultaneously in the pit and on electronic platforms, and, more recently, contracts that trade solely on electronic markets, such as the E-mini S&P. Electronic trading allows markets to trade for longer periods than is possible in an open outcry trading pit. The E-mini S&P, for example, trades for 23 hours and 15 minutes each weekday. As well as allowing extended trading times, electronic trading ensures markets are open simultaneously around the world, providing benefits for all market participants.

In 1998 the German derivatives exchange Deutsche Terminborse (DTB) and the Swiss Options and Financial Futures Exchange (SOFFEX) merged to establish the Eurex exchange. Eurex was one of the first exchanges to offer trading only via its electronic trading platform (there is no pit trading at all on Eurex).

Tip

In 2007 the CME and CBOT exchanges merged. They are now referred to as CME Group.

Today CME Group is the largest futures exchange in the US, with annual trading volumes in excess of 3 billion contracts, worth more than $10 trillion. It is one of the three largest futures exchanges in the world, along with the European-based Eurex exchange, with annual trading volumes of more than 2 billion contracts, and NYSE Euronext exchange (including LIFFE), with annual trading volumes in excess of 1 billion contracts.

Globally there are now more than 100 exchanges on which futures contracts are traded, ranging from behemoths such as CME Group to much more modest enterprises such as the Mercantile Exchange of Madagascar and the Sibex exchange in Romania.

Today's futures markets have far outgrown their agricultural origins, with financial contracts now accounting for well over 80 per cent of daily futures trading volume. Most futures contracts are now traded electronically via online platforms that offer a truly global marketplace. For example, more than 83 per cent of all trades on CME Group, and all trades on Eurex, are executed electronically.

From forwards to futures

As discussed, early forward contracts were vulnerable to default. Direct dealings between brokers were relatively simple when purchases and sales balanced, allowing the brokers to cash settle the differences between contract quantities. The problems began when, as was most often the case, the quantities didn't balance. If, for example, Broker A had purchased a 5000-bushel wheat contract from Broker B, and at a later date Broker B had bought a 6000-bushel wheat contract from Broker A, the two contracts could be offset at the settlement date if Broker B simply sold a 1000-bushel wheat contract to Broker A. The hassles really kicked in, though, if Broker B had also sold a 1000-bushel contract to Broker C, who had sold a 1000-bushel contract to Broker A. In this case, each broker's net position was offset, but all three had to meet in order to settle their obligations to one another. This was referred to as a 'ring settlement'. 'Transfer settlements', in which brokers transferred their mutual obligations to other brokers in order to balance out their forward contract obligations, were also common.

The clearing house

To resolve both the non-delivery issues and the complicated ring and transfer settlements, the exchanges introduced a system of cash deposits. Each party involved in a forward contract was required to deposit a sum of money with a neutral third party to help ensure that both parties honoured the agreement. If one party defaulted on the deal, the other would receive the cash deposit as reimbursement for any financial loss or inconvenience. Exchanges first began trialling these procedures in the 1880s, with the earliest recognised formal clearing house and offset procedures established by the Minneapolis Grain Exchange in 1891. The CME Clearing House, launched in 1919, formalised the role of the clearing house in all futures transactions and set the precedent that was to be followed by all recognised futures exchanges. As we'll discuss in chapter 2, the clearing house provides futures traders with a guarantee of settlement.

Futures contracts today

Present-day futures contracts evolved from standardised forward contracts. While they retain the basic features of the earlier contracts, they are much more specific and cover a remarkable range of markets and related products. Futures contracts are traded on registered exchanges, with the clearing house interposed between the counterparties to every futures contract. Every contract is fungible and may be either deliverable or cash settled. The only variable in the modern-day futures contract is the price. It is the constant process of price discovery that gives rise to changes in market prices for a huge range of futures contracts on exchanges all over the world, and it is this that makes futures trading the dynamic global industry it is today. In the next chapter we will look in more detail at the specifics of futures contracts and the role of the clearing house.

Chapter summary

⇒ The origins of the use of agreements to deliver a specific commodity at some future time for an agreed price date back to ancient Greek and Roman marketplaces.

⇒ Forward contracts were frequently not honoured by one or other party if market conditions — namely, price — had changed significantly from when the contract was first negotiated.

⇒ In 1865 the Chicago Board of Trade introduced standardised futures contracts for corn, wheat and oats. These contracts specified the quantity and quality of the commodity being traded and the delivery date, but not the price. These were followed by a range of agricultural products, then other natural commodities.

⇒ Growth of financial futures markets can be linked to the breakdown of the Bretton Woods agreement, the floating of major global currencies and the growth of the free market, which allowed financial instruments to be freely traded.

⇒ The history of futures trading has not been without controversy, and to this day there are those who argue that it is little more than glorified gambling. Mostly these attacks come from those who simply don't understand futures trading.

⇒ Originally all futures contracts were traded by open outcry in the trading 'pit', where brokers had evolved a unique system of hand gestures to facilitate trade execution.

⇒ As internet use expanded in the early 1990s exchanges began introducing electronic trading on futures contracts in off-exchange hours, and the transition from floor-based trading to electronic trading via computer terminals began.

⇒ Today's futures markets have far outgrown their agricultural origins, with financial contracts now accounting for well over 80 per cent of daily futures trading volume. Most futures contracts are now traded electronically via online platforms that offer a truly global marketplace.

⇒ Futures contracts are traded on registered exchanges, with the clearing house interposed between the counterparties to every futures contract. Every contract is fungible and may be either deliverable or cash settled. The only variable in the modern-day futures contract is price.

chapter 2

How futures work

Now we know how and where futures contracts evolved, it's time to acquire a better understanding of what futures are, how they work and how they trade. Equally important, why would we *want* to trade them and how are we going to profit from the exercise? In this chapter we will explore futures contracts more closely and also take a more detailed look at the role of the clearing house.

What exactly is a futures contract?

A futures contract is a legally binding, standardised agreement to buy or sell a commodity or financial instrument of specific quality and quantity on a specified future delivery date at a given location. The only variable is price, which is agreed upon at the time of the trade. Some futures contracts, such as wheat and live cattle, call for physical delivery, while others, such as Eurodollars and S&P 500, are cash settled.

All futures contracts are based on an underlying physical instrument—a physical commodity such as wheat or gold, or a financial instrument such as an equity index, a currency or an interest rate. A futures contract is an agreement between two parties to buy or sell a standardised quantity and quality of the underlying asset at a specified future date but at a price agreed on today. The contracts are negotiated on a registered exchange, which acts as intermediary between the two parties. The buyer of a futures contract is referred to as being 'long', which reflects their view that prices will increase. The seller of a futures contract is referred to as being 'short', which reflects their view that prices will decrease. Futures contracts can either be cash settled or provide for physical delivery of the underlying commodity or instrument.

Fungibility

An important consideration for any commodity or instrument considered for a futures contract is fungibility. Any commodity or instrument that is capable of mutual substitution is considered fungible. For example, a buyer of a 5000-bushel corn contract is not concerned with buying 5000 bushels of corn from a specific field on a specific farm in Ohio; he simply needs to know with certainty that the corn he buys will be as specified in the contract, regardless of its exact origin. Similarly, the buyer of CAN$ 100 000 doesn't need to specify the exact notes and denominations required at delivery; as long as they are genuine legal currency as specified in the contract, the contractual obligations of the seller will have been met. Both of the underlying instruments in these two examples are interchangeable, or fungible, in that any 5000 bushels of corn or any CAN$100 000 that meet the contract specifications can be used to honour the settlement under the terms of the contract.

Tip

On an everyday level, fungibility applies if we lend someone $10 or 20 litres of unleaded petrol. We don't need to receive in return the same $10 note or 20 litres of unleaded petrol from the same specific supplier in order to have the loan repaid. As long as we get back $10 in the same currency or 20 litres of unleaded petrol, regardless of the brand, we will consider the loan repaid in full.

Offsetting

Because futures contracts are fungible, many traders who never intend either to make or to take delivery of the underlying commodity can buy and sell futures contracts. Traders and speculators buy and sell futures contracts as a way of making a profit from price fluctuations as market conditions change. They are taking advantage of the other key feature of futures trading—the ability to eliminate an open position by buying or selling the opposite side of the existing open position before the expiry date, a process known as 'offsetting'. Every futures contract has a last trading date by which all open positions must be closed out. For physical-delivery futures contracts (such as wheat and lean hogs) and cash-settled futures contracts (such as Eurodollars or E-mini S&P), open positions are closed out by making an offsetting trade. If you are long wheat, for example, you simply sell the futures contract, profiting from the difference between the price you paid and the price you sold at, or accepting the loss if the price has moved against your open position. In this way you have 'offset' your open position. Figure 2.1 (overleaf) illustrates the offsetting process.

Figure 2.1: the offsetting process

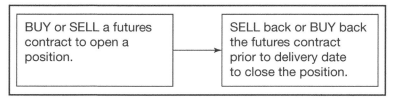

Offsetting allows traders and speculators with absolutely no interest in accepting delivery of the underlying instrument to participate actively in futures trading, knowing that before the delivery date they can simply close out any existing positions and either keep the profit or accept the losses from the trade.

Cash settled or physical delivery

Futures contracts may be divided into those that call for physical delivery of a particular commodity or financial instrument, and those that are cash settled. You can take or make delivery in the case of physical-delivery contracts, or have the position closed out by a final mark-to-market cash adjustment in the case of cash-settled contracts, which will result in a credit to your account if you have made a profit or a debit to your account if you have incurred a loss. Fewer than 5 per cent of all futures contracts actually result in physical delivery. The vast majority of market participants prefer to close out or offset their open positions prior to expiration date, as very few speculators have any desire to accept or make delivery of, say, 112 000 pounds of sugar or 40 000 pounds of hog carcasses. Of course, some producers and end-users do choose to take delivery (this will be discussed in chapter 3).

Despite the fact that few futures contracts result in actual physical delivery, the provision for physical delivery plays two important roles in the futures markets. First, it allows buyers and sellers to take or make delivery of the underlying commodity or instrument if they so choose. In this way, a large consumer of corn, for example, can use the futures market to accumulate corn for physical delivery if they believe the price of corn will rise before they actually require the grain for their manufacturing purposes. Similarly, a corn grower who has sold corn futures at a higher price than that prevailing in the market may choose to make delivery of the actual corn he has produced. Second, the fact that delivery can be made or taken ensures that futures prices accurately reflect the cash price being paid for the underlying commodity or instrument at the time of contract expiration. The two prices will converge as the contract expiration date approaches.

Cash-settled futures have no provision for delivery but are settled in cash when the contract expires. Stock index futures, for example, are cash settled, because to arrange delivery of the shares that make up the index would be impractical. At contract expiry the trader's account is simply debited or credited the difference between the value of the underlying instrument and the price of the futures contract. With cash-settled contracts, price convergence is automatic.

Role of the clearing house

To handle the offsetting of futures contracts, a method is needed to match the final buyer with the final seller. Futures exchanges developed clearing operations to record all transactions, to document transfer and delivery of futures contracts between buyers and sellers, to facilitate and regulate delivery if required, and to settle trading transactions. This clearing operation plays a third-party role in every transaction. The clearing house assumes the role of seller against the original seller and the role of buyer against the original buyer, and thereby ensures the integrity of all trades. It operates as if the seller has sold to the clearing house and the buyer has bought from the clearing house, and thus serves as the counterparty in every trade. It can do this because the number of long contracts is always equal to the number of short contracts.

> *Tip*
>
> *By serving as the counterparty in every transaction, the clearing house becomes 'the buyer to every seller and the seller to every buyer'. This substantially reduces the financial performance risk of every market participant and eliminates third-party counterparty risk.*

The leveraged nature of futures contracts adds to volatility and can lead to situations in which large losses are incurred by one party, which may be unable to honour its obligations at the settlement date. For a market to operate efficiently and effectively, market participants need to be assured that all transactions will be honoured, particularly in instances when prices may have moved significantly. If the buyer and seller were to deal directly with each other, running credit assessments, setting credit limits and arranging settlement would be messy, costly and time-consuming processes that would detract from the advantages of a centralised exchange. To avoid this, the clearing house intervenes between the two counterparties to guarantee that each trade will be settled as intended in the contract. This process, called 'novation', eliminates counterparty risk for traders. The clearing house is able to accept the risk through use of a margin requirement process.

Clearing house and OTC models compared

Figure 2.2 illustrates the difference between the clearing house model used by futures exchanges and the over-the-counter (OTC) dealing used for some other instruments, such as spot forex.

Figure 2.2: clearing house compared with OTC model

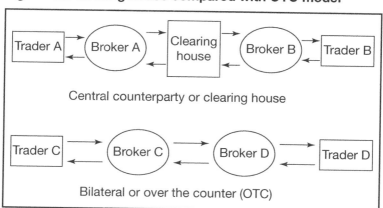

Central counterparty or clearing house

Bilateral or over the counter (OTC)

In the clearing house model, Trader A decides to buy a futures contract and instructs his broker (Broker A) accordingly. Trader B is a seller of the same futures contract through her broker (Broker B) at the same price at which Trader A is willing to buy. The transaction occurs on a registered futures exchange. As counterparty to both sides of the transaction, the clearing house becomes the seller to Trader A and the buyer from Trader B, through their respective brokers. Trader A and Trader B remain anonymous to each other, as do Broker A and Broker B, as they have effectively transacted with the clearing house. In this model, the brokers and their clients have no counterparty risk, as they are dealing with the clearing house rather than with each other. Third-party risk is mitigated through the clearing house's role as counterparty to each transaction.

In the OTC model, Trader C decides to buy and instructs his broker (Broker C) accordingly. Trader D is a seller of the same instrument through her broker (Broker D) at the same price at which Trader C is willing to buy. The trade occurs 'off-exchange' in an OTC market, such as the forex market. In this case, Broker C has dealt directly with Broker D as there is no counterparty through which to execute the trades. Both Broker C and Broker D and their respective clients are now exposed to counterparty risk. There is a chance that either party could face a credit or cash default that prevents them from meeting their obligations, and this would have a negative impact on the other party to the deal. If, for example, Broker D were to be bankrupted and default on the deal with Broker C, then Trader C would be negatively affected. Trader D would also incur a negative consequence, as her broker would no longer be in business.

The existence of a central counterparty or clearing house gives futures an important advantage over other derivatives markets in which the counterparties deal directly with each other 'over the counter' (OTC). An example of an OTC market is the spot forex or FX market. OTC transactions occur directly between two counterparties with no neutral central party to extend credit, guarantee performance or ensure agreements are honoured. Without this cover, market participants are exposed to the risk of default of the other party and to higher overall credit risk in these market environments.

Clearing house margin requirements

The clearing house charges two types of margin: the initial margin when a trade is opened, and the variation or mark-to-market margin on open positions. Trading futures allows you to use leverage to control large positions with a relatively small amount of your own capital. To enter a trade, only a fraction of the contract's full value is required. This margin deposit confers no rights of ownership; it is simply a security bond required to protect the financial integrity of the market.

Initial margin

The initial margin (also called a performance bond) is a security deposit required by the clearing house to ensure that traders have sufficient funds to meet any potential loss from a trade. This is essentially a 'good faith' deposit that you pay to indicate you will be able to fulfil your contractual obligations. These initial margin amounts are determined by the futures exchange and they are a function of the volatility of each futures contract, rather than a set percentage of the contract value. Brokers are permitted to request higher margin requirements from private clients, but never less than the minimum amount set by the exchange. If at any time your account dips below a specified maintenance level, you will be required to deposit more money to keep your account up to the initial margin requirement level. This is often referred to as a 'margin call'.

Variation or maintenance margin

Also called mark-to-market margin, this is an amount of the initial margin that must be maintained for each position before a margin call is generated and you have to add further funds to your account. At the end of each trading day your open positions are revalued at the day's closing price. The clearing house will add money to your margin balance if you are in profit and deduct money from your margin balance if you are in loss. If the loss is large enough that the balance in your margin account has fallen below the maintenance level, a margin call will be issued and you will have to replenish your account with extra cash or close out the position.

As an example, let's assume that the initial margin on a wheat futures contract is $1200 and the maintenance margin is $800. When you buy or sell one wheat futures contract, to open a position you will need to have $1200 set aside in your account for the initial margin. If the price of wheat moves against you by 10 cents per bushel or $500 per contract (5000-bushel contract × $0.10 per bushel), you have violated the maintenance margin level of $800 ($1200 − $500 = $700) and will need to move an additional $500 to your account to bring it back to the original maintenance level of $1200.

A margin call will be triggered when the value of your account drops below the maintenance level for all your open positions. Let's say, for example, you have six open positions with an initial margin requirement of $8000 and a maintenance margin requirement of $5000. If the value of your account drops to $4500, you will get a margin call for $3500 to bring your account back to the initial margin requirement. You can also liquidate positions and thus eliminate the margin call.

These margin requirements mean it is highly unlikely that a client will not be able to fulfil their obligations according to the futures contract. They also help ensure the financial integrity of the clearing house, the brokers and the exchange as a whole, and add to the appeal of trading futures.

Marking open positions to market each day also assists in the management of risk both at an individual client level and for the market as a whole, as it helps eliminate the accumulation of large losses or excess debt. Clients are informed every day of their open positions and the excess or deficit of margin requirements in their accounts. If a margin call is required it must usually be met within 24 hours either by the addition of extra cash or by the closure of enough open positions to bring the account back into line with the margin requirements.

Tip

The practice of 'mark to market' helps to ensure that individual trading accounts maintain sufficient working capital to be able to meet any margin requirements on a daily basis.

Price discovery process

Futures prices are determined through a competitive bidding or auction process. Originally this was determined through the 'open outcry' method on the exchange trading floors or pits, where brokers and their agents met to conduct this auction process. Since the late 1970s the process has also been undertaken via electronic trading platforms, with prices available electronically immediately and continuously around the globe. A number of contracts (such as the e-mini range of products) and exchanges (such as Eurex) now only undertake electronic trading. Traders are able to instruct their broker to execute orders on their behalf or, as is increasingly the case, they can execute their own orders to buy or sell through broker-supplied electronic platforms on their own computers from anywhere an internet connection is available. We will delve deeper into this topic in chapter 4. Figure 2.3 shows a typical dealing screen available to retail clients on their personal computer.

Figure 2.3: a typical dealing screen

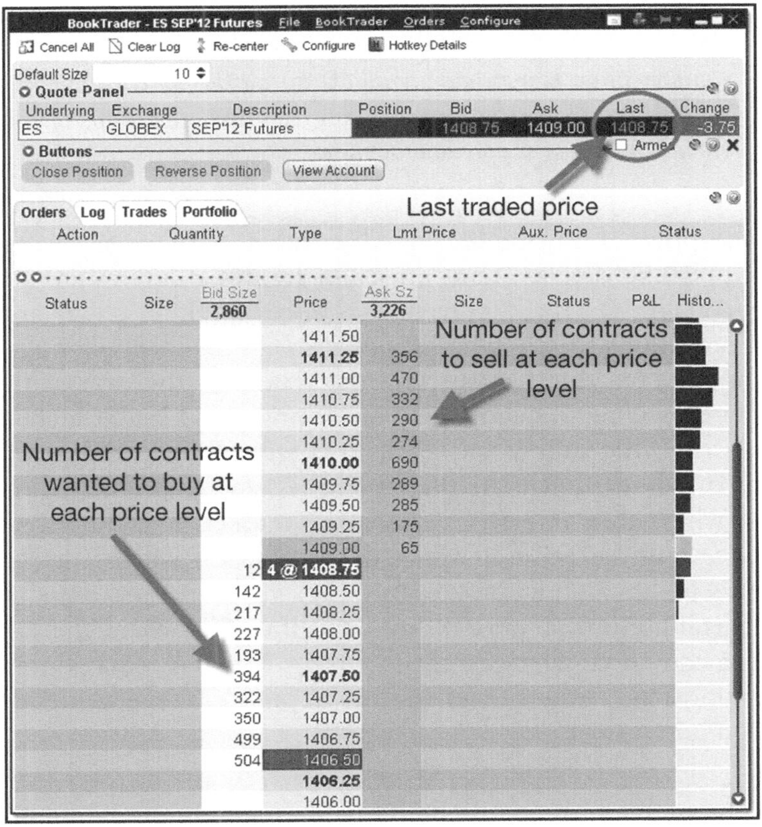

Source: Interactive Brokers LLC.

On this screen we can see the electronic auction process in action for the E-mini S&P 500 futures contract. The last traded price was 1408.75. There are 12 contracts being bid for at this price, and 65 contracts being offered to sell at 1409.00. For a new transaction to take place, either a seller has to adjust their price down to meet the bid price at 1408.75 or a buyer has to adjust their price up to meet the offer or sell price at 1409.00.

Tip

The price discovery or auction process is an ongoing and ever-changing one. Prices move up and down through the trading day in response to external events and new information being made available to market participants, resulting in prices being adjusted and the constant realignment of supply and demand.

The price of any product is 'discovered' by changes in its supply and demand, and prices for futures contracts are no exception. On the supply side, if prices are high sellers are more willing to sell, while at lower prices they will offer less for sale. On the demand side the reverse is the case, with buyers willing to buy more at lower prices and less at higher prices. If the supply and demand curves for any product or financial instrument are placed on the same graph, the point at which they intersect denotes the market or equilibrium price and the price at which the transaction will be made. This is shown in figure 2.4. In this example, price is initially in equilibrium at price P_1 and quantity Q_1, where the D_1 demand curve intersects the S_1 supply curve. A reduction in supply to Q_2 results in an increase in price to the new, higher equilibrium at P_2.

Figure 2.4: supply and demand and price equilibrium

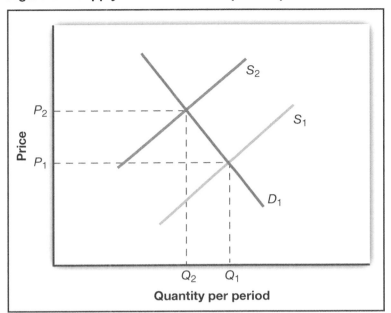

Supply and demand curves and thus equilibrium prices are constantly shifting as new information enters the markets. Futures market participants respond to these changes, a new equilibrium price is reached and new trades ensue. This equilibrium price can change minute by minute or even more frequently in fast-moving, volatile markets.

Tip

Supply and demand shifts create risk—for a corn grower, as the corn he plants today could be worth more or less by the time it is ready for harvest, just as for an equity portfolio fund manager, as the shares she buys today could be worth more or less in a few days' time. Shifts in supply and demand also create opportunity for speculators in any market to profit from adjustments to the equilibrium price.

Minimum price changes and daily price limits

To give some structure and guidance to the markets, futures exchanges determine the minimum price movements for individual futures contracts and the maximum daily price movement that can occur for some futures contracts.

Minimum price moves (ticks)

Each futures contract has a minimum amount by which it can move up or down. These minimum price moves are established by the exchange and vary with each instrument. Minimum price moves are called 'ticks'. On a gold futures contract, for example, a tick is 10 cents per ounce, so a one-tick move on a 100-ounce contract is worth $10 (10 cents per ounce × 100 ounces). In comparison, a tick on a grain futures contract is $0.0025 (¼ of 1 cent) per bushel. On a standard 5000-bushel wheat futures contract, that equals $12.50 per tick (5000 bushels × $0.0025 per bushel). It is important to know the tick moves for every futures contract you trade so you know how a price change will affect the value of the contract. This information is covered in detail when discussing specific contracts in parts II and III of this book.

Maximum daily price limits

Commodity exchanges also establish maximum daily price limits for futures contracts. These price limits are stated in terms of the previous day's closing price plus or minus a specified amount in cents or dollars per contract unit. Once a futures contract has increased or decreased in price by its daily limit, no more trading can take place until the next trading session; this is termed 'lock-limit'. If the daily limit for live cattle futures, for example, is 3 cents per pound on a 40 000-pound futures contract and the previous day's settlement price was 92 cents per pound, no trading can take place during the current trading session at any price above

95 cents per pound or below 89 cents per pound. Price is allowed to increase or decrease within the limit amount each day. These daily price limits can result in days when it is not possible to exit an existing futures position because the market is lock-limit. This can be both frustrating and costly if the market is moving against you or extremely beneficial if it is moving in the direction of your open position. In the live cattle example above, the daily 3-cents-per-pound limit equated to $1200 per futures contract (3 cents per pound × 40 000-pound contract).

These daily price limits are eliminated during the contract expiry month (also called the delivery or spot month) for some contracts, allowing price to trade according to supply and demand rather than being artificially curtailed by daily price limits. While daily limits are imposed by exchanges supposedly to provide order to the market, they are inefficient and can be frustrating for speculators. It would be far better to have no limit applied to these markets and to let price naturally find its own level. The professional use of stop-loss orders by traders would ensure positions could be liquidated much more efficiently.

Position limits

Exchanges and regulators also set limits on the maximum speculative position that any one person can have at any one time in any single futures contract. Maximum position limits are imposed to prevent any buyer or seller from being able to influence the price of a market through their buying and selling activities. These position limits are stated in total number of contracts or total units of the instrument or commodity.

Rollovers and delivery dates

All futures contracts have a specified month in which delivery or cash settlement must take place. Unlike shares, which have an indefinite life so long as the company remains solvent and listed on the exchange, all futures contracts are terminal. Prior to the expiration of the contract the trader is able either to offset their existing position and close out the trade or to roll over to another contract month.

Monthly expiry and rollover

For some contracts delivery dates are specified for every month, while for others delivery dates may be every second or third calendar month. Each calendar month is given an alphabetical symbol, as shown in table 2.1. The next available contract month is called the 'front month' or 'nearby month', while those further away are referred to as the 'back months'.

Table 2.1: delivery month symbols

Month	Symbol	Month	Symbol
January	F	July	N
February	G	August	Q
March	H	September	U
April	J	October	V
May	K	November	X
June	M	December	Z

When you are placing trades, these codes are used to specify the month you are trading. The monthly expiry of futures contracts gives rise to a process called 'rollover'. For example, you may be long cotton futures contracts and the delivery date is approaching for the contract month you have bought. You believe price will continue to rise and you want to capture more profit on the trade. To roll over to the next contract month you simply sell out of the contract month you are holding and buy the same number of contracts in the next month. This trade is done simultaneously and most brokers charge a reduced rate for specified rollovers.

First notice day and last trading day

Two important days for futures traders are first notice day (FND) and last trading day (LTD). First notice day is the first day prior to the expiration of a futures contract that the clearing house can give notice to the buyer of a futures contract of intent to deliver. It is the first 'warning' that they may be called upon to accept delivery. At any time after first notice day, a seller can be called on to make delivery and the buyer can be called on to accept delivery of the commodity or instrument specified in the contract. The clearing house randomly allocates holders of long positions (buyers) with holders of short positions (sellers) after first notice day.

Tip

First notice day applies only to contracts that call for physical delivery, as cash-settled contracts are automatically offset via a cash settlement at the contract expiry date.

To ensure that traders and speculators don't hold open positions past FND (unless they are in a position to take or make delivery), most brokers require their clients to close out or roll over their positions one to two days prior to FND so as to avoid any chance of being called on to accept or make delivery. In the case of electronic brokers with clients trading on electronic platforms and having no contact with a human broker, any positions still held by clients one to two days before FND can be automatically closed out to avoid any chance of delivery being called on to be made or accepted. This compulsory liquidation applies only to contracts calling for physical delivery.

Last trading day is simply the last business day on which a particular contract can be traded on the exchange, and corresponds with the expiration date for the contract.

In the case of contracts that specify physical delivery of the underlying commodity, this date will be relevant only to those wishing to participate in the delivery process, as all others will have already closed out or rolled over any open positions prior to FND. Cash-settled contracts can be traded up to last trading day, as any open positions at the expiry of the contract will be cash settled for the difference between the price of the futures contract and the price of the underlying instrument.

A typical futures contract

The live cattle futures contract in figure 2.5 shows all the features we have discussed so far. You can clearly see that this is a contract for the physical delivery of 40000 pounds of grade 3 steers, priced in cents per pound. The minimum tick move is $0.00025 per pound, or $10 per contract, and the daily price limit is 3 cents per pound. This contract is traded side-by-side on the Globex electronic platform and in the trading pit during pit hours. You can also see the contract months, the last trading day and the position limits, and that the contract calls for physical delivery of the specific quality and quantity of live cattle.

Leverage

Leverage is a major attraction for traders and speculators. Using leverage when trading allows your money to work much more efficiently than if you used only your own capital to trade with. You are able to control large amounts of a commodity or instrument for a fraction of its face value, as only a small initial deposit or margin (as discussed previously) is required to trade. As a result, a relatively small movement in price can produce large profits in relation to the initial margin. Leverage is a double-edged sword, however, and small movements in price against your position will also magnify losses.

Figure 2.5: live cattle futures contract

Contract Size	40,000 pounds (~18 metric tons)	
Product Description	55% Choice, 45% Select, Yield Grade 3 live steers	
Pricing Unit	Cents per pound	
Tick Size (minimum fluctuation)	$.00025 per pound (=$10 per contract)	
Daily Price Limits	$.03 per pound above or below the previous day's settlement price	
Trading Hours (All times listed are Central Time)	CME Globex (Electronic Platform)	MON 9:05 a.m. - FRI 1:55 p.m. Central Time Daily trading halts 4:00 p.m. - 5:00 p.m. Central Time
	Open Outcry (Trading Floor)	MON-FRI: 9:05 a.m. -1:00 p.m. Central Time
Last Trade Date/Time View Calendar	Last business day of the contract month, 12:00 p.m.	
Contract Months View Listings	Feb, Apr, Jun, Aug, Oct, Dec	
Settlement Procedure	Physical Delivery See CME Rule 10103.	
Position Limits	Non-Spot: 5,400 contracts in any contract month Spot: 450/300 contracts All months combined: n/a See CME Rule: 10102.E	
Ticker Symbol View Product Codes View Vendor Codes	CME Globex (Electronic Platform)	LE 48=Clearing
	Open Outcry (Trading Floor)	LC
Rulebook Chapter	101	
Exchange Rule	These contracts are listed with, and subject to, the rules and regulations of CME.	

Source: CME Group Inc.

At the time of writing, the initial margin requirement for the live cattle futures contract shown in figure 2.5 is $1080, on a contract with a face value of around $38000. This means we are able to initiate a position—either long or short—in this market by lodging just $1080 as margin with our futures broker, who in turn lodges it with the exchange. A 1-cent-per-pound move equates to $400 per futures contract. If the trade moves in our favour by 1 cent per pound, we have a $400 profit per contract or a 37 per cent return on our initial margin requirement ($400 profit on $1080). If we had to use all of our own capital to participate in the trade, the return would be just over 1 per cent ($400 profit on $38 000 contract value). Conversely, if the trade had moved against our position by 1 cent per pound, our losses would be equally magnified. Through the power of leverage, a 1 per cent move in the price of the futures contract results in a 37 per cent move in our margin account.

Tip

Buying and selling futures contracts has exactly the same profit or loss potential when measured in dollars and cents as does buying or selling the actual underlying commodity or financial instrument. The benefit comes from the low margin requirements (higher available leverage) when using futures contracts, as outlined in the live cattle trading example in figure 2.5 (see p. 33).

Trading using leverage is enormously beneficial to those who know and understand the benefits and pitfalls. Used wisely, and applying prudent money management and risk management principles, it can result in significant increases in return on capital. Used incorrectly, however, it can wipe out your trading capital. In addition to the necessary financial resources, futures trading requires a particular emotional temperament. While it may be a bit disappointing to see a $250 000 share portfolio lose 10 per cent of its value, or $25 000, it is rather more serious to have the same $25 000 wiped off a leveraged S&P 500 Index futures contract when your account balance is just $50 000 — for a loss of 50 per cent of your trading capital.

In the next chapter we will look at who trades futures and why, and discover the role and importance of both hedgers and speculators in the futures markets—as well as exploring how money is made (and lost) when trading futures.

Chapter summary

⇒ A futures contract is a legally binding, standardised agreement to buy or sell a commodity or financial instrument of specific quality and quantity on a specified future delivery date at a given location. The only variable is price, which is agreed upon at the time of the trade.

⇒ Futures contracts are fungible, as they may be mutually substituted.

⇒ In futures trading, open positions are offset to close them out by buying or selling the opposite side of the existing open position before the expiry date.

⇒ Futures contracts may be divided into those that call for physical delivery of a particular commodity (delivery can be taken or made), and those that are cash settled (the position is closed out by a final mark-to-market cash adjustment).

⇒ The clearing house ensures the integrity of all trades by assuming the role of seller against the original seller and the role of buyer against the original buyer. It operates as if the seller has sold to the clearing house and the buyer has bought from the clearing house, and thus serves as the counterparty in every trade.

⇒ Futures prices are determined through a competitive bidding or auction process. Originally this was determined through the 'open outcry' method on the exchange trading floor. Most trading now occurs via electronic trading platforms, with prices available electronically immediately and continuously around the globe.

⇒ Each futures contract has a minimum amount by which it can move up or down. These minimum price moves (called 'ticks') are established by the exchange and vary with each instrument.

⇒ Commodity exchanges also establish maximum daily price limits for futures contracts. These price limits are stated in terms of the previous day's closing price plus or minus a specified amount in cents or dollars per contract unit.

⇒ Futures contracts are traded for specified delivery months. For some contracts these are every month, while for others they may be every second or third calendar month.

⇒ First notice day (FND) is the first day prior to the expiration of a futures contract that the clearing house can give notice to the buyer of a futures contract of intent to deliver. Last trading day (LTD) is the last business day on which a particular contract can be traded and corresponds with the expiration date for the contract.

⇒ Using leverage when trading allows your money to work much more efficiently than if you used only your own capital to trade with. You are able to control large amounts of a commodity or instrument for a fraction of its face value.

chapter 3

Who trades futures and why

Participants in the futures markets range from small retail clients trading single-lot contracts to giant hedge funds trading vast numbers of contracts. Futures traders cover a very broad spectrum, but each has their own reasons for participating in this global marketplace. In this chapter we identify these market participants and examine some of the reasons why they are trading futures. Futures markets traders can be classified broadly according to two modus operandi—hedging or speculating. While some indulge in both hedging and speculating, their reasons for undertaking activities in each area are often quite different.

Hedging

One of the primary economic functions of the futures markets is to manage price risk. Hedging is the practice of offsetting price risk in a cash market by taking equal and opposite positions in the futures market. Hedging is based on the principle that the cash market price for a commodity or financial instrument and the futures market price for that same product will tend to move up and down more or less in unison. By taking opposite positions, hedging allows losses incurred in one market to be offset by gains in the other. In this way the hedger is able to establish a known price level for a cash market transaction weeks or months in advance.

Tip

When undertaking a hedging strategy, the hedger willingly gives up the opportunity to benefit from a favourable price move in order to protect themselves against any unfavourable price move.

The range of hedging possibilities is virtually limitless. A wheat farmer can hedge against a decline in wheat prices, while a biscuit maker can hedge against an increase in the price of wheat. A lender can hedge against a potential fall in interest rates, while a borrower can hedge against an interest rate rise. The following examples of hedging indicate how the strategy is used in a couple of different scenarios.

The 'short' hedge

The seller of a commodity, such as a farmer growing soybeans, can hedge (or protect) against falling soybean prices by short selling futures contracts. Having planted his crop, the farmer may determine that soybean prices are currently high by normal seasonal standards, owing to any number of conditions ranging from a drought the previous year to increased demand from stock-feeders. The farmer observes that December soybean futures are trading at $9.50 per bushel, while the best bid in the cash market for December delivery is $9.10 — 40 cents per bushel lower than the December futures contract, but still higher than in previous years. The farmer decides to hedge his potential soybean crop:

he sells short six soybean futures contracts, or 30 000 bushels (each contract is for 5000 bushels), at $9.50 per bushel. The farmer has willingly given up the opportunity to benefit from an increase in the price of soybeans in order to protect himself from a decrease in the price prior to his anticipated delivery date. He has locked in a price of $9.50 per bushel for 30 000 bushels of soybeans.

If, come December, the cash price for soybeans has fallen to, say, $8.50 per bushel, the farmer has benefited to the tune of $1.00 per bushel from undertaking this simple hedging strategy in one of two ways. Having sold short six futures contracts at $9.50 per bushel, he could offset his short position by buying back or 'covering' his short position at $8.50 per bushel for a gain of $1.00 per bushel less brokerage and costs, and then deliver his soybeans to the market at $8.50 per bushel. The transaction details are displayed in figure 3.1 (overleaf). Alternatively, he could arrange to make physical delivery of the soybeans at the contract price of $9.50 per bushel, as physical delivery is specified in the soybean futures contract. Either way, he has 'locked in' a guaranteed price for his soybeans.

Without the hedge in place, the farmer would have simply delivered his soybeans at harvest and received the prevailing cash market price of $8.50 per bushel for a total return of $255 000.00.

If, however, the price of soybeans increases to $10.50 per bushel, the farmer will have given up the opportunity to sell his soybeans for the higher price, as he is locked in to sell at $9.50 per bushel, effectively reducing his return by $1.00 per bushel. Having short sold six futures contracts at $9.50 per bushel, he could offset this short position by buying back his short-sold contracts at $10.50 per bushel for a loss of $1.00 per bushel, then delivering his soybeans to the market at $10.50 per bushel. The transaction details are displayed in figure 3.2 (overleaf). Alternatively, he could arrange to make physical delivery of the soybeans at the contract price of $9.50 per bushel.

Figure 3.1: results of short hedge when price declines

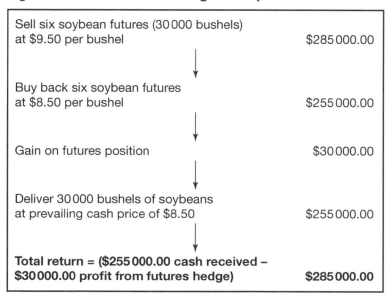

Figure 3.2: results of short hedge when price increases

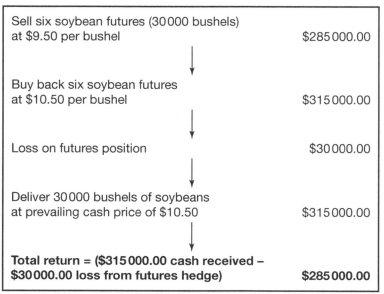

Without the hedge in place, the farmer would have simply delivered his soybeans at harvest and received the prevailing cash price of $10.50 per bushel for a total return of $315 000.00.

Both examples assume that the cash price and the futures price are identical at the time of delivery, and do not include any brokerage or other transaction costs.

These examples show the workings of a short hedge as a protection mechanism for a commodity producer. Regardless of the price movement, the soybean producer has been able to lock in a known return for his soybean crop. Without the hedge in place the farmer would have incurred a $30 000 loss if the price of soybeans had declined by $1 per bushel, but would have made an additional $30 000 if the price of soybeans had risen by $1 per bushel.

The 'long' hedge

As the buyer of a commodity, a jewellery manufacturer who uses gold can hedge (or protect) against rising gold prices by buying futures contracts. The manufacturer knows she will need to buy more gold in six months' time to fulfil production requirements for orders already placed at prices based on the current price of gold. She is concerned that a rising gold price could easily erode any profit on the existing deal. The manufacturer observes that March gold futures are trading at $1208.70 per troy ounce, a slight discount to the prevailing cash market price of $1214.50 per troy ounce. She decides to hedge her known gold quantity requirements of 300 troy ounces (each gold futures contract is for 100 troy ounces of gold) and buys three March gold futures contracts at $1208.70. The manufacturer has willingly given up the opportunity to benefit from a fall in the price of gold in order to protect herself from any increase in the price of gold. She has locked in a fixed purchase price of $1208.70 per troy ounce of gold.

If, come March, the cash price of gold has risen to, say, $1397.00 per troy ounce, the manufacturer has successfully protected herself from the surge in the gold price. She can now offset her long position in the futures market by selling her futures contracts at $1397.00 per troy ounce for a gain of $188.30 per troy ounce, then buying the required amount of gold in the cash market at $1397.00 per troy ounce. The transaction details are displayed in figure 3.3. Alternatively, she could arrange to take physical delivery of the gold at $1208.70 per troy ounce, as physical delivery is specified in the gold futures contract. Either way, she has locked in a guaranteed price for the purchase of her gold requirements.

Figure 3.3: results of long hedge when price rises

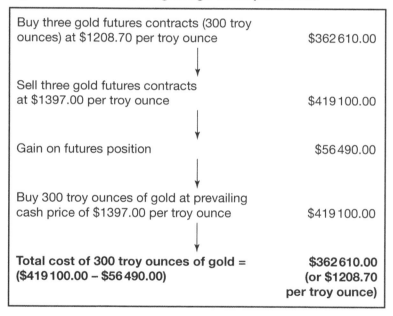

Buy three gold futures contracts (300 troy ounces) at $1208.70 per troy ounce	$362 610.00
Sell three gold futures contracts at $1397.00 per troy ounce	$419 100.00
Gain on futures position	$56 490.00
Buy 300 troy ounces of gold at prevailing cash price of $1397.00 per troy ounce	$419 100.00
Total cost of 300 troy ounces of gold = **($419 100.00 – $56 490.00)**	**$362 610.00** **(or $1208.70** **per troy ounce)**

Without the hedge in place the jewellery manufacturer would have paid the prevailing market price of $1397.00 per troy ounce, effectively reducing her overall profit on the deal by $56 490.00, as she had costed the forward product order at the prevailing market price for gold when the order was placed ($1208.70 per troy ounce).

If, however, the price of gold declines to $1020.40 per troy ounce, the manufacturer has given up the opportunity to buy gold at a much lower price, as she has locked in a purchase price of $1208.70 per troy ounce, effectively reducing her potential return by $188.30 per troy ounce. Having bought long three futures contracts at $1208.70 per troy ounce, the manufacturer could offset this long position by selling three contracts at $1020.40 per troy ounce, for a loss of $188.30 per troy ounce, and then buying gold in the cash market for $1020.40 per troy ounce. The transaction details are displayed in figure 3.4. Alternatively, she could take physical delivery of the gold at $1208.70 under the terms of the futures contract. Either way, the cost of the gold is locked in at $1208.70 per troy ounce.

Figure 3.4: results of long hedge when price falls

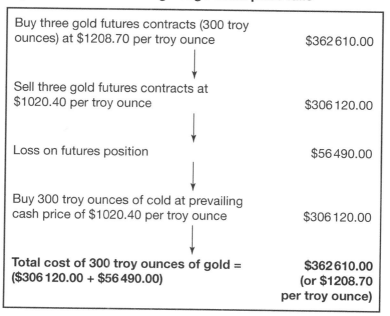

Buy three gold futures contracts (300 troy ounces) at $1208.70 per troy ounce	$362 610.00
Sell three gold futures contracts at $1020.40 per troy ounce	$306 120.00
Loss on futures position	$56 490.00
Buy 300 troy ounces of cold at prevailing cash price of $1020.40 per troy ounce	$306 120.00
Total cost of 300 troy ounces of gold = **($306 120.00 + $56 490.00)**	**$362 610.00** **(or $1208.70** **per troy ounce)**

Without the hedge in place, the jewellery manufacturer would have simply purchased 300 troy ounces of gold at the prevailing cash price of $1020.40 per troy ounce, effectively increasing her profit on the deal by $56 490.00.

Both examples assume that the cash price and the futures price are identical at the time of delivery, and do not include any brokerage or other transaction costs.

These examples show the workings of a long hedge as a protection mechanism for a commodity buyer, in this case a jewellery manufacturer. Regardless of the price movement, the gold buyer has been able to lock in a known cost for her gold requirements. Without the hedge in place, the gold buyer would have incurred a $56 490.00 loss if the price of gold had risen by $188.30 per troy ounce, or would have made an additional $56 490.00 profit if the price of gold had fallen by $188.30 per troy ounce.

Who are hedgers?

Just as the range of hedging opportunities is virtually limitless, depending on the desired outcome in virtually any market under a range of market conditions, so too is the range of market participants using these hedging concepts. These participants range from small operators hedging one or two contracts to much larger organisations hedging substantially larger positions in both the natural commodities and financial markets.

Commodity producers

From farmers growing corn, wheat or soybeans, to soybean oil manufacturers and cattle feed-lotters, to gold-mining companies and crude oil producing companies—all commodity producers can use short-hedging strategies to manage price risk and hedge against a fall in prices for the commodity they produce.

Commodity buyers

On the other side of the coin, commodity consumers such as food processors and manufacturers, jewellery makers, supermarket chains concerned about rising meat prices, and major users of energy products such as airlines and large transport companies can use long hedging strategies to manage risk and set a known cost base for core ingredients, thus stabilising their input prices.

Portfolio managers

Portfolio managers include the investment fund manager seeking to protect the assets of mutual funds, superannuation funds, managed equity funds, managed share or futures portfolios, and even individual investors with large share or other financial instrument portfolios. Hedging strategies can be used to increase or decrease the overall market exposure of an investment portfolio and to safeguard an investment portfolio that may have been built up over many years. Someone with a large share portfolio, for example, can short sell equity index futures such as S&P 500 Index futures to protect their total portfolio, rather than sell out of stocks within the portfolio in the event of a market downturn.

Hedge funds

As managers of diverse, often highly leveraged portfolios using advanced investment strategies and techniques to maximise returns for their investors, hedge funds use hundreds of different strategies to achieve their investment objectives. The futures market allows these funds to use combinations of hedging strategies in order to both manage risk and increase overall returns.

Speculating

Futures markets facilitate the transfer of risk from hedgers to speculators. Speculators take on the risk that hedgers hope to avoid, or at least to minimise, by aiming to profit from anticipated increases or decreases in futures prices. By their willingness to take and hold the opposite side of a hedger's position, speculators add capital to the market that helps to limit a hedger's exposure to price fluctuations and price risk. If it were not for speculators and their willingness to accept risk, hedgers would find it difficult to implement their strategies, as short hedgers would be able to trade only with long hedgers. They would also face the difficult challenge of finding someone who was prepared to take exactly the opposite side of their transaction.

Speculators add liquidity to the futures markets. Liquidity refers to the number of contracts or units outstanding at any one time. The more liquid a futures contract, the easier it is for large transactions to occur without causing a major change in price. If the markets were limited to those undertaking hedging activities, liquidity in all markets would be significantly less. The actions of speculators add to the win–win nature of futures markets; hedgers win through increased liquidity, and speculators win through the opportunity to participate in the futures markets in order to generate profits from their trading and investing activities.

Speculators employ a wide variety of analysis techniques, methodologies and strategies for engaging the markets. They rarely set out to take or make delivery of the underlying commodity or instrument, and this also adds to liquidity to the markets. Through offsetting long positions by selling them and offsetting short positions by buying them back, speculators are able to enter and exit markets quickly and easily, providing greater liquidity for hedgers.

Speculators bring additional and different information to the futures markets, thus enhancing the price discovery role of these markets; and, having many different reasons for buying and selling at varying price points, they contribute to the price discovery process.

Buying a futures contract — 'going long'

Someone who expects a futures price to increase will buy or 'go long' a futures contract. If their analysis proves to be correct and the market rises (price increases), the futures contract can be sold for a higher price, offsetting their original long position and resulting in a profit. If their analysis proves to be incorrect and the market falls (price decreases), they can just as easily offset the original long position by selling at a lower price and incurring a loss on the trade.

A trader's analysis may suggest that crude oil futures will increase in price. As the trader is not interested in taking delivery of the underlying crude oil, but only in selling out of the futures contract at a higher price over the medium term, she will look at the front-month contract in order to determine her entry price, stop-loss and profit target. The trader enters the trade by buying a September crude oil futures contract at $95.18 per barrel. The trader has now entered a contract to buy 1000 barrels of crude oil under the terms specified in the futures contract, at $95.18 per barrel, for a total contract value of $95 180.00. With the leverage available in the futures market, the trader has to lodge an initial margin (as determined and specified by the exchange) of around $6500.00. At the time of entering the trade, she also enters her designated stop-loss (the price at which she will exit the trade if price declines and proves her assessment of the market to be incorrect) and a predetermined profit target. Ten days later the price of crude oil has increased, reaching the trader's profit objective of $101.50 per barrel and generating a profit of $6.32 per barrel ($101.50 − $95.18 = $6.32 per barrel). The overall profit on the trade (excluding brokerage and costs) is $6320.00. The transaction details are displayed in figure 3.5 (overleaf).

Figure 3.5: profitable long trade

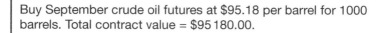

Buy September crude oil futures at $95.18 per barrel for 1000 barrels. Total contract value = $95 180.00.

Sell (to offset) September crude oil futures at $101.50 per barrel for 1000 barrels. Total contract value = $101 500.00

Trade profit = $101 500.00 (sell price) – $95 180.00 (buy price) = $6320.00 (excluding brokerage charges and costs)

By making use of the leverage available in the futures markets, the trader in this example has achieved a profitable return of $6320 on an initial margin requirement of $6500 in 10 trading days. This equates to just over a 97 per cent return on the margin required to enter the trade. The overall return on equity will depend on the trader's account size at the time of executing the trade. If we assume an account size of $100 000, she will have achieved a positive return of 6.32 per cent over 10 days.

Perhaps, however, the trader's analysis proves incorrect and the price for crude oil falls rather than rises as expected. As an educated and disciplined trader, though, she has a stop-loss in place, limiting her overall loss on the trade to a manageable level of her available capital. With a stop-loss set at $1700.00, the trader has a predetermined exit point should her analysis prove incorrect and the market decline. This $1700.00 total stop-loss amount equates to $1.70 per barrel ($1700.00 ÷ 1000 barrels = $1.70 per barrel). The trader sets her stop-loss at $93.48 per barrel ($95.18 entry price − $1.70 = $93.48). Four days later, following a fall in the price of crude oil, the stop-loss price is reached and the trade is closed out for a $1700.00 loss. The transaction details are displayed in figure 3.6.

Figure 3.6: losing long trade

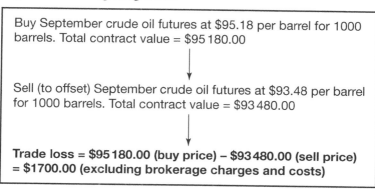

By making use of the leverage available in the futures markets, the trader in this example has achieved a negative return of $1700 on an initial margin requirement of $6500 in four trading days. This equates to just over a 26 per cent loss on the margin required to enter the trade. The overall return on equity will depend on the trader's account size at the time of executing the trade. If we assume an account size of $100 000, she will have achieved a negative return of 1.7 per cent over four days.

Short selling a futures contract — 'going short'

Someone who expects a futures contract to fall in price can initiate a short or sold position by selling a futures contract. If they are proven correct in their analysis and the market falls (price decreases), the futures contract can be bought back at a lower price, offsetting their original short position and resulting in a profit. If their analysis proves incorrect and the market rises (price increases), they can just as easily offset their original short position by buying back at a higher price, incurring a loss on the trade.

The essence of short selling is that a position can be initiated by selling, as opposed to the process of first buying something to establish a position.

Tip

A major benefit of futures trading is the ability to short sell or 'go short' futures contracts just as easily as buying or going long. Prospective traders need to familiarise themselves with the process of short selling in order to benefit from the advantages of trading in downtrending markets.

A trader's analysis may indicate that the price of feeder cattle futures will decrease. As the trader is not interested in making delivery of the underlying feeder cattle, but only in buying back the futures contract at a lower price over the medium term, he will look at the front-month contract in order to determine his entry price, stop-loss and profit target. The trader enters the trade by selling an August feeder cattle futures contract at 156.375 cents per pound. The trader has now entered a contract to sell 50 000 pounds of feeder cattle under the terms specified in the futures contract, at 156.375 cents per pound, for a total contract value of $78 187.50 (50 000 pounds × 156.375 cents per pound). With the leverage available in the futures market, the trader has to lodge an initial margin (as determined and specified by the exchange) of around $2000.00. At the time of entering the trade, he also enters his designated stop-loss (the price at which he will exit the trade if price rises and proves his assessment of the market to be incorrect) and a predetermined profit target. Seven days later the price of feeder cattle has decreased, reaching the trader's profit objective of 152.150 cents per pound and generating a profit of 4.225 cents per pound (156.375 − 152.150 = 4.225 cents per pound). The overall profit on the trade (excluding brokerage and costs) is $2112.50. The transaction details are displayed in figure 3.7.

Figure 3.7: profitable short trade

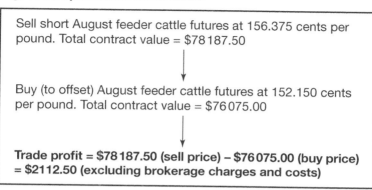

Sell short August feeder cattle futures at 156.375 cents per pound. Total contract value = $78 187.50

Buy (to offset) August feeder cattle futures at 152.150 cents per pound. Total contract value = $76 075.00

Trade profit = $78 187.50 (sell price) – $76 075.00 (buy price) = $2112.50 (excluding brokerage charges and costs)

By making use of the leverage available in the futures markets, the trader in this example has achieved a profitable return of $2112.50 on an initial margin requirement of $2000.00 in seven trading days. This equates to just over a 105 per cent return on the margin required to enter the trade. The overall return on equity will depend on the trader's account size at the time of executing the trade. If we assume an account size of $100 000.00, he will have achieved a positive return of 2.1 per cent over seven days.

The trader's analysis may have proved incorrect, however, and the price of feeder cattle risen rather than fallen as expected. As an educated and disciplined trader, though, he has a stop-loss in place, limiting his overall loss on the trade to a manageable level of his available capital. With a stop-loss set at $925.00, the trader has a predetermined exit point should his analysis prove incorrect and the market rise. This $925.00 total stop-loss amount equates to 1.85 cents per pound ($925.00 ÷ 50 000 pounds = 1.85 cents per pound). The trader sets his stop-loss at 158.225 cents per pound (156.375 entry price plus 1.85 = 158.225). Three days later, following a rise in the price of feeder cattle, the stop-loss price is reached and the trade is closed out for a $925.00 loss. The transaction details are displayed in figure 3.8 (overleaf).

Figure 3.8: losing short trade

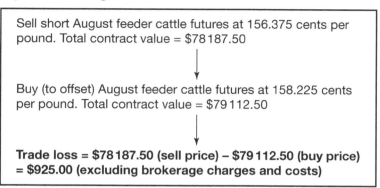

Sell short August feeder cattle futures at 156.375 cents per pound. Total contract value = $78187.50

Buy (to offset) August feeder cattle futures at 158.225 cents per pound. Total contract value = $79112.50

Trade loss = $78187.50 (sell price) – $79112.50 (buy price) = $925.00 (excluding brokerage charges and costs)

By making use of the leverage available in the futures markets, the trader has incurred a loss in this example of $925 on an initial margin requirement of $2000 in three trading days. This equates to just over a 46 per cent loss on the margin required to enter the trade. The overall return on equity will depend on the trader's account size at the time of executing the trade. If we assume an account size of $100000, he will have achieved a negative return of 0.9 per cent over three days.

Who are speculators?

Just as there are any number of reasons for hedgers to enter the futures markets, there are myriad reasons for speculators to do so. Their trading activities range from small, one-lot orders to much larger, multiple contract buy-and-sell orders. The traders speculating in the futures markets may be fundamental analysts whose decision making is based on market reports, crop reports, interest rate announcements and the like, or they may be technical analysts who use charting and mathematical models and systems to generate their trading orders. This diversity in both participants and trading approaches fosters the constant market action of buying and selling, adds liquidity to the markets and aids significantly in the price discovery process.

Independent traders

Many speculators are individuals trading their own funds. They range from small, single-lot traders to those with larger accounts trading several contracts at a time, seeking to generate profits from directional trading activities — going long when they expect prices to rise, and selling short when they expect prices to decline. Electronic trading has improved access to price and trade information for independent traders, who can now access this information on personal computers anywhere with an internet connection.

Prop traders

Proprietary trading firms supply their traders with the capital they need to execute trades according to a specified system or strategy. By using the capital provided by the firm, the traders are able to trade larger positions than if they were trading their own account. These 'prop traders' have a business relationship with the firm regarding profit sharing, performance bonuses and other remuneration possibilities.

Hedge funds and other managed investment funds

Hedge funds and other managed funds are active speculative traders seeking to generate profits from directional trading strategies, just like independent traders but with a much greater number of contracts traded at any one time. Funds are also active hedgers in futures markets.

Market makers

Trading firms that are contracted to add liquidity to the markets by continually providing bid-and-offer prices are referred to as market makers. They provide market liquidity, particularly in some electronic markets, which allows large transactions to take place without causing a major price shift. Market makers generate their profits from capturing small differences in the bid/offer spread over a large number of transactions.

Speculative trading styles

Speculative traders may also be classified according to the time frame over which their trades unfold, or by their method of arriving at their trading decisions.

Position traders

Traders who initiate a futures trade with the intention of holding it open over several days, weeks or even months are referred to as position traders. Position traders tend to be 'trend-followers', buying or selling in the direction of the prevailing price trend with the expectation of capturing large price moves on a few of these trends. They are often stopped out of trades for relatively small losing amounts until a new major trend allows them to recover these small losses and reap a few large winning trades. Position traders use 'trailing stops' to protect their profits, raising the price at which they will be stopped out of a long trade, or lowering the price at which they will be stopped out of a short trade, when the trend comes to an end and price retraces. Trailing stops allow the position trader to let their profitable winning trades run for as long as the trend continues. By trailing the stop-loss level they aim to continually lock in an increasing amount of profit. When the trend does finally reverse they will inevitably give back some of their theoretical profit. Figure 3.9 shows a chart of gold in a clear uptrend. As the price climbs steadily, the trailing stop is continually raised. Eventually the price retraces through the trailing stop and the trade is closed out for a significant profit.

Tip

The key to the successful application of a long-term trend-following approach is the discipline to use a trailing stop and let the trend unfold over an extended period of time.

Figure 3.9: medium-term gold trend-trade with trailing stops

Source: Trade Navigator / Genesis Financial Technologies Inc.

Not all position traders are interested in capturing large trend moves using trailing stops. Many use the existing trend to capture smaller moves in the direction of that trend, getting in and out of the market several times as the trend develops. These traders will use profit targets or objectives and will re-enter trades several times within the life of the prevailing trend. Figure 3.10 (overleaf) shows an example of a trading system capturing several short-selling opportunities within an existing downtrend in coffee futures.

Tip

The key to the successful application of a strategy like this is the discipline to re-enter the trade, seizing trading opportunities as they occur, and to follow the rules of the system or strategy being used.

Day traders

As the name suggests, day traders are interested in holding open market positions only for the trading day in which they are entered. They will exit the market at the close of each trading day. Their objective is to capture the price move, either long or short, on the day. By closing out all their open positions at the end of each trading day, they aim to avoid any adverse overnight price moves. The downside is that they can miss out on significant medium- and long-term trends if they develop.

Figure 3.10: short selling in coffee downtrend

Source: Trade Navigator / Genesis Financial Technologies Inc.

Scalpers

Originally limited to trading their own accounts in the open outcry trading pits or trading floors, many scalpers now also trade on electronic trading platforms as prop traders. The scalper's technique is to trade minimum price fluctuations on large numbers of contracts, generating small profits and smaller losses on a large number of trades. Scalpers continually 'buy the bid and sell the offer' with the aim of being right more times than they are wrong and generating their profits from a high volume of trades.

Fundamental or technical?

Beyond their chosen time frame or trading style, speculators can also be divided into those using fundamental analysis and those using technical analysis to arrive at their trading decisions.

Fundamental analysts

Those traders using supply and demand information, such as crop reports, analysis of economic conditions, changes in government regulations or levels of market intervention, geopolitical events, weather conditions, and any other news or forecasts that might lead to changes in price, are referred to as fundamental analysts. They undertake detailed analysis of the underlying fundamentals that might bring about change in the conditions of supply and demand and cause prices to respond accordingly. Fundamental analysis requires an understanding of, and an ability to interpret, a wide range of news, figures and data, and to extrapolate this into useable information upon which to form a rational decision on an appropriate course of action. This is a very time-consuming process.

Tip

It is important to differentiate between true fundamental analysis and simply reacting to news and other reports. True fundamental analysis involves the detailed examination and interpretation of a range of issues that have the potential to alter the supply and demand equilibrium, and thus cause a major change in price. It should never be confused with reacting to news reports and other information reported in the press. It is impossible to consistently make money in the markets simply by reading the fundamentals and news reports in the daily newspaper and other sources and making decisions to buy or sell based on that information. Not only is it too late by the time this information is in the newspaper or on the seven o'clock news, but everyone else has seen it too!

One of the drawbacks with using fundamental analysis is that much of the news can be 'old' by the time it is fully available, analysis is conducted and an opinion formed. There can also be a time lag between when events occur and when they are reported, during which conditions can change dramatically. Often the market has already factored in and reacted to the prevailing or expected conditions well ahead of the information reaching the public domain. (The internet and other electronic media have mitigated this time lag to some extent as news reports and events are now transmitted around the world with much greater speed and efficiency.)

Overall market conditions or perceptions of market conditions will also greatly affect prices and markets. If the consensus of market participants is positive or bullish, then even a minor change in fundamental conditions can cause prices to rise sharply. If the market consensus is gloomy and the majority of participants are negative, then the same announcement may have little effect on prices, or a minor negative news report will send prices tumbling.

Technical analysts

Technical analysis is the study of price and volume relationships to form a view on future price direction, and thus make a profit from trading in the direction of that view — going long if the trader expects price to increase and selling short if the expectation is for price to decrease. Technical analysts study this price action on charts that display price and other information in a graphical format. They also use a range of technical indicators derived from the interrelationship between price, time and volume to aid in their analysis. Technical analysis searches past data and information for patterns and relationships that may be replicated in the future, allowing the trader to interact with the market according to these patterns and base their decision making regarding trade entry and exit on a system of rules.

Tip

Technical analysis is based on the concept that the marketplace, and the participants that constitute that market, consider ALL the information known about that market, including the fundamental information, and then determine fair value through the process of price discovery.

Now accepted and used by a huge number of traders and investors, technical analysis is conducted using specialised computer software programs that are preconfigured with a range of technical indicators and analysis tools, such as Trade Navigator from Genesis Financial Technologies (www.genesisft.com). These programs are fast and easy to use, and have opened up the world of technical analysis to vast numbers of market participants. When combined with electronic trading platforms, complex trading systems using mathematical algorithms and combinations of complex processes can be used to generate high-speed, high-volume trading strategies that are fully automated and execute trades according to the rules of the particular system without any human intervention in the trading process. These systems are especially suited to the fast-moving, highly liquid and often volatile financial futures markets.

For the short- to medium-term trader, technical analysis is without doubt the preferred way to locate and prioritise potential trading opportunities and determine entry and exit techniques. It is also used to define stop-loss levels and to set profit targets and adjust trailing stops if required.

More often than not, technical analysts have little or no interest in the underlying commodity or financial instrument, its fundamentals or the actual reasons behind the price move. They simply react to the information displayed on their charts, in conjunction with the use of their chosen technical indicators, and take action according to a set of predefined rules or parameters. They are not concerned with 'why' prices are moving up or down. They are concerned only with the direction of the move, and then entering a trade in that direction with the aim of exiting at a profit at some point in the future—which may be in hours, days or weeks, depending on their time frame and view of the market.

Spreading

Most speculators engage in directional trading strategies that focus on either buying futures contracts to profit from an increase in price or short selling to profit from a decrease in price. Spread trading or 'spreading' involves simultaneously buying one futures contract and selling another. The spreader's goal is to profit from an expected change in the price relationship between the two contracts.

Spreaders aim to take advantage of the wide range of price spread relationships that exist in the futures markets. These shifting spread relationships include those:

⇒ between the price of the same commodity on the same exchange in different delivery months (for example, buying March soybeans and selling November soybeans). These are referred to as *interdelivery spreads* or calendar spreads. They are intramarket spreads, as they occur in the same market.

⇒ between different but related futures contracts (for example, buying March feeder cattle and selling March live cattle). These are referred to as *intercommodity spreads.*

⇒ between the price of the same commodity trading on different exchanges (for example, buying ICE-traded cocoa and selling NYSE Euronext cocoa). These are referred to as *intermarket spreads.*

⇒ between the cash price and the futures price of the same commodity in the same delivery period. These are referred to as *basis spreads.*

Tip

'Buying a spread' involves buying the higher priced futures contract and selling the lower priced contract with the expectation that the price difference, or spread, will continue to widen. 'Selling a spread' involves selling the higher priced futures contract and buying the lower priced contract in the expectation that the price difference between the two will narrow or converge.

In all these examples, there are 'normal' seasonal relationships that reflect normal market conditions. When these price patterns deviate from their typical pattern the spreader's actions will involve buying one futures contract and selling another in order to profit as the market corrects back to the norm. There are also seasonal-specific spreading strategies, which aim to take advantage of historical seasonal patterns between the prices of futures contracts.

Tip

There are three possible ways to achieve a profit when 'buying a spread':
⇒ The price for both contracts increases, with the bought leg or contract month increasing by more than the sold leg or contract month.
⇒ The price for both contracts decreases, with the bought leg decreasing by less than the sold leg.
⇒ The bought leg increases and the sold leg decreases.

One of the most commonly used spreads, the calendar spread, involves taking advantage of price differences between two delivery months of the same futures contract.

A trader's analysis may indicate that a seasonal pattern exists in the corn market between the months of March and December, in which the price spread between these two months widens. In this case, the trader would buy the spread, as he expects the price differential to increase. To open the position he buys the March corn futures contract at 610.00 cents per bushel and sells the December corn futures contract at 579.75 cents per bushel, for a difference (or spread) of 30.25 cents per bushel (610.00 − 579.75 = 30.25). Two months later the price of the March contract has increased by 38.75 cents per bushel to 648.75 cents per bushel, and the price of the December contract has increased by only 14.5 cents per bushel to 594.25 cents per bushel. To close the position the trader now offsets both legs of the spread by selling the March contract at 648.75 cents per bushel and buying back the December contract at 594.25 cents per bushel for a spread difference of 54.50 cents per bushel (648.75 − 594.25 = 54.50). The trader's profit on the spread trade is 24.25 cents per bushel (54.50 exit price − 30.25 entry price = 24.25) or $1212.50 (24.25 cents per bushel × $50 per 1 cent = $1212.50), excluding brokerage and costs. The transaction details are displayed in table 3.1.

Table 3.1: profitable calendar spread example

			Spread
Month A	Buy March corn @ 610 cents/ bushel	Sell December corn @ 579.75 cents/ bushel	30.25 cents
Month C	Sell March corn @ 648.75 cents/ bushel	Buy December corn @ 594.25 cents/ bushel	54.50 cents
	38.75 cents gain	14.50 cents loss	24.25 cents profit
Overall profit = 24.25 cents per bushel @ $50.00 = $1212.50 (excluding brokerage and charges).			

The trader's analysis could have proven incorrect and the price spread between the two selected months may have actually decreased rather than increased as expected, resulting in a losing trade. The price of the March corn contract may have fallen to 595 cents per bushel, and the price of the December contract may have actually risen to 587.25 cents per bushel—causing a loss on both legs of the spread—for an overall loss of 22.50 cents per bushel. The transaction details are shown in table 3.2.

Table 3.2: losing calendar spread example

			Spread
Month A	Buy March corn @ 610 cents/ bushel	Sell December corn @ 579.75 cents/ bushel	30.25 cents
Month C	Sell March corn @ 595 cents/ bushel	Buy December corn @ 587.25 cents/ bushel	7.75 cents
	15.00 cents loss	7.50 cents loss	22.50 cents loss
Overall loss = 22.50 cents per bushel @ $50.00 = $1125.00 (excluding brokerage and charges).			

Tip

Spread trading involves double the amount of brokerage of a simple long or short trade, as each spread trade actually involves four transactions.

Spread trading is often considered a more conservative and less risky approach than having outright long or short positions, as profits and losses occur only as a result of changes in the price differential between the two contracts. However, while this may generally be the case, the losses from spread trades can be greater than those incurred when trading an outright futures position. It is possible to experience losses on both legs of a spread trade (as in table 3.2), which can actually magnify losses.

Futures markets offer a virtually unlimited array of spread trading possibilities, from the simple to the very complex, which are beyond the scope of this book. In the next chapter we will look at the actual mechanics of futures trading, including the various order types used when trading futures, placing orders on electronic trading platforms or verbally with a broker, choosing a futures broker, and selecting computer hardware and software for your trading business.

Chapter summary

⇒ One of the primary economic functions of the futures markets is to manage price risk.

⇒ Hedging is the practice of offsetting price risk in a cash market by taking equal and opposite positions in the futures market.

⇒ Hedgers include commodity producers, commodity buyers, portfolio managers and hedge funds.

⇒ Speculators include independent traders, prop traders, managed investment funds and market makers.

⇒ Speculators aim to profit from anticipated increases or decreases in futures prices, taking on the risk that hedgers hope to avoid.

⇒ Someone who expects a futures price to increase will buy or 'go long' a futures contract. Someone who expects a futures contract to fall in price can initiate a short or sold position by selling a futures contract.

⇒ Speculative trading styles include position trading, day trading and scalping.

⇒ Technical analysis is the study of price and volume relationships to form a view on future price direction. Technical analysts use a range of technical indicators derived from the interrelationship between price, time and volume to aid in their analysis.

⟹ Fundamental analysis involves detailed analysis of the underlying fundamentals that might bring about change in supply and demand, in an attempt to determine how this will impact on price.

⟹ Spreading involves simultaneously buying one futures contract and selling another, with the aim of profiting from any expected change in the price relationship between the two.

⟹ In a calendar spread, the trader seeks to take advantage of price differences between two delivery months of the same futures contract.

chapter 4

Trading mechanics

We now know what futures are and understand the important aspects of a futures contract, understand the role of hedgers and speculators, and the concepts involved in buying and selling futures in order to generate a profit. In this chapter we will look at the actual mechanics of placing trades, as well as order types, broker selection and the trading process.

Trading futures contracts — long and short

One of the key attributes of futures trading is that it allows us to sell short in expectation of further price falls as well as to buy long in expectation of further price rises. So we may open a trade by *selling* to enter the market (going short) just as readily as we open a trade by buying to enter the market (going long). Similarly, we do not always sell to close trades, as exiting a short position involves *buying* to close the trade. Grasping the concept of short selling is important, as it allows the trader to participate in trades in a variety of market conditions. You are no longer restricted to buying in anticipation of further price rises in an uptrending market, because you can also actively participate in downtrending markets by selling short in the expectation of further price falls. (The concept of short selling was introduced in chapter 3.)

Tip

In futures trading it matters little if a market is in an uptrend or a downtrend; what matters is that you have the necessary skills and confidence to trade any market in either direction.

Understanding the concept of short selling and being able to undertake short trades confidently will open up fantastic profit-making opportunities. Markets do not always go up and can spend significant periods of time declining, providing trading opportunities during these downtrending periods. Having spent a considerable time increasing in price, markets can very often decline much faster, and such falls can be very sharp. Knowing how to benefit from these opportunities can significantly enhance your trading and profit-making potential.

Figure 4.1 shows a chart of the natural gas futures market in a downtrend providing some ideal opportunities to profit by shorting the market—selling at a high price and buying back for a profit to offset the trade when price declines.

Figure 4.2 shows a steady uptrend followed by a steep downtrend in the price of orange juice. The market had risen from around 100 cents per pound to more than 200 cents per pound over a period of 24 months. The decline from 200 back to 100 took just over four months.

Figure 4.1: natural gas downtrend

Source: Trade Navigator / Genesis Financial Technologies Inc.

Figure 4.2: weekly orange juice

Source: Trade Navigator / Genesis Financial Technologies Inc.

There are also plenty of opportunities to trade the long side of the market. Figure 4.3 (overleaf) is a chart of 10-year notes in an uptrend providing some ideal opportunities to profit by going long in this market—buying at a low price and selling out of the position for a profit to offset the trade when the price increases.

Figure 4.3: 10-year notes uptrend

Source: Trade Navigator / Genesis Financial Technologies Inc.

Order types

Competency with the various order types that apply to the futures markets is an essential skill to acquire and master for those wanting to participate in these markets. In a fast-moving market with rapidly changing prices, understanding which order type is appropriate and when to place that order is crucial to the successful trading of futures contracts. Correct order placement saves time, effort and money, and will let you engage the market with confidence.

Every trade is made up of at least two orders—one to enter and one to exit the trade. If a trade is entered with a buy order (to go long), then it will be closed or exited with a sell order—for either a profit or a loss. If a trade is entered or opened with a sell order (to go short), then it will be closed with a buy order—for either a profit or a loss. Traders can use a range of different order types in various combinations.

Tip

These order types apply regardless of whether you are placing your orders verbally through your broker or executing your own trades through the use of an online trading platform.

Orders fall into two categories—*market orders*, which are intended to trade immediately, and *limit orders* and *stop orders*, which are standing orders to trade when certain conditions are met.

Market orders

A market order, also referred to as an 'at best' order, is an order to buy or sell at the current market price. It will result in a trade being filled immediately at the best price possible. If you are buying at market you are prepared to pay the price being offered by the lowest seller. This is referred to as 'hitting the offer'. If you are selling at market you are prepared to accept the current highest bid or buy price. This is referred to as 'hitting the bid'. In a fast-moving market the price you receive for your 'at market' order may differ from the price you see on your computer screen or the price your broker quotes you. By the time the order is placed and sent through to the market, prices may have moved, resulting in a different 'fill' price for your order.

Tip

Market orders trade immediately and unconditionally at either the current market price or the next available market price.

In figure 4.4 (overleaf) you can see that the bid price (the price at which we could sell at market) for crude oil is 87.43, while the offer price (the price at which we could buy at market) is 87.46. A market order to buy would be filled at 87.46. A market order to sell would be filled at 87.43.

Figure 4.4: crude oil bid and offer at market

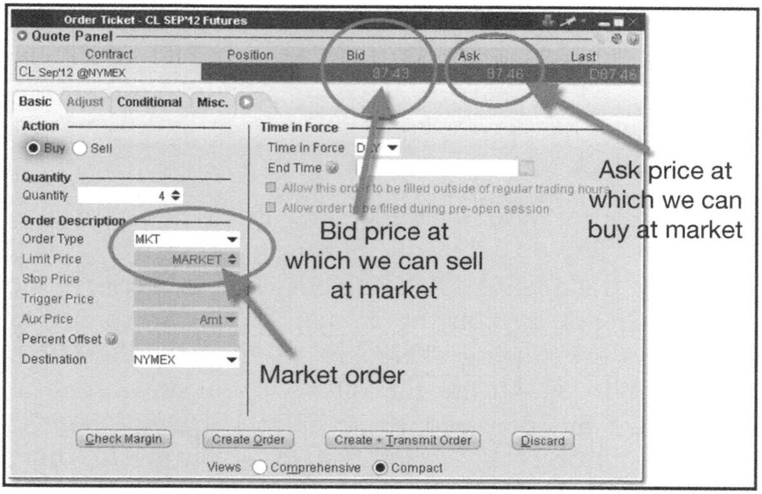

Source: Interactive Brokers LLC.

Tip

It is important to remember that we may open a trade by selling at market (going short) just as easily as we may open a trade by buying at market (going long), and that we are not always selling to close a trade, as exiting a short position involves a buy order to close the trade.

Market on close (MOC)

Market on close orders will be filled during the final moments of trading—usually within the last 30 seconds—at whatever price is available.

Market on open (MOO)

Market on open orders will be filled during the opening range of trading—usually within the first 30 seconds—at the best price available. Not all exchanges recognise MOO orders.

Limit orders for trade entry

Limit orders are designed to execute a trade at some time in the future if a certain price condition is met. Limit orders are used to enter long trades below the current market price or short trades above the current market price. Since the market may not trade at the designated limit price, these orders may not always be filled.

Using our crude oil example again, with the market trading at 87.46, a buy limit order could be placed, for example at 87.25, as shown in figure 4.5 (overleaf). This means the price would have to fall back by 0.21 (87.46 − 87.25 = 0.21) to reach the desired entry price. Once crude oil trades at 87.25 the trade would be executed and you would now be long at this price. If the price of crude oil continues to rise, and the price doesn't pull back to the limit price at 87.25, the order will not be filled and the trade entry will be missed.

Tip

A limit order to buy to enter a trade will always trigger from above, as it requires the price to fall to the limit you have set before the trade will be entered.

Similarly, a sell limit could be used to enter the market to the short side. With the market trading at 87.40, a sell limit order could be placed, for example, at 87.75, as shown in figure 4.6 (overleaf). This means the price would have to rise by 0.35 (87.75 − 87.40 = 0.35) to reach the desired entry price. Once crude oil trades at 87.75 the trade would be executed and you would now be short at this price. If the price of crude oil continues to fall, and the price doesn't move up to the limit price at 87.75, the order will not be filled and the trade entry will be missed.

Tip

A limit order to sell to enter a trade will always trigger from below, as it requires the price to rise to the limit you have set before the trade will be entered.

Figure 4.5: buying to enter with a limit order

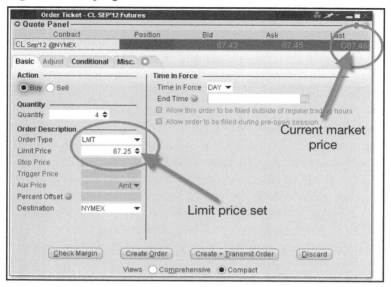

Source: Interactive Brokers LLC.

Figure 4.6: selling to enter with a limit order

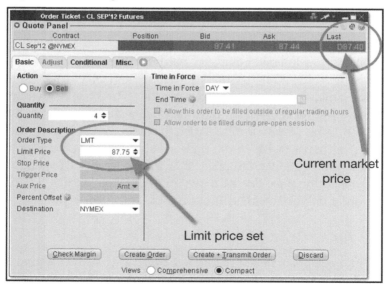

Source: Interactive Brokers LLC.

Stop orders for trade entry

Like limit orders, stop or 'on stop' orders are used to execute a trade at some point in the future when a certain price condition is met. Whereas limit orders are used to enter a long trade if price falls, and to enter a short trade if price rises, stop orders do exactly the opposite: buy stop orders are used to enter a long trade as price rises and sell stop orders are used to enter a short trade as price falls. Once the stop price is touched, the order is treated like a market order and will be filled at the next available price.

> *Tip*
>
> *Stop entry orders are used to enter long trades above the current market price or short trades below the current market price.*

Using our crude oil example again, with the market trading at 87.46 a buy stop order could be placed, for example, at 87.75, as shown in figure 4.7 (overleaf). This means the price would have to rise by 0.29 (87.75 − 87.46 = 0.29) to reach the desired entry price. Once crude oil trades at 87.75 the order becomes a market order and the trade would be executed at the next available price. In most cases the use of a stop entry order will result in trades being filled at the specified entry level. Sometimes though, in fast-moving markets or 'thin' markets with low volume and/or poor liquidity, fill prices may be higher than the specified price. This is referred to as 'slippage'.

> *Tip*
>
> *A buy stop order to enter a long trade will always trigger from below, as it requires the price to rise to the specified stop price you have set before the trade will be entered.*

Figure 4.7: buying to enter with a stop order

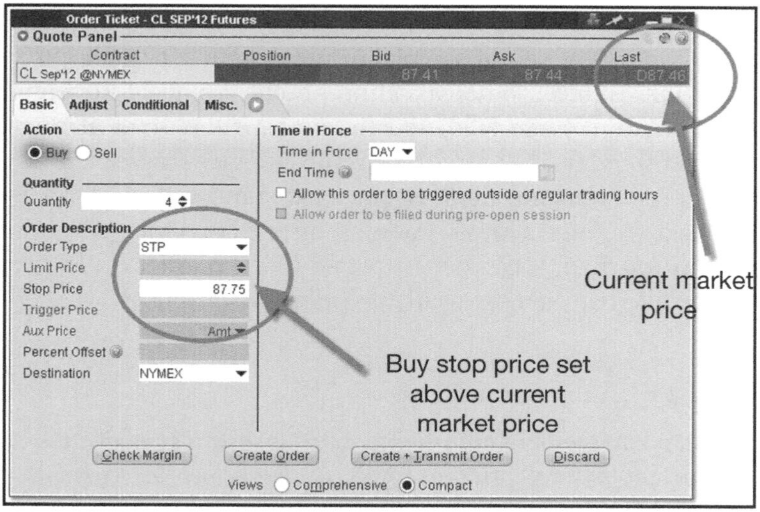

Source: Interactive Brokers LLC.

Similarly, a sell stop could be used to enter the market to the short side. With the market trading at 87.39 a sell stop order could be placed, for example, at 87.25, as shown in figure 4.8. This means the price would have to fall by 0.14 (87.39 − 87.25 = 0.14) to reach the desired entry price. Once crude oil trades at 87.25 the order becomes a market order and the trade would be executed at the next available price.

Tip

A sell stop order to enter a short trade will always trigger from above, as it requires the price to fall to the specified stop price you have set before the trade will be entered.

Figure 4.8: selling to enter with a stop order

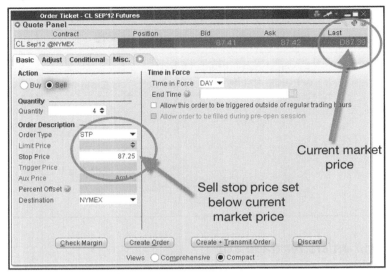

Source: Interactive Brokers LLC.

The placement of buy limit and buy stop orders to enter a trade is shown diagrammatically in figure 4.9.

Figure 4.9: buy limit and buy stop entry orders

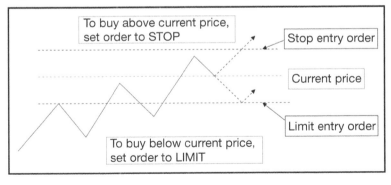

The placement of sell limit and sell stop orders to enter a trade is shown diagrammatically in figure 4.10.

Figure 4.10: sell limit and sell stop entry orders

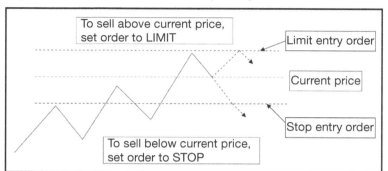

To sell above current price, set order to LIMIT

Limit entry order

Current price

Stop entry order

To sell below current price, set order to STOP

Limit orders for trade exit

Limit orders are also used to exit trades at a designated price or profit target. For long trades this is above the entry price once the trade has been entered. For short trades this is below the entry price once the trade has been entered. Limit orders to exit existing trades are also referred to as 'profit targets' or targets. They allow traders to place their desired profit target or trade exit with their broker or on their trading platform at this predefined level. The use of limit orders to exit profitable trades eliminates the need to watch the screen and then have to exit the trade by manually placing a market order when the desired exit price is met.

Using our crude oil example again, and assuming we have entered a long trade at 87.46 and have decided on a profit target of 87.75, a sell limit order would be placed at 87.75, as shown in figure 4.11. This means the price would have to rise by 0.29 (87.75 − 87.46 = 0.29) to reach the desired exit price. Once crude oil trades at 87.75 the trade would be executed and you would exit the long trade for a profit of 0.29 points, or $290.00 less brokerage and costs.

Figure 4.11: sell limit order to exit a long trade

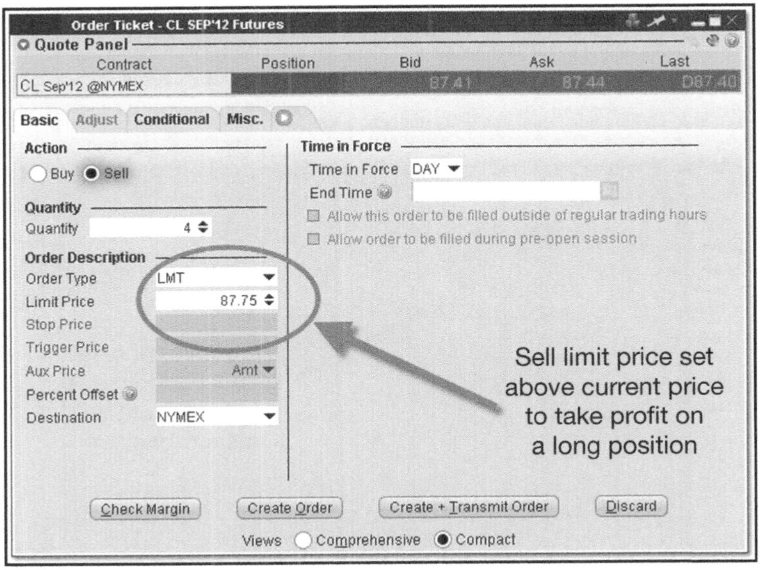

Source: Interactive Brokers LLC.

Similarly, a buy limit order could be used to exit an existing short trade at a predefined profit target. Assuming we have entered a short trade in crude oil at, say, 87.40 and have decided on a profit target at 87.25, a buy limit order would be placed at 87.25, as shown in figure 4.12 (overleaf). This means the price would have to fall by 0.15 (87.40 − 87.25 = 0.15) to reach the desired exit price. Once crude oil trades at 87.25 the trade would be executed and you would exit the short trade for a profit of 0.15 points, or $150.00 less brokerage and costs.

Tip

A limit order to buy to exit an existing short trade will always trigger from above, as it requires the price to fall to the limit you have set before the trade will be exited.

Figure 4.12: buy limit order to exit a short trade

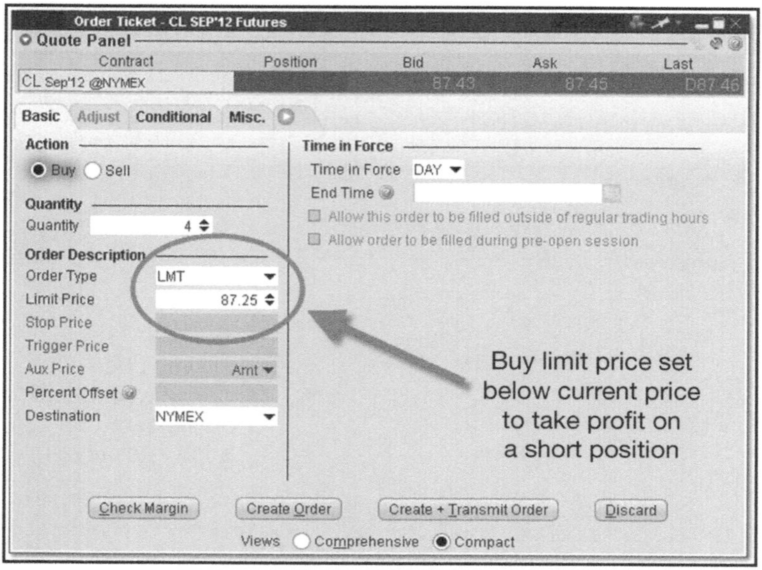

Source: Interactive Brokers LLC.

Stop orders for trade exit

Like limit orders, stop or 'on stop' orders are used to exit a trade at some point in the future when a certain price condition is met. Whereas limit orders are used to exit a long trade at a predefined profit target price when the price rises and to exit a short trade at a predefined profit target price when the price falls, stop orders do exactly the opposite: buy stop orders are used to exit a long trade if the price falls and sell stop orders are used to exit a short trade if the price rises. Once the stop price is touched, the order is treated like a market order and will be filled at the next available price. In this context they are called 'stop-loss' orders, as they are set at a predefined price at which you will exit a losing trade according to your risk management and money management rules. Stop-loss orders are used to exit losing trades. They are a trader's protection mechanism to aid the preservation of trading capital, to limit the amount lost to predetermined and predefined levels, and to ensure losing trades don't spiral out of control. Stop-loss orders work hand in hand with the trading mantra of 'letting profits run and cutting losses': by using them in all trades, predefined loss levels are placed into the market, which reduces the emotional attachment to the outcome of the trade and the need to constantly monitor any open position.

Tip

Stop exit or stop-loss orders are used to exit long trades below the current market price or short trades above the current market price.

Referring again to our crude oil example, and assuming we have entered a long trade at 87.46 and have decided on a stop-loss at 87.25, a sell stop order would be placed at 87.25, as shown in figure 4.13 (overleaf). This means if the price falls by 0.21 (87.46 − 87.25 = 0.21) to 87.25 the stop-loss order would be triggered. Once crude oil trades at 87.25 the order becomes a market order and would be filled at the next available price.

Tip

A stop order to sell to exit an existing long trade (stop-loss) will always trigger from above, as it requires the price to fall to the stop price you have set before the trade will be exited.

Figure 4.13: sell stop order to exit an existing long trade

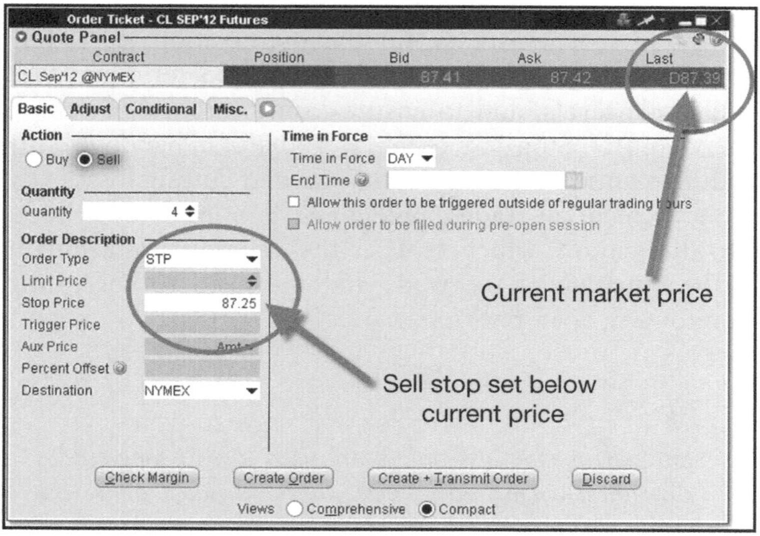

Source: Interactive Brokers LLC.

Similarly, a buy stop order can be used as a stop-loss to exit an existing short trade at a predefined loss level. Assuming we have entered a short trade in crude oil at, say, 87.46 and have decided on a stop-loss at 87.75, a buy stop order would be placed at 87.75, as shown in figure 4.14. This means if the price rises by 0.29 (87.75 − 87.46 = 0.29) the stop-loss order would be triggered. Once crude oil trades at 87.75 the trade would become a market order and would be filled at the next available price.

> *Tip*
>
> *A stop order to buy to exit an existing short trade (stop-loss) will always trigger from below, as it requires the price to rise to the stop price you have set before the trade will be exited.*

Figure 4.14: buy stop order to exit an existing short trade

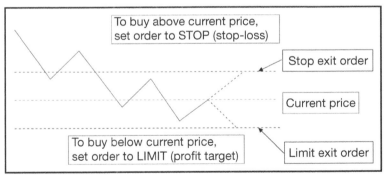

Source: Interactive Brokers LLC.

The placement of buy limit and buy stop orders to exit an existing short trade is shown diagrammatically in figure 4.15.

Figure 4.15: buy limit and buy stop orders to exit an existing short position

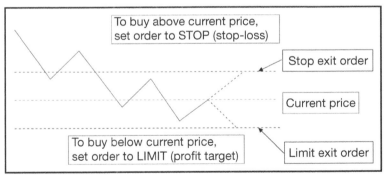

The placement of sell limit and sell stop orders to exit an existing long trade is shown diagrammatically in figure 4.16 (overleaf).

Figure 4.16: sell limit and sell stop orders to exit an existing long position

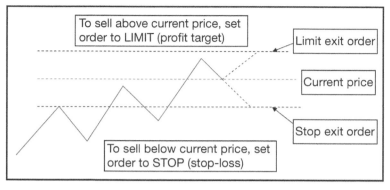

Using stop orders as trailing stops

Once you have entered a trade, stop orders are initially used as stop-loss orders as described, and act as a capital protection mechanism, ensuring that losing trades are closed out at a predefined maximum loss level. Stop orders are also used to protect profits once a trade has moved into profit. Primarily the domain of trend followers, the stop order is trailed along underneath a long trade and above a short trade as the trade moves with the trend of the market. By using stops in this way, the trend follower aims to capture large trend moves, continually 'locking in' profits as the trade moves in their favour. Eventually the trend will reverse and the trade will be stopped out, but with a large portion of the profit still intact. Figure 4.17 shows an example of a trailing stop in action. As the price declines, the trailing stop (shown as the thick line above the price bars) moves down according to the defined parameters, allowing profit in the trade to be protected. Eventually the downtrend ends, price reverses back up through the trailing stop level, and the trade is exited.

Figure 4.17: trailing stop

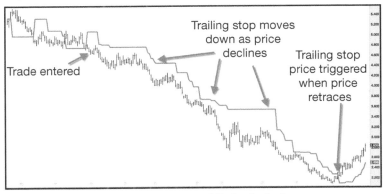

Source: Trade Navigator / Genesis Financial Technologies Inc.

Slippage

In most cases the use of a stop order will result in trades being filled at the specified price level. In fast-moving markets or 'thin' markets with low volume and/or poor liquidity, there may not be an opportunity to execute the order at the specified stop price, and the next available price at which the order can be filled may be significantly different from the specified price. This is referred to as 'slippage' or 'slip'. The upside of slippage when using stop orders as a stop-loss is that at least you are able to exit the trade somewhere near the price specified and not suffer as great a loss as you would if you had no protection mechanism in place. The upside of slippage when using a stop order to enter a trade is that it may mean it is a healthy start to the trade continuing to move in the anticipated direction.

Tip

The reality of trading futures is that slippage will occur—it is part and parcel of the business we have chosen to be involved in.

The chart shown in figure 4.18 is an example of price slippage occurring in the corn market. Stop orders working around the price indicated (around 586 cents per bushel) would have been filled at a much higher price when the market experienced a huge gap (at 621 cents per bushel). This is a difference of 35 cents per bushel, or $1750 per contract (35 cents per bushel × $50 per 1 cent). Traders who were short corn and working a stop exit order would have experienced a much greater loss per contract than they were expecting as a result of this price gap. On the other hand, traders wanting to buy corn and working a stop entry order would have experienced a significantly worse fill than they were expecting for their trade entry.

Figure 4.18: price slippage in corn market

Source: Trade Navigator / Genesis Financial Technologies Inc.

Price slippage can also occur in fast-moving markets when it is simply not possible to fill an order quickly enough owing to the speed at which the market and prices are moving.

The move to electronic markets that are open for much longer periods of time has reduced the incidence of large price gaps and the associated slippage that can occur between when a market closes and when it reopens, particularly if a significant event or market announcement has occurred while the market is closed. With markets open for longer and more market-sensitive information now available to more market participants through the internet and other forms of electronic media, the ability of the floor traders to manipulate prices is now virtually a thing of the past. Price discovery is a much more sophisticated and informed process as a result of these technological advances. Price gaps and slippage can still occur, though, as seen in the soybean price chart of July 2012 in figure 4.19. Typically, these moves occur after a weekend or holiday period—as in this example, where the first gap occurs between the close on Friday and the open the following Monday, and the second gap occurs between the close on Tuesday before a holiday on Wednesday and the market's reopening on Thursday morning.

Figure 4.19: price gaps in July 2012 soybean market

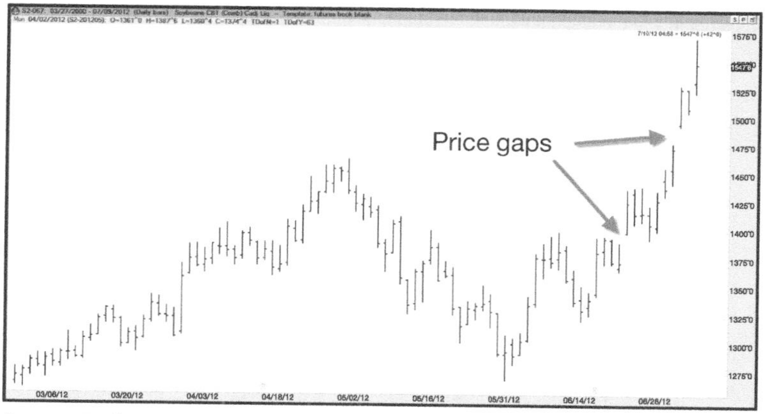

Source: Trade Navigator / Genesis Financial Technologies Inc.

Lock-limit

In markets that utilise a maximum daily price limit, it is possible that trading can cease when the market reaches this daily price limit. This is known as a 'lock-limit' market (also covered in chapter 2). When a market is lock-limit, no further trading is allowed. It is also possible that underlying conditions may give rise to extreme price pressure that results in a market being lock-limit for more than one day. This can mean significant losses, as it is impossible to liquidate a losing position, and it may cause serious damage to your trading account. Once again, improvements in price discovery and order flow as a result of the use of electronic markets, coupled with the removal of maximum daily price limits on the delivery or front-month contracts, have reduced the incidence of lock-limit markets, but they can potentially still occur.

Figure 4.20 shows a market being lock-limit for several days in a row. This is a chart of coffee way back in 1977. While it is not relevant to traders today, it does serve to show the potential for damage when a market 'locks' for several days in a row. In this example, coffee was lock-limit for six days in a row, traded freely for five days and was then lock-limit again for another five days.

Figure 4.20: coffee market at lock-limit

Source: Trade Navigator / Genesis Financial Technologies Inc.

Stop limit orders

A stop limit entry order contains two prices. The aim is to gain more control over the price at which a stop order is filled. In the event of a large price gap or a fast-moving market that could result in a large amount of slippage, a stop limit order will specify the amount over a buy stop and under a sell stop that you are willing to accept. A stop limit order indicates that once the stop price is triggered, you do not want your order filled beyond the limit you have set.

Figure 4.21 shows an example of a buy stop limit order in gold futures. With the market trading at 1592.00, a buy stop entry order is placed at 1595.00, three points above the current price. A limit of 1595.50 is also set. This means that if the price of gold reaches 1595.00, the buy stop order will become active up to a maximum price of 1595.50. In this way we have set the maximum amount of slippage that we will be prepared to accept on our buy stop order. If the price moves quickly through this price or gaps over 1595.50, the buy stop order will not be filled.

Figure 4.21: buy stop limit order

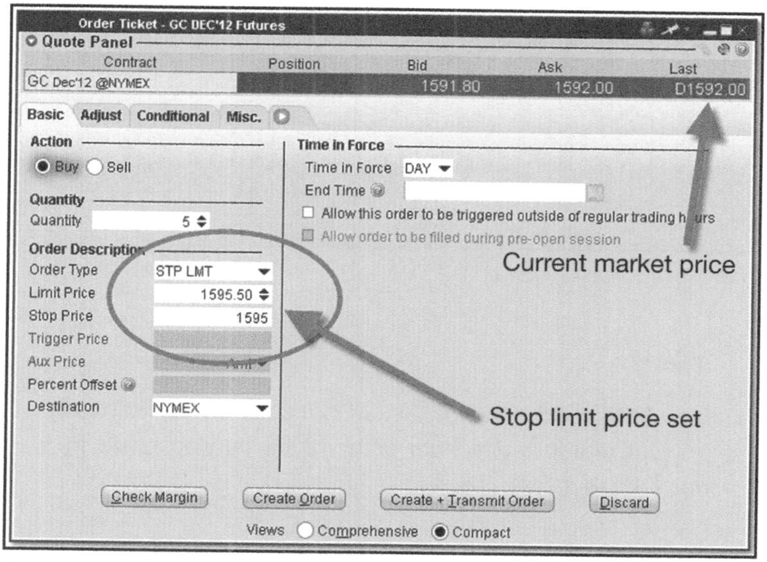

Source: Interactive Brokers LLC.

Figure 4.22 shows an example of a sell stop limit order in gold futures. With the market trading at 1592.00, a sell stop entry order is placed at 1585.00, seven points below the current price. A limit of 1584.50 is also set. This means that if the price of gold reaches 1585.00, the sell stop order will become active up to a maximum price of 1584.50. In this way we have set the maximum amount of slippage we will be prepared to accept on our sell stop order. If the price moves quickly through this price or gaps over 1584.50, the sell stop order will not be filled.

Figure 4.22: sell stop limit order

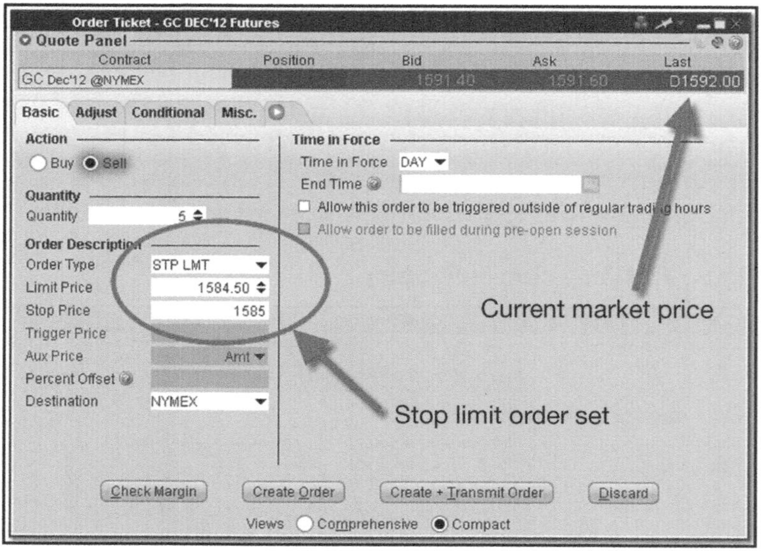

Source: Interactive Brokers LLC.

Tip

Stop limit orders are not used to exit positions as they could prevent a stop order from being filled, only to result in a much greater loss.

Order cancels order, or one cancels other (OCO)

Also referred to as linked orders, OCOs allow us to bracket our orders so our entry order, the stop loss and the profit target are all placed at the same time. An OCO means that once the trade entry is filled the stop-loss and profit target (limit order) are active in the market, waiting for the specified price condition to be met. When one of these orders is filled, the other order is automatically cancelled. The OCO legs, or trades, become active only when the initial entry order is filled.

OCO orders are a powerful tool for futures traders for a number of reasons. They allow maximum loss levels to be set via the use of the stop-loss function. They allow profit targets to be set via the use of the limit order, thus ensuring that when the target is reached it will become active in the market, which alleviates the need to watch the market in order to exit trades. They also reduce the emotional need to constantly watch the market. The order is simply placed in the market and then left to its own devices. The stop-loss can be adjusted as the trade moves in the intended direction, but the profit target should never be altered.

Figure 4.23 (overleaf) shows a buy OCO order in the corn market. In this example the stop entry order to buy long is placed at 725.00, above the current bid/offer of 717.00/717.50. For the buy stop entry order to become active, corn would need to rally up to this price. Once the entry order is triggered, the trader is working a stop-loss order to sell at 715.00, 10 points below the entry price of 725.00 (725.00 − 715.00 = 10.00), and a limit order to sell to take profit at 740.00, 15 points above the entry price (740.00 − 725.00 = 15.00). If the price of corn were to fall back to 715.00, the trade would automatically be stopped out for a 10-point loss, and the limit order to sell at 740.00 would be automatically cancelled. If the price of corn were to rally up to 740.00, the trade would automatically be closed out at 740.00 for a 15-point profit, and the stop order to sell at 715.00 would be automatically cancelled.

Figure 4.23: buy OCO order

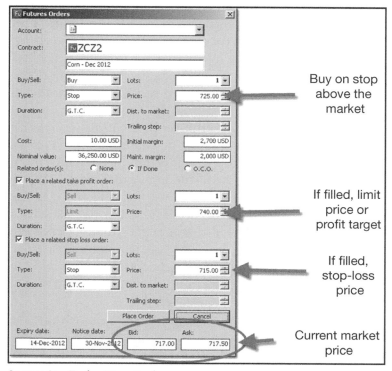

Source: SaxoTrader / Saxo Bank.

Figure 4.24 illustrates placing a sell OCO order in the corn market. In this example the stop entry order to sell short is placed at 710.00, below the current bid/offer of 717.00/717.25. For the sell stop entry order to become active, corn would need to fall to this price. Once the entry order is triggered, the trader is working a stop-loss order to buy back at 725.00, 15 points above the entry price of 710.00 (725.00 − 710.00 = 15.00), and a limit order to buy to take profit at 690.00, 20 points below the entry price (710.00 − 690.00 = 20.00). If the price of corn were to rally to 725.00, the trade would automatically be stopped out for a 15-point loss, and the limit order to buy at 690.00 would automatically be cancelled. If the price of corn were to fall to 690.00, the trade would automatically be closed out at 690.00 for a 20-point profit, and the stop order to buy at 725.00 would automatically be cancelled.

Figure 4.24: sell OCO order

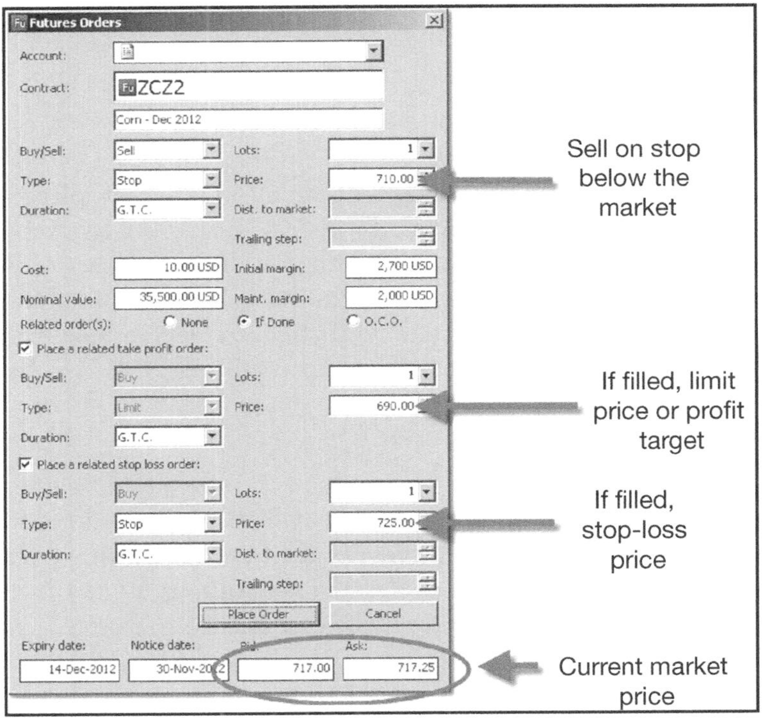

Source: SaxoTrader / Saxo Bank.

Good until cancelled (GTC)

Used in conjunction with stop orders and limit orders, GTC means the order will remain valid until it is cancelled. GTCs are used when a trader may want entry at a specified price within a certain time period. If the trade is not entered it must be manually cancelled. It is handy to make notes about the placement of GTC orders, as if they are forgotten you may inadvertently find yourself in a trade at some point in the future because you forgot to cancel a previously placed GTC order!

Tip

GTC orders do not cancel automatically; they must be cancelled manually.

The use of GTC orders can be seen in figure 4.24 on p. 93, where the stop and limit orders of the OCO order are placed GTC. Once the trade is entered the OCO orders are working until such time as either side is filled (when the other will automatically be cancelled), or the levels are amended or changed. If the original trade entry requirement is not met and the trade is cancelled, then the OCO legs will also be cancelled automatically.

Good for day, or day order

If a trade is not specified as GTC it will be considered a day order and will remain valid only for the trading day on which it is placed in the market. If the trade conditions are not met on that day, it will automatically be cancelled.

Good all markets (GAM)

With the advent of electronic trading it is now important to place GAM orders so they are working in both pit hours and on the electronic market. While this is a bit of a hangover from the years when markets were making the transition from pit-only trade execution during floor trading hours to two separate trading sessions that involved the floor session and then an after-market electronic session, it is still important to check to make sure all orders are working across all markets. The vast majority of markets now offer side-by-side trading, which means the electronic market is trading simultaneously with the floor session, and electronic platforms default to the electronic market — so orders are virtually always assumed to be working GAM, but it still pays to check.

Tip

The big S&P 500 futures market is currently one of the only markets that still runs two separate trading sessions. While the floor trading session is active there is no electronic platform trading; when floor trading ceases the electronic market reopens after a short break. Traders in this market need to ensure that their orders are working GAM.

Iceberg orders

Any market participant with a large order to buy or sell can divide their order into smaller parcels so only a small portion of the total can be seen at any one time — just as the tip of an iceberg suggests a much larger mass of ice beneath the surface. Iceberg orders can be used whenever a large order at a particular price may be enough to move the market or to cause price slippage to occur. By using an iceberg order the trader can gradually enter or exit the position at or near the specified price without influencing the market via one large order quantity.

Figure 4.25 (overleaf) is an example of an iceberg buy limit order for 50 contracts of platinum. The platinum market could easily be moved with an order for 50 contracts if they were all placed at the one time. To avoid this, an iceberg order to feed in five contracts at a time is created. With the market currently trading at 1513.0, the order is to buy 50 contracts at a limit of 1512.0, one point under the current market price.

Figure 4.25: iceberg order

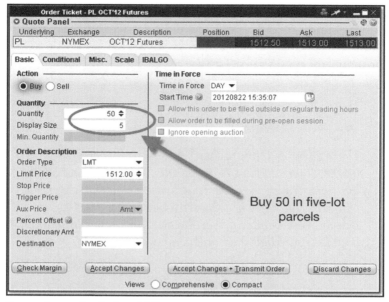

Source: Interactive Brokers LLC.

Placing an order verbally

While many traders will place their orders independently via online trading platforms such as the three we have shown in the preceding examples, many may still wish to place orders verbally with their chosen futures broker. When speaking with a broker it is important to use clear and concise terminology and to ensure you use the correct orders for trade placement and order execution. Most brokers will be patient and guide you through the process at the outset, but the more you know and understand before placing your first few orders, the better it will be for both of you. There will be times when your broker is extremely busy, or when a market price is close to your entry requirements, so speed and clarity will be very important.

Referring back to the corn futures long entry OCO trade in figure 4.23 on p. 92, let's now look at how we would place an order verbally with a broker. Let's assume that it is August 2012 and we have decided to go long (buy) one contract. The front month is December, which has the symbol Z. The current price is bid 717.00 cents per bushel, offer 717.50 cents per bushel. We wish to buy into a rising market when the price reaches 725.00 cents per bushel. Our trading strategy dictates a profit target at 15.00 cents above the entry price. Our risk management rules dictate a stop-loss 10.00 cents under the entry price, or $500.00 (10.00 cents per bushel at $50.00 per 1 cent).

The verbal order to our broker would therefore be:

BUY 1 December 2012 Corn contract at 725.00 ON STOP. If filled sell 1 at 715.00 On Stop OCO sell 1 at 725.00 Limit GTC GAM.

Similarly, if we wished to place a sell order to enter a short trade in expectation of a further price fall, as shown in figure 4.24 on p. 93, our verbal order would read:

SELL 1 December 2012 Corn contract at 710.00 On Stop. If filled buy 1 at 725.00 On Stop OCO buy 1 at 690.00 Limit GTC GAM.

Choosing a broker

You can place trades with a broker by phoning or emailing your order instructions, or you can place them yourself via an online trading platform. Either way, you will first need to open an account by completing the necessary paperwork, and depositing funds into your account for use as a margin when you open positions. Brokers charge a fee for executing trades when you buy and sell futures contracts.

Electronic trading via the internet is considerably cheaper than using a traditional voice broker, but you need to be confident that you can place orders competently and quickly yourself. Electronic trading has 'levelled the playing field' for retail traders, as transactions can be executed in a transparent environment where market makers and floor traders can no longer use inside knowledge to manipulate price, front-run large orders or hold back small orders.

Finding a broker you can work with is an essential part of becoming a successful futures trader, as they are an important link between you and the global financial markets on which you will be trading. Your broker is an integral part of your trading business and will become an important part of your team if you stick at it for a long time. It may take a few attempts to find the 'right' broker for you, but moving from one to another is not a complex or onerous task today. In short, if you don't like the one you have, or they can't provide the service or technology you need or expect, change to one who does!

If you have your own trading software and strategies and are computer and technology savvy, then a cheap online low-service broker may meet all your needs. Alternatively, you might prefer the services of a broker who will take your orders verbally, execute your trades and provide you with a higher level of service, for which you will pay higher commissions.

Here are some of the points you may wish to consider when choosing your futures broker:

⇒ *the level of service you require*. Are you confident placing your orders yourself on an electronic trading platform, or do you prefer a broker to place them for you according to your instructions?

⇒ *the quality and ease of use of the electronic platform if you are self-executing your trades*. Trading platforms should be user-friendly and easy to navigate. A platform that is difficult to use may put you at a disadvantage when you are placing orders in a pressure situation.

⇒ *the quality of the people involved*. Are the staff helpful, courteous and professional, or are they a band of 'young guns' with huge egos who can't really be bothered with your orders? It may sound trivial but if you are going to develop a long-term relationship with your broker, it needs to be with someone you can communicate with comfortably at all levels.

⇒ *do they provide a 24-hour service?* This may be important if you are placing trades verbally and need the services of a broker outside regular market hours. It may also be important to those trading online if they suffer a computer or internet malfunction and need a broker to access trades on their online platform.

⇒ *order types*. Will the broker accept and 'work' the order types you need to use? This may include price-specific orders, time-specific orders or orders that require certain conditions to be met before they are placed.

⇒ *account size and balance*. Does the broker require a minimum account size?

⇒ *trade size*. Are there minimum or maximum order sizes they will accept?

⇒ *available markets*. Does the broker have access to all the markets and all the exchanges on which you want to trade?

⇒ *brokerage rates*. While cheap brokerage means lower costs for you, the cheapest brokerage rate is not always the best option. Cheap rates may indicate a much lower level of service, restricted market access, no after-hours service and poor trade execution. If poor trade execution or a missed order results in a loss of $500 of your money, but you saved $5 on brokerage, you might begin to think that the equation doesn't really add up! 'You pay peanuts, you get monkeys.'

⇒ *how your money is held.* Is it in a client-segregated account or pooled with the company's funds in one account? The rules on client fund segregation vary from country to country, so you may wish to check the rules to ensure you are happy with the way your trading funds are held.

⇒ *account reporting.* Are your trading statements and other reports easy to access and understand, and is the information freely available from the broker when you request it?

Hardware, software and data providers

Your choice of computer equipment will depend to a large extent on your choice of order placement method. Traders using end-of-day data and placing orders with a voice broker will need much less sophisticated equipment than those trading short term and firing orders into the market from their own computer. In order to confidently execute trades via the internet it is essential to have high-quality equipment and software to ensure fast and efficient market access and order execution.

A high-speed, reliable internet connection is essential, as is a fast and reliable computer. Ideally, for short-term and intraday traders, this computer should be dedicated to trading. Use another computer for emails, web browsing, data storage and so on. Your trade execution platform, which provides live prices and quotes, must also be fast and reliable.

Market analysis, chart studies, system design and back testing are all carried out on charting software programs designed specifically for these purposes. It is essential that this software analysis program is reliable, provides you with a range of indicators and analysis techniques, and allows you to design and test your own trading strategies across a wide range of markets. My choice is Trade Navigator from Genesis Financial Technologies. A 30-day free trial is available for download at www.genesisft.com/landing.php?v=webwisdom.

> ### Tip
>
> *Futures trading exposes you to a true global economy that, with the use of robust trading strategies and sound risk management and money management, can provide great opportunities and returns for the disciplined and consistent trader. In the words of Michelangelo, 'The greatest danger for most of us lies not in setting our aim too high and falling short; but in setting our aim too low, and achieving our mark'.*

In the next chapter we will take a look at money management for futures traders. As with all trading endeavours, managing risk is the key to long-term success. Inappropriate use of the leverage available in the futures markets will result in the destruction of your trading account. Knowing how to use leverage and other money management tools is paramount to your success as a futures trader.

Chapter summary

⇒ A key attribute of futures trading is that it allows us to sell short in expectation of further price falls as well as to buy long in expectation of further price rises.

⇒ Understanding the concept of short selling opens up great profit-making opportunities.

⇒ Orders fall into two categories — *market orders*, which trade immediately at best current price, and *limit orders* and *stop orders*, which trade when certain price conditions are met.

⇒ Stop orders are used to limit losses on losing trades and protect profits once a trade has moved into profit.

⇒ In fast-moving or 'thin' markets, when orders are not executed at the specified stop price some slippage is inevitable, although more sophisticated electronic markets have reduced this problem.

⇒ In markets that utilise a maximum daily price limit, trading can cease when this daily price limit is reached. This is known as a 'lock-limit' market. When a market is lock-limit is reached, no further trading is allowed.

⇒ Limit orders are designed to execute a trade at some time in the future if a certain price condition is met. Limit orders are used to enter long trades below the current market price or short trades above the current market price.

⇒ Buy stop orders are used to enter a long trade as price rises; sell stop orders are used to enter a short trade as price falls.

⇒ A stop limit entry order contains two prices, indicating that once the stop price is triggered you do not want the order to be filled beyond the limit you have set.

⇒ OCOs allow us to bracket our orders so our entry order, the stop-loss and the profit target are all placed at the same time. Once the trade entry is filled the stop-loss and profit target (limit order) are active in the market, waiting for the specified price condition to be met. When one of these orders is filled, the other order is automatically cancelled.

⇒ Finding a broker you can work with is an essential part of becoming a successful futures trader, as your broker is an important link between you and the global financial markets on which you will be trading.

⇒ Your choice of computer equipment will depend to a large extent on your choice of order placement method.

⇒ Market analysis, chart studies, system design and back testing are all carried out on charting software programs designed specifically for these purposes.

chapter 5

Risk and money management

In previous chapters we have focused on developing an understanding of futures contracts and how they are traded. Now, in perhaps the most important chapter, we will discuss the risks and rewards associated with the futures markets, and the importance of risk and money management.

Although similar and related, these two concepts need to be understood as quite separate. Risk management involves identifying the amount of capital you are prepared to risk (lose) on a trade, placing stop-loss limits as appropriate for this maximum risk per trade, identifying the number of open positions that fit within your defined risk parameters, and addressing other factors associated with risk such as volatility and market risk. Money management concerns all factors associated with the growth of your trading account balance over time, including position sizing, deciding when to add contracts in line with increases to your capital and when to reduce the number of contracts traded in a drawdown, techniques for measuring drawdowns, and overall equity management.

Tip

All trading, regardless of the market or the specific instrument, involves risk. As either speculators or investors, we are seeking risk in order to generate profits from our trading operations. Quite simply, if we are not prepared to accept risk, we cannot expect to generate any reward.

Shares vs futures—six common fallacies

Most traders tend to start out in the sharemarket. They gravitate to the futures markets once they start to gain an appreciation of the many factors that impact on the sharemarket—factors such as prices for crude oil and other energy products, base metal prices, and the interaction and impact of currency price movements. Once their interest is piqued and they begin to notice and experience some of these effects, they start to explore futures in greater depth. Many are also drawn to futures when they come to recognise the value of trading both the long and short side of the markets with the same degree of ease, which is difficult to accomplish in the sharemarket given the impediments to short selling. (Although this issue has been addressed to some degree with the use of Contracts for Difference (CFDs), these too have their shortcomings—a topic that is beyond discussion in this book.) Many traders find they need the ability to diversify their trading across different markets and different market conditions. Restricting your trading activities to the sharemarket limits your profit-making opportunities, particularly during periods when the market is stuck in a sideways pattern or trend.

Tip

Trading futures opens up a world of opportunity to traders, and while it is essentially 'just another market', it is important to understand the differences in the underlying market structure—the actual trading mechanics—and the risks involved.

For many traders who start out trading shares, futures are perceived as risky. Many are led to believe that share trading is 'safer' and therefore the best place to start. They are encouraged to begin their trading in the sharemarket, and think that only when they have developed a level of understanding and trading experience in this market should they look to other markets such as futures and forex. This mistaken advice stems from misunderstandings in relation to a number of factors.

First is the idea that trading or investing in the sharemarket gives you something tangible (ownership of a small piece of a publicly listed company), while futures trading involves speculating on something intangible (the future price of something according to its value on paper, based on what may or may not happen before the contract expiry date). The apparent logic here is that even if you get the timing of your buying wrong and have to hang on to the shares, you will still have a tangible asset in a company. The counter-argument is that while shares in a company may appear to be tangible, their value can deteriorate significantly for those unprepared to exit losing trades promptly. Shares can and do fall to zero. Countless companies have come and gone from the sharemarket over the years, the value of their shares reduced to nothing. In recent times, post global financial crisis (GFC), there are many, many examples of companies that have declared bankruptcy and been delisted from stock exchanges around the world. There is nothing 'tangible' about these delisted companies. Futures contracts, on the other hand, are based on real things—coffee, wheat, Treasury bonds, crude oil and Aussie dollars, for example.

Tip

The underlying instrument or commodity on which a futures contract is based is real. The value may rise and fall, but it is backed by a product that cannot go bankrupt or reach zero value.

Second, the apparent value of shares in a company can also be built on 'intangibles', such as intellectual property, ideas and goodwill. Again, there are numerous examples of share-price values skyrocketing due to speculation concerning these intangibles, only to plummet once market participants realise that the claims are not supported by any real evidence or results. Figure 5.1 illustrates such an occurrence. Often rapid price increases are based on public announcements from the company or its directors. The price rise is further fuelled when speculators discover the trend and price action unfolding and decide to seize a potential profit opportunity. Unfortunately for the punters, the whole house of cards comes crashing down when the market realises that there is nothing tangible to the initial claims, and so the value of the company collapses, sometimes to zero.

Figure 5.1: ABC Learning share price collapse

Source: Beyond Charts Pty Ltd / www.beyondcharts.com.

Third, there is nothing intangible about a futures contract in wheat, platinum or 30-year Treasury bonds. The prices may rise and fall, and at times be driven by speculative trading, but the underlying products do exist and will always have some value. Unlike share prices in dubious companies, commodity price values will never go to zero. If prices fall below the cost of production, producers will shift resources to other areas or (perhaps temporarily) cease production. This, in turn, will result in a shortage of supply, causing prices to recover.

Tip

Futures prices are based on the underlying need for the commodity or instrument on which the contract is based.

The world simply cannot do without these products. The global economy needs crude oil and natural gas to fuel vehicles and industry. We need cotton for clothes, meat and wheat for food, financial futures for price risk and interest rates, and currency markets for global trade and investment. It would be a cold, hungry and diminished world without these products. On the other hand, the world could function well enough if major global companies such as Microsoft, Apple, BHP or Caterpillar went bankrupt and were delisted from the stock exchange. While their collapse might cause some inconvenience, the products they offered would quickly be supplied by other companies—and life would go on.

Fourth, there is an almost inbuilt belief in many sharemarket participants in the need to identify and buy 'good' companies. The definition of 'good' varies but tends to include such principles as 'low-risk', a 'sound' balance sheet, 'solid' management and a 'high return' on equity. These fine-sounding attributes are often spoken about without any real objective measurement. How can a value be placed on 'sound' or 'solid', and what exactly is a 'high return'? Many share traders and investors were persuaded by these depictions during the long-term bull market, or uptrend, that lasted for decades prior to the events of the GFC in 2008. The sharemarket lulled many into believing that share prices in 'blue-chip' companies would increase no matter what, and that their continuing patience would eventually be rewarded as prices steadily increased. Investors who bought into many of these 'good' companies in late 2007 are now lamenting this decision, as many such shares have decreased in value by more than 50 per cent. The chart of ASX-listed company Rio Tinto shown in figure 5.2 offers one such example.

Figure 5.2: chart of Rio Tinto

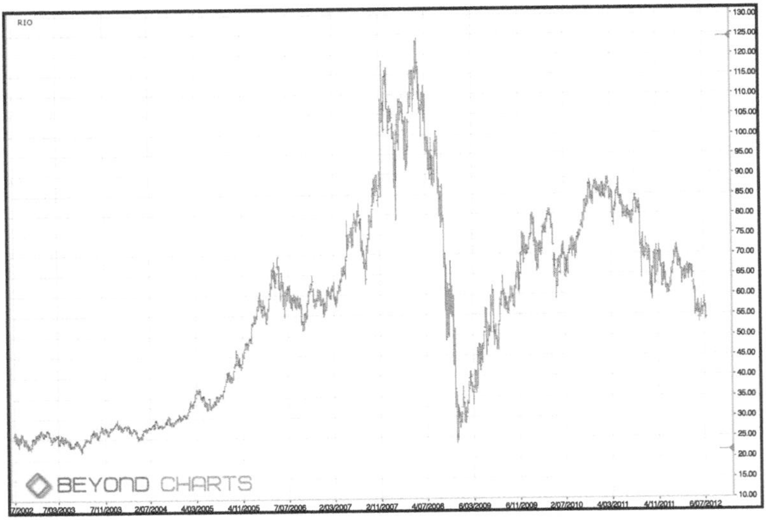

Source: Beyond Charts Pty Ltd / www.beyondcharts.com.

Tip

The reality is that sharemarket traders using the buy-and-hold approach can have their money tied up in these long-term positions for extended periods of time, during which their only return on these funds is any dividend paid by the company!

There really is no such thing as a 'good' company. There are only companies that are increasing in value, in which we need to buy shares, and companies that are falling in value, in which we either need to go short to profit from the downtrend or get out of the market while the decline occurs. Similarly, in the futures markets there isn't a 'good' commodity—it is either rising in value or falling in value. If prices are increasing, then to make a profit we need to be buyers in these uptrends. If prices are falling, then we need to be short sellers to make a profit from the downtrend. As we have noted, the ease of trading either long or short is one of the major appeals of the futures markets. Figure 5.3 shows directional moves in sugar futures—long in the uptrends and short in the downtrends.

Figure 5.3: long and short in sugar futures

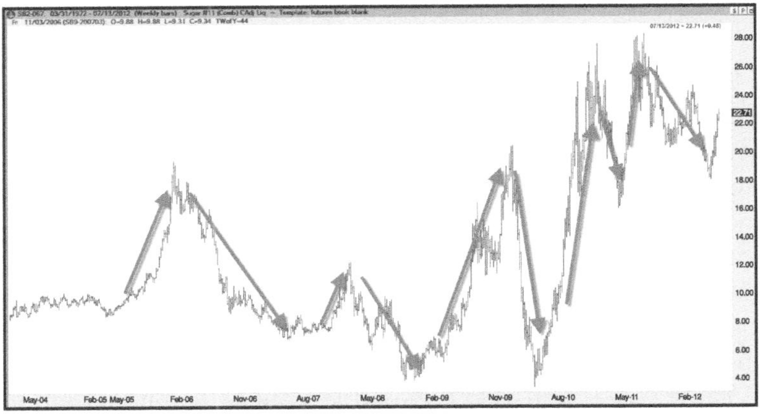

Source: Trade Navigator / Genesis Financial Technologies Inc.

Fifth, unlike prices for shares, which are often driven by emotion and sentimentality, the initial drivers of price moves in the commodity markets are real issues of supply and demand. Factors contributing to changes in the supply/ demand equilibrium, as discussed in chapter 2, are the initial reasons behind price moves in these markets. An oversupply of soybeans, for example, coupled with large carryover stock levels from the previous year and reduced current demand, will drive prices down. Once the trend begins, speculators of all types will attempt to profit from falling prices by selling short soybean futures, thus adding more selling pressure to the market and contributing to further price declines. On the other hand, a drought in the Corn Belt during the growing season that threatens to have a serious impact on production can lead to a sharp rise in prices. Once the uptrend begins speculators are drawn to the long side of the market, buying corn futures in anticipation of further price rises.

Tip

The underlying reason for the initial price moves and the development of the subsequent price trend is a change in supply and/or demand.

A sixth factor in favour of futures markets over sharemarkets is the longer periods of time that global futures markets are open for trading. Traders benefit from being able to enter and exit the market whenever it is open for trading. With almost all futures markets now traded on electronic trading platforms, typical trading hours are often in excess of 20 hours per day. Compare this with equity markets, which may be open for only six to eight hours each day. These extended trading times reduce the potential for markets to 'gap' (as discussed in chapter 4). Because the sharemarket is closed for longer than it is open, it is particularly vulnerable to price gaps. The ASX, for example, which is open from 9.50 am to 4.00 pm each weekday, is subject to massive price gaps, as it is heavily influenced by the trading action that occurs in the Northern Hemisphere markets while the ASX is closed. Such price gaps can be detrimental to stop levels and hence to traders' profitability. Arguably, these gaps can be beneficial if you are on the right side of the price move! They do, however, add considerably to the volatility and uncertainty of these markets. Figure 5.4, a chart of ASX-listed

BHP shares, clearly shows the price gaps that regularly occur in this market.

Figure 5.4: BHP gaps everywhere

Source: Beyond Charts Pty Ltd / www.beyondcharts.com.

Compare the BHP chart with one for feeder cattle, shown in figure 5.5, during the same time period. Despite being a futures contract considered notorious for price gaps, it is nothing like the chart for BHP.

Figure 5.5: feeder cattle — comparatively few gaps

Source: Trade Navigator / Genesis Financial Technologies Inc.

All the preceding points contradict the misplaced belief that futures are risky when compared with shares, and that they are too volatile and unpredictable for the 'average' trader. As in all markets, there is volatility and risk when trading futures. The key is to learn about and understand the markets, and to grow from being an 'average' trader to being an educated and informed one with a strict set of rules for engaging the market on your terms, according to your rules.

Using leverage to your advantage

Futures traders can come undone through inappropriate use of the leverage available in these markets, and it is here that the risk management and money management strategies you use will contribute most to your ultimate success or failure. As discussed in chapter 2, futures contracts are traded with the use of leverage via a margin account. With leverage you can use a relatively small amount of your own funds to control a much larger face-value position. The initial margin is the amount you must put up in order to enter a trade, either long or short. It is essentially a 'good faith' deposit that allows you to trade on a commodity exchange. Brokers may insist that clients put up a greater amount of margin than is actually required by the exchange, but they can never let their clients put up less than the minimum required by the exchange. An exchange can raise or lower these minimum margin requirements at any time. Upward changes in margin requirements generally occur only during periods of extreme volatility and/or large price movements. Once the market settles down and volatility decreases, margin requirements will be lowered.

Let's examine a hypothetical wheat trade to illustrate the workings of trading on margin. We will assume that the price of wheat is $7.05 per bushel and that the initial margin requirement is $1000.00 per 5000-bushel wheat contract. This implies that with $1000.00 in your trading account, you could potentially trade one contract. It doesn't mean that your risk is limited to $1000.00, nor would this be advisable. Here's why. Each 1 cent per bushel move in the price of wheat equates to $50.00 on a futures contract. With wheat trading at $7.05 per bushel, the contract is worth (has a face value of) $35 250.00 (5000 bushels × $7.05 per bushel). If the price of wheat increases by 30 cents to $7.35 per bushel, and the trade is long, the trader will have made a profit of $1500.00 less brokerage and charges (30 cents per bushel × $50.00 = $1500.00). This represents a return on the $1000.00 margin requirement of 150 per cent — a fantastic result! *But* if the price of wheat falls by 30 cents per bushel to $6.75, the trader will incur a loss of $1500.00, wiping out the initial $1000.00 plus a further $500.00 that they are required to submit to the broker — a 150 per cent loss from one trade. This scenario is highly unlikely to occur, as the broker would require an account size of more than $1000.00 to enter the trade, but it serves to highlight the effects of margin trading.

A scenario like this is improbable because of the second type of margin required by futures exchanges — maintenance margin. Maintenance margin is the minimum amount a trader must maintain in their account to be allowed by both the relevant exchange and the broker to keep an open position in any given market. If the trader's account falls below this amount, they will receive a margin call requesting either the input of more funds into the account, or that one or more open positions be closed out to bring the account back into line with the required margin amounts. In the case of our wheat trader in the above example, let's assume the maintenance margin for wheat is $700. If, after an initial move in the trader's favour, the price of wheat then started to decline and the long trade moved into a loss situation, the trader would be required to post additional funds to maintain the open position, or alternatively to close the open position. In this example, this would occur as soon as the amount of money in the account dropped below $700, the required maintenance margin for this wheat trade. If a trader fails to meet a margin call within a specified period of time, then the broker can automatically liquidate open positions to return the account to a positive margin balance. In this example, the trader has used the leverage available in the futures markets to increase their exposure to a market, in this case the wheat market. They have put up $1000 of their own cash to gain access to a contract with a value of $35250, less than 3 per cent of the contract value. This represents leverage of 35:1. As this example shows, leverage is a double-edged sword—great when it works in your favour but potentially catastrophic if you use it incorrectly.

This example offers a very raw illustration of using low account balances when trading futures. It highlights the need to trade with a well-funded account and to understand the workings of both initial margin and maintenance margin. A more likely scenario with this wheat trade is that a much larger account size is required to enter the trade in the first place. If, for example, the trader were to have $20000 rather than $1000 in the account, the scenario would be completely different. The $1500 loss would represent only 7.5 per cent of the account—not ideal, but a loss that could be recovered over time.

The other way margin is incorrectly used is when traders over-margin their accounts. Let's take an example of a trader with a $40000.00 trading account. She is an experienced share trader but, having only ever traded shares with leverage of 1:1, she doesn't fully understand the leverage available in the futures markets. Traditionally, she allocates $20000.00 of capital to each new position in the sharemarket. If she chooses to buy into XYZ Company, trading at $4.00 per share, she simply buys 5000 shares in order to be fully invested (5000 shares × $4.00 per share = $20000.00). Using this same philosophy, our trader allocates $20000.00 to the wheat trade discussed above and decides to go long. Seeing that the margin requirement for wheat is $1000.00 per contract, she buys 20 futures contracts at $7.05 per bushel. Her total outlay is the initial margin requirement of $20 000.00, but her risk is much greater. She now has exposure to 100 000 bushels of wheat (20 contracts × 5000 bushels per contract) worth $705 000.00 (20 contracts × 5000 bushels per contract × $7.05 per bushel = $705 000.00). She also has a maintenance margin requirement of $14 000.00 (20 contracts × $700.00 maintenance margin per contract = $14 000.00). If at some point the money in her account falls below this figure she will receive a margin call. If the price of wheat rallies by 30 cents per bushel, she will of course generate a significant profit of $30 000.00 (100 000 bushels × 30 cents per bushel = $30 000.00). This would represent a 150 per cent return on the $20 000.00 initial margin requirement, and a 75 per cent return on her $40 000.00 account. If the price of wheat were to fall by 30 cents per bushel, she would incur a loss of $30 000.00 or 150 per cent of the initial margin requirement, and 75 per cent of her account balance, leaving her with just $10 000.00 in her trading account. She might also receive a margin call on the account when the available funds fell below the required maintenance margin of $14 000.00. The trader has wiped out 75 per cent of her account, even though the price of wheat declined by only 4.25 per cent ($7.05 − 0.30 = $6.75). If the trader had restricted her exposure to just one contract, the results would be significantly less devastating: a loss of just $1500.00 (5000 bushels × 30 cents = $1500.00), or 3.75 per cent of her account balance of $40 000.00.

Tip

Both of these examples highlight the importance of understanding risk management and money management when trading futures, and understanding the power of the leverage available in these markets. Used correctly, it is a tool that can greatly enhance profits. Used incorrectly, it can wipe you out.

Using stop-losses and position sizing

As illustrated in table 5.1, the percentage return needed to recover from large losses increases in line with the percentage of trading capital lost. A trader who risks 1 per cent of their trading capital on a trade that produces a loss has to earn a return of 1.01 per cent to regain the capital level at which they started. A trader who loses 50 per cent of their trading capital needs to return 100 per cent on their remaining capital just to return their account to the amount with which they started out. In the wheat trade detailed above, our trader lost 75 per cent of her trading capital through incorrect position sizing and a failure to understand the effects of leverage. She would need to earn a 300 per cent return on her remaining $10 000 to restore her trading account to the $40 000 she started with.

Table 5.1: percentage gain needed to recover trading losses

% loss of capital	% return needed to recover
1.00	1.01
2.00	2.04
5.00	5.30
10.00	11.10
20.00	25.00
25.00	33.00
50.00	100.00
60.00	150.00
75.00	300.00

Table 5.1 highlights the importance of capital preservation and of containing losses to amounts that can be recovered. If you lose your capital you can't trade anymore. If you take risks that are too large for your account size you can lose your trading capital. In order to contain losses to within manageable limits, all traders need to set stop-loss levels on every trade *before* they enter it so they know exactly how much of their trading capital is at risk and can afford to

lose if the trade fails to work out as they anticipate. It is for this reason that traders are advised to limit their losses to between 1 and 2 per cent of their account balance.

Once you have decided on the percentage of your capital that you are prepared to risk on each trade, this becomes your stop-loss level and you can calculate your position size to within this maximum loss level. As shown in table 5.1, it is much easier to recover from a 2 per cent loss than from a 10 per cent loss. Our wheat trader would have been much better off with a maximum stop-loss level of 2 per cent of her trading account, or $800 ($40 000 × 2% = $800). In reality, as her trading strategy dictated that she needed to use a stop-loss level of 30 cents per bushel, she would have been unable to take this wheat trade because the stop-loss level is outside the maximum loss allowable under the 2 per cent rule. A stop-loss level of 30 cents per bushel on a 5000-bushel contract equals $1500, which is almost double the $800 maximum allowable under the 2 per cent rule. Her alternative might have been to use a tighter stop-loss of, say, 15 cents per bushel as this would have kept her within the maximum allowable loss of $800 (15 cents per bushel × 5000 bushels = $750), but this might have subjected her to being stopped out anyway if the market was volatile.

Tip

The point at which a trade will be exited for an initial loss is referred to as a stop-loss. It is the point at which the amount of money we can afford to lose on any trade is reached and the trade is cut or exited in order to stop any further loss of capital.

Even if our wheat trader had a higher risk tolerance and was prepared to accept a 5 per cent loss on the trade, the mechanics for calculating the number of contracts would remain the same. A 5 per cent risk on her $40 000 account equals $2000. With a $2000 maximum allowable loss, she would be able to take one futures contract if her stop-loss remained at 30 cents per bushel or $1500 per contract, as this would fall within the maximum $2000 loss she has defined. While she won't get rich from this one trade if it works in her favour, she will have achieved a profit. The saving grace is that in the event the trade is a loser she has dusted only $1500, and with a profitable trading system she will be able to move on, continue trading and recover from the loss.

Tip

Your personality, and especially your aversion to or acceptance of risk, will help you define the percentage risk you are prepared to apply to your trading account and position sizing. For some, 2 per cent may be more than they can accept, while for others it may be too small. This is a personal choice and one that can be arrived at by the 'sleep test'. If you can put a trade on and go to sleep at night unconcerned about the outcome, then you have your risk management and position sizing aligned with your personality and trading style. You need to be able to accept the outcome of every trade — win, lose or draw — without experiencing emotional turmoil.

To work effectively, stop-loss levels must be clearly defined for each trade *before* the trade is placed. Every trade must be entered into knowing exactly where it will be exited if it goes the wrong way. This ensures we know how much money we are prepared to lose on a trade and the price at which this will occur. Once that price point is reached the trade is exited immediately without a second thought or any emotional concern. If you are wrong, move on — there's no point trying to hang on to a losing trade to make a point or to prove to the market or anyone else that you know what you are doing. No-one gets every trade right. Even the greatest traders in the world have losing trades. What makes them great traders is that they know they will sometimes lose, they accept their losses and they know precisely where these trades will be exited. This process allows them to continually probe the market in search of profitable opportunities. By cutting losing trades early, they are able to reallocate the capital to another potentially profitable opportunity, unburdened by any attachment to the outcome of any one trade.

Tip

The number one trading rule is to always set an initial stop-loss and to define it before you open every new trade.

The initial stop-loss must be set before you enter every single trade. Stop-losses can be determined a number of ways, and you may wish to research the most appropriate method for you. Methods include:

⇒ using a maximum dollar amount expressed as a percentage of your trading account. If you have a $10 000 account, for example, you may wish to set 3 per cent or $300 as the maximum loss you are prepared to accept on any losing trade. Generally, the larger your account size, the smaller this amount is in percentage terms. Someone with a $100 000 account, for example, may want to risk only 1 per cent or $1000.

⇒ using chart patterns and price to place stop-losses—under a swing point low in the case of a long trade, or above a swing point high in the case of a short trade

⇒ using areas of support and resistance

⇒ using volatility to determine appropriate stop-loss levels far enough away from the current price to allow the trade a degree of freedom to move around, but not so far away that the stop-loss is too large

⇒ using other tools or indicators that you may develop over time from your own experience.

Learning to lose

One of the most critical mistakes many traders make is failing to clearly define the amount of capital they are prepared to lose on each trade. While they spend a huge amount of time and effort on defining their trade entry rules and requirements, the concept of trade exit is often overlooked or, at best, given only minor consideration. Always defining the point at which a trade will be exited separates the real traders from the punters.

Tip

Knowing how to accept losing trades through the application of clearly defined exit rules will contribute significantly to your long-term trading success.

Having clearly defined exit rules simply means knowing when to admit a trade is not working out as planned, accepting the market has moved against you and cutting your losses by exiting the trade. It's all about accepting that on this occasion you are wrong and moving on to the next trade. There's no point hanging on to losing positions in the hope that they will turn around and move back in your favour. Not only does this tie up capital you could put to better use in another potentially profitable trade, but it also wastes mental energy as you spend precious time agonising over what to do and when to do it. Far better to cut the losing trade early and unemotionally and move on.

Success as a futures trader requires an acceptance of losing, sometimes several times in a row, when trades go against you. Strings or runs of losing trades will happen. No trader can consistently make money from the markets without experiencing these periods. A losing streak doesn't mean you are stupid or shouldn't be trading. You need to be realistic in your expectations, and to focus on the trading process and money management over the long term rather than the desire to get every trade right. Some win, some lose, so what! It is how you manage your capital through position sizing and the use of stop-losses that determines whether you get to fight another day. If you blow all your trading capital, the game is up. If you cut your losses and manage the risk, you stay in the game.

Conservative levels of leverage, adequate account capitalisation, and the judicious application of stop-losses and position sizing will ensure losses are kept to a minimum, enabling you to adhere to the number one priority of all trading activities—capital preservation. As long as you can survive the losing trades and remain solvent you can continue to participate in the endless stream of trading opportunities that the global futures markets offer. In the following chapters we will introduce and examine in detail some of the most significant futures contracts in the natural commodities markets (chapters 6 to 10) and in the financial markets (chapters 11 and 12).

Chapter summary

⇒ Risk management involves identifying the amount of capital you are prepared to risk (lose) on a trade.

⇒ Money management concerns all factors associated with the growth of your trading account balance over time.

⇒ Many uneducated traders perceive trading futures as more 'risky' than trading shares because of a number of misconceptions, including:

   ✧ that share trading involves 'tangible' assets; in fact, futures contracts are based on real commodities that never reach zero value

   ✧ that share value can be fuelled by intangibles; in fact, it can equally quickly lose this notional value

   ✧ that solid 'blue-chip' companies are the most reliable investment vehicles; in fact, a quick examination of the share prices of some major companies since the GFC will reveal the reality

   ✧ that time needs to be spent identifying 'good' companies; in fact, even these can perform poorly

   ✧ that a 'buy and hold' investment strategy works over the long term; in fact, profits can be made in the futures markets by trading in both rising and falling markets.

⇒ Futures contracts are traded with the use of leverage via a margin account. With leverage you can use a relatively small amount of your own funds to control a much larger face value position.

⇒ Leverage is a double-edged sword: used correctly it can allow you to multiply profits and grow your trading account; used incorrectly it can wipe you out.

⇒ The initial margin is the amount you must put up in order to enter a trade, either long or short. It is essentially a 'good faith' deposit that allows you to trade on a commodity exchange.

⇒ Maintenance margin is the minimum amount a trader must maintain in their account to be allowed by both the relevant exchange and the broker to continue to hold an open position in any given market.

⇒ To contain losses to within manageable limits, all traders need to set stop-loss levels on every trade before they enter it, so they know exactly how much of their trading capital is at risk.

⇒ By only taking position sizes that fall within your maximum capital loss rules you will alleviate any mental and emotional stress associated with trading.

⇒ Success as a futures trader requires an acceptance of losing, sometimes several times in a row, when trades go against you. Strings or runs of losing trades will happen.

Part II

Natural commodity futures contracts

Having covered the principles and practice of trading futures it is now time to examine the major global futures contracts in detail. In this part of the book we look at the global natural commodity futures contracts that trade the largest volumes and are of greatest interest to most traders. A brief history and overview of each commodity is followed by a discussion of the major factors influencing the price of that commodity. A historical price chart and a contract specifications sheet, as well as pricing details and examples of a long trade and a short trade, are also included.

chapter 6

Grains

The most actively traded grains are often referred to as the food and feed grains because they are used throughout the world to feed both people and livestock. Corn and oats tend to be used primarily as feed grains, with some use in the food industry. Rice and wheat are mainly food grains, although wheat is also used as a feed source when other feeds such as corn or oats are in short supply. The soybean complex (soybeans, soybean meal and soybean oil) is considered both a feed and a food grain. The most actively traded grain futures contracts are corn, wheat and the soybean complex, and these are discussed here. There is insufficient space in this book to examine the less actively traded contracts of oats, rough rice, barley and canola.

Bushel weights

Because of variations in moisture content and grain size, cereal grains are measured using a volume measurement called a bushel. A bushel is the amount of grain that will fill a volume cylinder of 2150.42 cubic inches or 35.2391 litres. Bushels can be used as a measure of weight when a standard bushel weight at a specific moisture content is used. Futures contract sizes for grains are quoted in bushels. The standard bushel weights at the specified moisture contents are shown in table 6.1.

Table 6.1: standard bushel weights and moisture contents

Grain	Standard bushel weight	Kilogram equivalent
Corn	56 lb @ 15.5% moisture	25.4012 kg
Wheat	60 lb @ 13.5% moisture	27.2155 kg
Soybeans	60 lb @ 13.0% moisture	27.2155 kg
Oats	32 lb @ 14% moisture	14.5152 kg
Rough rice	45 lb @ 13.5% moisture	20.4119 kg

Using these standardised bushel weights allows for futures contracts quoted in bushels to be converted to metric tonne equivalents for delivery and hedging purposes. A 5000-bushel corn contract, for example, converts to 127 metric tonnes (5000 bushels × 25.4012 kg per bushel).

Corn

Corn, or maize, is a cereal grain grown throughout the world. The Food and Agriculture Organization of the United Nations estimated world production of corn in 2009 at 817 million tonnes, making it the most-produced grain crop in the world. Of this the United States produces around 40 per cent, or just under 330 million tonnes. China is the world's second-largest producer. Other major producers include Brazil, Mexico, Indonesia, India and France.

Corn is used as a food source as well as in many food products such as cornmeal, starch, bread and breakfast cereals. Corn oil is used in cooking and in other food products such as margarines and salad dressings. Corn starch is used in the paper industry. The greatest use of corn is as a feed for livestock and meat production. The ever-expanding ethanol fuel industry is now a major user of corn, contributing to an increase in area planted to corn over the past several years. As crude oil prices rise, and demand for ethanol increases, the area planted to corn, particularly in the US, is expected to increase to satisfy this demand. According to figures available from the United States Department of Agriculture (USDA) and the Renewable Fuels Association, of the 12.45 billion bushels of corn produced in the US in 2010, 5350 billion bushels (43 per cent) was used as livestock feed and 4650 billion bushels (37 per cent) was used in ethanol production, with the balance used in a variety of ways. The amount of corn used in ethanol production has increased from approximately 11 per cent of total production in 2003.

Tip

The increase in demand for corn from the expanding Chinese economy and the increasing use of corn in ethanol fuels continues to boost the global demand for corn.

Factors affecting price

Factors affecting the price of corn include the following:

⇒ Hot, dry weather during pollination and the growing season can adversely affect the size and quality of the corn crop. While this applies directly to the US as the major world corn producer, weather conditions during pollination in the other major producing countries, such as China and Brazil, can also have an impact on the price of US corn. Reduced production in these and other countries can lead to increased demand for corn produced in the US, adding price pressure to this market. Similarly, in years when growing conditions are good and pollination occurs under stable weather conditions, yields and quality will be above average. This can put downward pressure on prices, particularly if growing and pollination conditions in the other major producing countries have also been favourable.

⇒ The size of grain-fed livestock herds both in the US domestic market and in other countries can also affect corn prices. Because of its high starch content, corn is ideal for fattening livestock and poultry. Large numbers of livestock on feed will increase the demand for corn, while lower numbers will decrease the demand for corn. If an increase in corn-fed livestock numbers corresponds with reduced production due to weather-related issues, corn prices can rise significantly.

⇒ As feed is the largest cost item when feeding livestock, the profitability of using corn (or any other feed grain, for that matter) will be determined by the cost of the grain relative to the price of meat. This is referred to as the livestock–corn ratio. When this ratio is low, livestock feeders will make adjustments by feeding less corn, reducing the number of animals on feed, or shortening the amount of time animals are kept on feed.

⇒ The level of 'carryover' stocks of corn from the previous harvest can also affect price. If a large amount of corn is still held in storage and the current season crop is above average, this indicates further stocks will be added to those already existing, which may adversely affect price. This is becoming less significant for corn because of its increased use in ethanol fuel production, which tends to absorb any excess corn stocks.

Figure 6.1 shows a weekly price chart of corn futures from 1987 to 2011. The sharp rises and falls that can occur in the corn market are easily visible.

Pricing

Corn futures are traded on the Chicago Board of Trade (CBOT). Corn futures contracts are quoted in cents per bushel on a 5000-bushel contract. A 1-cent-per-bushel move in the price of corn equates to $50.00 on the futures contract (5000 bushels × $0.01 = $50.00). The minimum price move, or tick, is $0.0025 (¼ cent) or $12.50 (5000 bushels × $0.0025 = $12.50).

Figure 6.1: CBOT weekly corn futures chart, 1987–2011

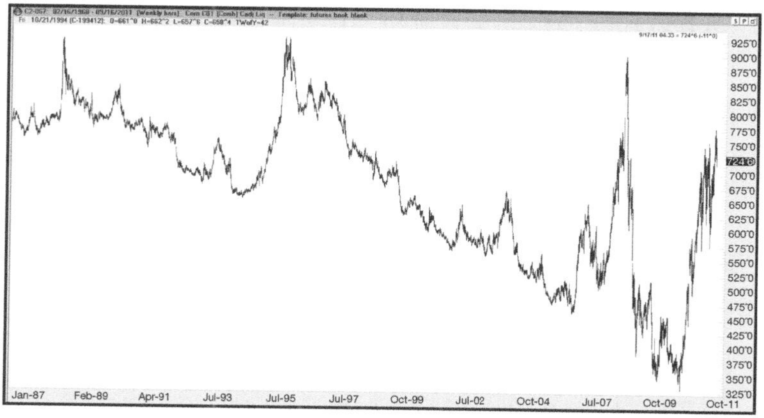

Source: Trade Navigator / Genesis Financial Technologies Inc.

Trading examples

Expecting the price of corn to rise, a trader would BUY (go long) a futures contract. Let's say the long position is initiated at 722.25 cents per bushel and the market rises to 766.00 cents per bushel, a move of 43.75 cents per bushel, or 175 ticks (43.75 ÷ 0.25 or ¼ cent). The trader's profit (excluding brokerage and costs) would be $2187.50 (175 ticks × $12.50 per tick = $2187.50).

> 766.00 cents per bushel (sell price) − 722.25 cents per bushel (buy price) = 43.75 cents per bushel × $50.00 per 1 cent = $2187.50

Expecting the price of corn to fall, a trader would SELL (go short) a futures contract. Let's say the short position is initiated at 728.25 cents per bushel and the market falls to 671.50 cents per bushel, a move of 56.75 cents per bushel, or 227 ticks (56.75 ÷ 0.25 or ¼ cent). The trader's profit (excluding brokerage and costs) would be $2837.50 (227 ticks × $12.50 per tick = $2837.50).

728.25 cents per bushel (sell price) − 671.50 cents per bushel (buy price) = 56.75 cents per bushel × $50.00 per 1 cent = $2837.50

Contract specifications

Full contract specifications for the CBOT corn futures contract are shown in figure 6.2.

Figure 6.2: CBOT corn futures contract specifications

Contract Size	5,000 bushels (~ 127 Metric Tons)	
Deliverable Grade	#2 Yellow at contract Price, #1 Yellow at a 1.5 cent/bushel premium #3 Yellow at a 1.5 cent/bushel discount	
Pricing Unit	Cents per bushel	
Tick Size (minimum fluctuation)	1/4 of one cent per bushel ($12.50 per contract)	
Contract Months/Symbols	March (H), May (K), July (N), September (U) & December (Z)	
Trading Hours	CME Globex (Electronic Platform)	5:00 pm - 2:00 pm, Sunday - Friday Central Time
	Open Outcry (Trading Floor)	9:30 am - 1:15 pm Monday - Friday Central Time
Daily Price Limit	$0.40 per bushel expandable to $0.60 when the market closes at limit bid or limit offer. There shall be no price limits on the current month contract on or after the second business day preceding the first day of the delivery month.	
Settlement Procedure	Physical Delivery	
Last Trade Date	The business day prior to the 15th calendar day of the contract month.	
Last Delivery Date	Second business day following the last trading day of the delivery month.	
Product Ticker Symbols	CME Globex (Electronic Platform)	ZC C=Clearing
	Open Outcry (Trading Floor)	C
Exchange Rule	These contracts are listed with, and subject to, the rules and regulations of CBOT.	

Source: CME Group Inc.

Trading hours

Corn futures contracts are traded electronically 21 hours per day on CME's electronic Globex platform from 5.00 pm each day until 2.00 pm (Chicago time) the following day, beginning at 5.00 pm on Sunday night. There is a three-hour gap in trading each day between 2.00 pm and 5.00 pm, Monday to Thursday. Corn futures are also traded on the CBOT in the traditional open outcry session between 9.30 am and 2.00 pm each weekday. The pit trading session occurs in conjunction with electronic trading during the pit session times. Figure 6.3 displays the trading session times for corn and all the CBOT-traded grain futures markets.

Figure 6.3: trading hours for CBOT grain markets

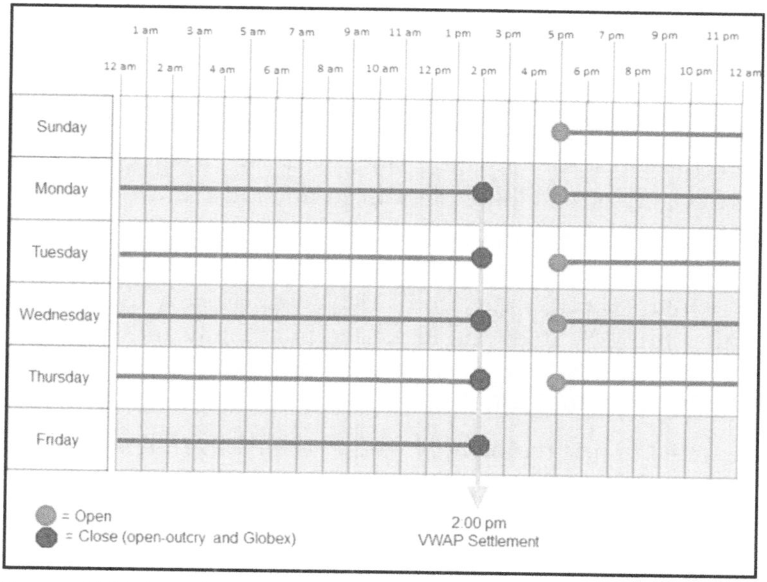

Source: CME Group Inc.

Wheat

Wheat is one of the oldest and most widely used food crops, having been first cultivated in Asia over 9000 years ago. Wheat is now grown on every continent on Earth except Antarctica and is a vital worldwide food grain. Of the approximately 670 million tonnes of wheat harvested in 2009, the European Union produced 22 per cent, followed by China, India, the United States, Russia, Canada, Australia and Pakistan. Wheat is second only to rice as a cereal food source for humans, being used in a huge variety of ways for human consumption, including for flour, bread, pasta, breakfast cereals and many other food items. Wheat can also used as a feed source for livestock, although it is not typically a preferred option.

In the Northern Hemisphere there are two distinct growing seasons for wheat. Winter wheat, which accounts for around 75 per cent of US wheat production, is planted in autumn, usually during September. It remains dormant through the winter months when a blanket of snow covers and insulates the young plants. Growth resumes in the spring, and harvest takes place in summer, usually in late May through to July, depending on the season. Spring wheat is grown in the northern United States as winters are too severe for winter wheat to survive. It is planted as early as possible in the spring (March) and harvested in late July and August.

Factors affecting price

Factors affecting the price of wheat include the following:

⇒ Because of its role in human food products, wheat
  demand tends to remain fairly constant. As a result, the
  main factors affecting the wheat price tend to relate to the
  supply side and are mainly weather driven, as extreme
  heatwaves or cold snaps during various stages of crop
  development can have a huge impact on production.
  Lack of adequate snow cover can adversely affect winter
  wheat dormancy. Extreme drought and heatwave
  conditions can affect spring wheat growing cycles.

⇒ Weather conditions in the other major wheat-growing countries can also affect supply and impact on the world wheat price. Drought conditions in China or India, for example, will affect wheat production in these countries, requiring them to import wheat, which places upward pressure on price. Similarly, in years where production is unaffected by these weather factors, import demand will be less and worldwide wheat prices will fall.

⇒ Government policies such as farmer subsidies and tariffs or other protectionist policies can also impact on both domestic and international wheat prices.

Figure 6.4 shows a weekly price chart of wheat futures from 1987 to 2011. The sharp rises and falls that can occur in the wheat market largely as a response to weather conditions are easily visible.

Figure 6.4: CBOT weekly wheat futures chart, 1987–2011

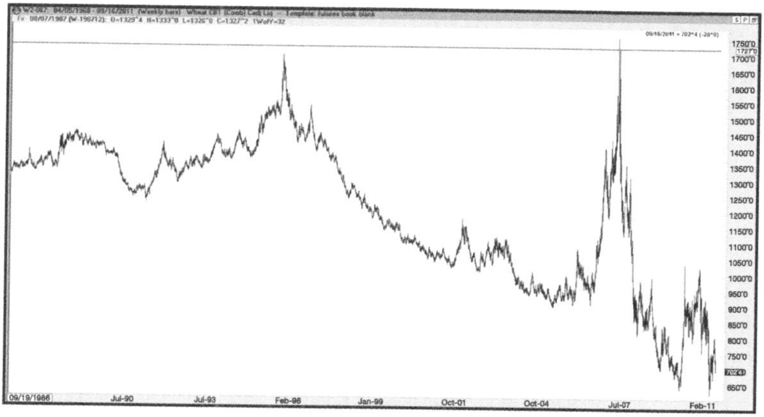

Source: Trade Navigator / Genesis Financial Technologies Inc.

Pricing

Because of the range of wheat types and variety of growing conditions, wheat futures are traded on three exchanges in the United States: the Chicago Board of Trade (soft red winter wheat), the Kansas City Board of Trade (hard red winter wheat) and the Minneapolis Grain Exchange (spring wheat). Contracts on all three exchanges are for 5000 bushels. As soft red winter wheat is by far the most heavily produced wheat in the US and hence trades the highest volume of futures contracts, details are provided here for this contract only.

Wheat futures contracts are quoted in cents per bushel on a 5000-bushel contract. A 1-cent-per-bushel move in the price of wheat equates to $50.00 on the futures contract (5000 bushels × $0.01 = $50.00). The minimum price move or tick is $0.0025 (¼ cent) or $12.50 (5000 bushels × $0.0025 = $12.50).

Trading examples

Expecting the price of wheat to rise, a trader would BUY (go long) a futures contract. Let's say the long position is initiated at 753.00 cents per bushel, and the market rises to 817.25 cents per bushel, a move of 64.25 cents per bushel, or 257 ticks (64.25 ÷ 0.25 or ¼ cent). The trader's profit (excluding brokerage and costs) would be $3212.50 (257 ticks × $12.50 per tick = $3212.50).

817.25 cents per bushel (sell price) − 753.00 cents per bushel (buy price) = 64.25 cents per bushel × $50.00 per 1 cent = $3212.50

Expecting the price of wheat to fall, a trader would SELL (go short) a futures contract. Let's say the short position is initiated at 743.75 cents per bushel and the market falls to 659.00 cents per bushel, a move of 84.75 cents per bushel, or 339 ticks (84.75 ÷ 0.25 or ¼ cent). The trader's profit (excluding brokerage and costs) would be $4237.50 (339 ticks × $12.50 per tick).

743.75 cents per bushel (sell price) − 659.00 cents per bushel (buy price) = 84.75 cents per bushel × $50.00 per 1 cent = $4237.50

Contract specifications

Full contract specifications for the CBOT wheat futures contract are shown in figure 6.5.

Figure 6.5: CBOT wheat futures contract specifications

Contract Size	5,000 bushels (~ 136 Metric Tons)	
Deliverable Grade	#2 Soft Red Winter at contract price, #1 Soft Red Winter at a 3 cent premium, other deliverable grades listed in Rule 14104.	
Pricing Unit	Cents per bushel	
Tick Size (minimum fluctuation)	1/4 of one cent per bushel ($12.50 per contract)	
Contract Months/Symbols	March (H), May (K), July (N), September (U) & December (Z)	
Trading Hours	CME Globex (Electronic Platform)	5:00 pm - 2:00 pm, Sunday - Friday Central Time
	Open Outcry (Trading Floor)	9:30 am - 1:15 pm Central Time, Monday - Friday
Daily Price Limit	$0.60 per bushel expandable to $0.90 and then to $1.35 when the market closes at limit bid or limit offer. There shall be no price limits on the current month contract on or after the second business day preceding the first day of the delivery month.	
Settlement Procedure	Daily Wheat Settlement Procedures (PDF)	
Last Trade Date	The business day prior to the 15th calendar day of the contract month.	
Last Delivery Date	Second business day following the last trading day of the delivery month.	
Product Ticker Symbols	CME Globex (Electronic Platform)	ZW W=Clearing
	Open Outcry (Trading Floor)	W
Exchange Rule	These contracts are listed with, and subject to, the rules and regulations of CBOT.	

Source: CME Group Inc.

Trading hours

Wheat futures contracts are traded electronically 21 hours per day on CME's electronic Globex platform, from 5.00 pm each day until 2.00 pm (Chicago time) the following day, beginning at 5.00 pm on Sunday night. There is a three-hour gap in trading each day between 2.00 pm and 5.00 pm Monday to Thursday. Wheat futures are also traded on the CBOT in the traditional open outcry session between 9.30 am and 1.15 pm each weekday. The pit trading session occurs in conjunction with electronic trading during the pit session times.

Australian wheat futures

Australian traders may also be interested in trading Australian Securities Exchange (ASX) wheat futures contracts. Details of the contract specifications are provided in figure 6.6. As a basis for comparison, average monthly traded volume of CBOT wheat futures contracts is around 2 000 000 contracts compared with around 22 000 on the ASX. The ASX wheat futures contract tends to be used more by hedgers, including end users and producers, than by speculators, due to the relatively low traded volumes.

Figure 6.6: ASX wheat futures contract specifications

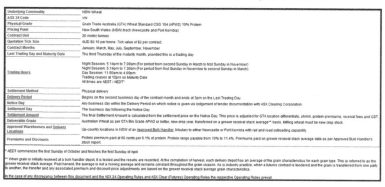

The soybean complex

Although technically an oil seed, soybeans are grouped with the other 'grains' as they are a legume crop. Soybeans are grown mostly for the soybean meal and soybean oil that is produced when the soybean is crushed. As such, the three 'products'—soybeans, soybean meal and soybean oil—are very closely related. This interrelationship is referred to as the *soybean complex* or the *soy complex*. Approximately 85 per cent of global soybean production is processed into soybean meal and soybean oil, with the remaining 15 per cent used in human food products.

Soybeans

Initially grown throughout China and Asia as a human food source, large-scale production of soybeans in the United States and other countries began only in the early 1900s. In the 1930s a trade embargo by China cut off supplies of soybeans to the US. This embargo, coupled with planting restrictions on wheat, corn and cotton due to a huge oversupply of these commodities, led to an increase in soybean plantings. Soybean oil became a substitute for cotton seed oil and soybean meal found uses as a feed source in livestock production. Following World War II demand for vegetable oils continued to rise. Population growth and increased affluence in many countries led to increased demand for red meat, poultry and eggs. Soybean meal as a high-protein feed source became an important component in livestock feeding.

According to the USDA, just under 211 million tonnes of soybeans were produced globally in 2009, with the United States producing almost 81 million tonnes, or 38 per cent. This was followed by Brazil with 57 million tonnes, then Argentina, China and India. Together, these five countries account for more than 90 per cent of the global soybean crop. Production of soybeans in China continues to expand in line with increased demand for meat and poultry products.

Tip

Soybeans are a cheap and useful source of protein. They produce more protein per hectare than any other source.

The soybean plant is photoperiodic—that is, the flowering and opening of the seed pods is controlled by the amount of daylight. Soybean plants will thus mature within a few days of a given calendar date, regardless of planting time. This feature has prompted the use of shorter-life hybrid varieties of soybeans in crop rotation programs, allowing farmers to 'double crop' in rotation with other crops. This has contributed to increased planting of soybeans and increased production of soybean meal and soybean oil.

Tip

Soybeans tend to be the most volatile of all the grains. Prices can rise and fall sharply in line with weather patterns and conditions, particularly during July and August when the plants are emerging.

Factors affecting price

Factors affecting the price of soybeans include the following:

⇒ As for all agricultural crops, soybeans require good rainfall during the growing season. Periods of hot, dry weather (drought conditions) can have an adverse affect on the soybean plant and therefore the production of soybeans. Prolonged wet weather can also cause problems for the growing plant and affect bean production.

⇒ The demand for poultry meat and eggs also impacts on the price for soybeans. As soybean meal is a primary source of protein in poultry feed, an increase in demand for poultry products leads to increased demand for soybeans, from which soybean meal is derived.

⇒ The availability and price of other feed commodities such as corn will also impact on soybean prices. If a large supply of corn is available at a cheaper price then livestock farmers will make use of it, reducing the demand for soybeans and thus lowering the price. If there is little supply of alternative feed sources then prices for soybeans will rise.

⇒ Consumer preferences for soy milk and other edible soy products can have a slight impact on soybean prices.

⇒ Increased demand for soybeans, soybean meal and soybean oil from the expanding Chinese economy is also impacting on the price of soybeans. The increased demand for livestock feed requirements to meet the need for greater meat production is increasing demand for soybean meal in particular. As this growth continues, China may well need to import more feed grains and protein meals to meet greater food and feed requirements. Weather conditions in the Chinese growing season will also have a significant impact on global soybean and other grain prices. If Chinese domestic production is adversely affected, then it will need to import its requirements from the US and other producers, potentially pushing prices higher.

⇒ The level of exports from the United States and the level of stocks carried over from the previous year's production will affect soybean prices. If export demand is high, prices will rise to reflect this overseas buying of US soybeans. If there was little carryover from the previous year (that is, a low volume of soybeans held in storage), then upward pressure on soybean prices may occur. If low carryover stock levels are coupled with a drought and high levels of export demand, then prices can rally higher quickly in response to such a situation.

Tip

The relationships between carryover stock levels, export demand, livestock feed requirements and the ever-present impact of the weather on the production of all grain crops can cause sharp upward and downward price spikes in the grain markets.

Figure 6.7 shows a weekly price chart of CBOT soybeans futures from 1987 to 2011. Sharp and sudden rises and falls in price in response to many of the issues discussed here are clearly visible.

Figure 6.7: CBOT weekly soybeans futures chart, 1987–2011

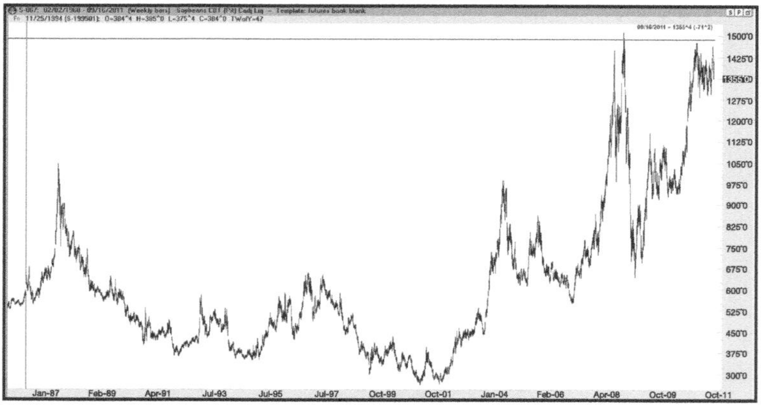

Source: Trade Navigator / Genesis Financial Technologies Inc.

Pricing

Soybean futures are traded on the CBOT. Soybean futures contracts are quoted in cents per bushel on a 5000-bushel contract. A 1-cent-per-bushel move in the price of soybeans equates to $50.00 on the futures contract (5000 bushels × $0.01 = $50.00). The minimum price move or tick is $0.0025 (¼ cent) or $12.50 (5000 bushels × $0.0025 = $12.50).

Trading examples

Expecting the price of soybeans to rise, a trader would BUY (go long) a futures contract. Let's say the long position is initiated at 1238.50 cents per bushel and the market rises to 1299.75 cents per bushel, a move of 61.25 cents per bushel, or 245 ticks (61.25 ÷ 0.25 or ¼ cent). The trader's profit (excluding brokerage and costs) would be $3062.50 (245 ticks × $12.50 per tick = $3062.50).

> 1299.75 cents per bushel (sell price) − 1238.50 cents per bushel (buy price) = 61.25 cents per bushel × $50.00 per 1 cent = $3062.50

Expecting the price of soybeans to fall, a trader would SELL (go short) a futures contract. Let's say the short position is initiated at 1385.75 cents per bushel and the market falls to 1300.50 cents per bushel, a move of 85.25 cents per bushel, or 341 ticks (85.25 ÷ 0.25 or ¼ cent). The trader's profit (excluding brokerage and costs) would be $4262.50 (341 ticks × $12.50 per tick = $4262.50).

> 1385.75 cents per bushel (sell price) − 1300.50 cents per bushel (buy price) = 85.25 cents per bushel × $50.00 per 1 cent = $4262.50

Contract specifications

Full contract specifications for the soybean futures contract are shown in figure 6.8 (overleaf).

Trading hours

Soybean futures contracts are traded electronically 21 hours per day on CME's electronic Globex platform, from 5.00 pm each day until 2.00 pm (Chicago time) the following day, beginning at 5.00 pm on Sunday night. There is a three-hour gap in trading each day between 2.00 pm and 5.00 pm Monday to Thursday. Soybean futures are also traded on the CBOT in the traditional open outcry session between 9.30 am and 1.15 pm each weekday. The pit trading session occurs in conjunction with electronic trading during the pit session times.

Figure 6.8: CBOT soybean futures contract specifications

Contract Size	5,000 bushels (~136 metric tons)	
Deliverable Grade	#2 Yellow at contract price, #1 Yellow at a 6 cent/bushel premium, #3 Yellow at a 6 cent/bushel discount	
Pricing Unit	Cents per bushel	
Tick Size (minimum fluctuation)	1/4 of one cent per bushel ($12.50 per contract)	
Contract Months/Symbols	January (F), March (H), May (K), July (N), August (Q), September (U) & November (X)	
Trading Hours	CME Globex (Electronic Platform)	5:00 pm - 2:00 pm, Sunday - Friday Central Time
	Open Outcry (Trading Floor)	9:30 am - 1:15 pm Central Time, Monday - Friday
Daily Price Limit	$0.70 per bushel expandable to $1.05 and then to $1.60 when the market closes at limit bid or limit offer. There shall be no price limits on the current month contract on or after the second business day preceding the first day of the delivery month.	
Settlement Procedure	Physical Delivery	
Last Trade Date	The business day prior to the 15th calendar day of the contract month.	
Last Delivery Date	Second business day following the last trading day of the delivery month.	
Product Ticker Symbols	CME Globex (Electronic Platform)	ZS S=Clearing
	Open Outcry (Trading Floor)	S
Exchange Rule	These contracts are listed with, and subject to, the rules and regulations of CBOT.	

Source: CME Group Inc.

Soybean meal

By far the greatest use of soybeans is in the form of soybean meal for use in livestock feeding. Approximately 98 per cent of soybean meal produced is used in the livestock feed industry because of its high protein and amino acid levels.

Soybean meal is the most widely used high-protein livestock feed in the world, accounting for around two-thirds of global protein meal consumption, according to USDA figures. As the largest producers of soybeans, the US and China also produce the largest amount of soybean meal. Argentina, Brazil and India are also important producers.

Soybean meal faces competition from other animal and vegetable protein meal products, which can be substituted for soybean meal by livestock producers when they are more favourably priced. Some of these alternative vegetable protein meals include canola meal, cottonseed and sunflower meal. Fishmeal and other animal byproduct meals can also be used in some circumstances if they are priced competitively.

Soybean meal is extracted from soybeans using a chemical extraction process known as hexane-solvent extraction, or simply solvent extraction. The soybeans are crushed mechanically into flakes. The solvent is then used to chemically extract soybean oil from these flakes. The remaining flake is then 'toasted' (heat treated using high-pressure moist steam) and ground into soybean meal containing 48 per cent protein. The remaining hulls can also be mixed back into the meal, producing a 44 per cent protein soybean meal.

Tip

Prices for soybean meal are highly correlated with the price of soybeans.

Factors affecting price

Factors affecting the price of soybean meal include the following:

⇒ Prices for soybean meal are directly linked with the price of soybeans, so any adverse weather conditions that impact on soybean prices will also impact on the price for soybean meal.

⇒ Meal prices will also be affected by the number of livestock and poultry consuming high-protein meals in their daily feed rations, both in the United States and in other countries with a large livestock feeding industry, such as China. Increased demand for meat and livestock products for human consumption leads to increased demand for high-protein feeds such as soybean meal. Prices for soybean meal in the United States, the largest exporter of soybeans and soy-related products, can be impacted by high levels of demand on the export market.

⇒ The availability and price of alternative high-protein feed sources can impact on the price of soybean meal. A plentiful supply of an alternative protein meal will allow animal producers to substitute the cheaper one, thus lowering the demand for, and the price of, soybean meal.

Figure 6.9 shows a weekly price chart of CBOT soybean meal futures from 1987 to 2012. The similarities between this chart and the chart for soybeans in figure 6.7 (see p. 144) show the close relationship between the price of soybean meal and the price of soybeans.

Figure 6.9: CBOT weekly soybean meal futures chart, 1987–2012

Source: Trade Navigator / Genesis Financial Technologies Inc.

Pricing

Soybean meal futures are traded on the CBOT. Soybean meal futures contracts are quoted in dollars and cents per Imperial ton or 'short ton' on a 100-ton contract. A 1-cent-per-ton move in the price of soybean meal equates to $1.00 on the futures contract (100 tons × $0.01 = $1). The minimum price move, or tick, is 10 cents or $10.00 per contract (100 tons × $0.10 = $10.00).

Tip

A 'short ton' is equivalent to 910 kg, making a 100 short ton soybean meal contract the equivalent of 91 metric tonnes.

Trading examples

Expecting the price of soybean meal to rise, a trader would BUY (go long) a futures contract. Let's say the long position is initiated at $299.40 per short ton and the market rises to $317.30 per short ton, a move of $17.90 per short ton, or 179 ticks (17.90 ÷ 0.10). The trader's profit (excluding brokerage and costs) would be $1790.00 (179 ticks × $10 per tick = $1790.00).

$317.30 per short ton (sell price) − $299.40 per short ton (buy price) = $17.90 per short ton × 100 tons per contract = $1790.00

Expecting the price of soybean meal to fall, a trader would SELL (go short) a futures contract. Let's say the short position is initiated at $357.60 per short ton and the market falls to $319.20 per short ton, a move of $38.40 per short ton, or 384 ticks (38.40 ÷ 0.10). The trader's profit (excluding brokerage and costs) would be $3840.00 (384 ticks × $10 per tick = $3840.00).

$357.60 per short ton (sell price) − $319.20 per short ton (buy price) = $38.40 per short ton × 100 tons per contract = $3840.00

Contract specifications

Full contract specifications for the soybean meal futures contract are shown in figure 6.10.

Figure 6.10: CBOT soybean meal futures contract specifications

Contract Size	100 Short Tons (~ 91 metric tons)	
Deliverable Grade	48% Protein Soybean Meal, meeting the requirements listed in the CBOT Rules and Regulations	
Pricing Unit	Dollars and Cents per short ton	
Tick Size (minimum fluctuation)	10 cents per short ton ($10.00 per contract)	
Contract Months/Symbols	January (F), March (H), May (K), July (N), August (Q), September (U), October (V) & December (Z)	
Trading Hours	CME Globex (Electronic Platform)	5:00 pm - 2:00 pm, Sunday - Friday Central Time
	Open Outcry (Trading Floor)	9:30 am - 1:15 pm Central Time, Monday - Friday
Daily Price Limit	$20 per short ton expandable to $30 and then to $45 when the market closes at limit bid or limit offer. There shall be no price limits on the current month contract on or after the second business day preceding the first day of the delivery month.	
Settlement Procedure	Physical Delivery	
Last Trade Date	The business day prior to the 15th calendar day of the contract month.	
Last Delivery Date	Second business day following the last trading day of the delivery month.	
Product Ticker Symbols	CME Globex (Electronic Platform)	ZM 06=Clearing
	Open Outcry (Trading Floor)	SM
Exchange Rule	These contracts are listed with, and subject to, the rules and regulations of CBOT.	

Source: CME Group Inc.

Trading hours

Soybean meal futures contracts are traded electronically 21 hours per day on CME's electronic Globex platform, from 5.00 pm each day until 2.00 pm (Chicago time) the following day, beginning at 5.00 pm on Sunday night. There is a three-hour gap in trading each day between 2.00 pm and 5.00 pm Monday to Thursday. Soybean meal futures are also traded on the CBOT in the traditional open outcry session between 9.30 am and 1.15 pm each weekday. The pit trading session occurs in conjunction with electronic trading during the pit session times.

Soybean oil

Soybean oil or *bean oil* is extracted from soybeans using the solvent extraction method described on p. 147. Soybean seeds contain around 19 per cent oil. Bean oil is one of the world's major edible-oils, accounting for around 50 per cent of total world edible oil consumption according to the UN Food and Agriculture Organization. As the largest producer of soybeans, the United States is also the largest global producer of bean oil.

Tip

Although soybean meal and soybean oil are related, prices can move independently as a result of short-term differences in demand for the two products.

Factors affecting price

Factors affecting the price of soybean oil include the following:

⇒ The demand for soybean meal has a direct impact on the production and supply of bean oil, as bean oil is often considered a byproduct of the production of soybean meal. If demand for soybean meal is high for use in the stock-feed industry, then it follows that production of bean oil will increase as a result of the increased crush of soybeans to meet the increased demand for soybean meal. If demand for bean oil is low at the same time, then prices for bean oil could potentially move lower, even though prices for beans and soybean meal are rising.

⇒ This can also be influenced by the supply of alternative edible vegetable oils on global markets, such as sunflower oil, cottonseed oil and palm oil. If these are in greater supply then downward price pressure may occur for bean oil if it too is in plentiful supply.

⇒ Weather conditions and the overall supply of soybeans will also affect the price of bean oil.

The soybean crush spread and reverse crush spread

In order to make a profit, soybean processors must be able to purchase soybeans at a lower cost than the combined sales income they will receive from soybean meal and soybean oil. This difference is called the gross processing margin, or GPM. If the GPM is high enough, processors will commit to buying soybeans, knowing they can make a profit from processing the beans into soybean meal and soybean oil. The price interrelationship between the three products can be complex at times and may hinge on the sale price of soybean meal or soybean oil rather than on the outright purchase price of the soybeans. These prices are in turn influenced by the demand for meal and/or oil. By applying the GPM to the futures markets, soybean processors may buy soybean futures to hedge cash purchases of soybeans in the physical market, while at the same time selling soybean meal and soybean oil futures to hedge later sales of these products once the processing is complete. This is known as the *crush spread*.

A distortion in normal price patterns occurs when the cost of buying soybeans is higher than the combined sales value of soybean meal and bean oil, resulting in a negative GPM and making it unprofitable for the soybean processors to produce meal and oil. In this instance, processors may sell soybean futures and buy soybean meal and bean oil futures.

This is known as the *reverse crush spread*. At the same time, processors may slow down or completely stop the crushing process. This decline in soybean processing can ease the demand for beans and can either slow the rising price for beans or cause prices to decline. At the same time, the reduction in production of soybean meal and soybean oil will lead to a tightening in supply and can cause prices to rise. The net result is a reversion to a more favourable GPM, allowing soybean processing to resume.

Figure 6.11 shows a weekly price chart of CBOT soybean oil futures from 1987 to 2012.

Figure 6.11: CBOT weekly soybean oil futures chart, 1987–2012

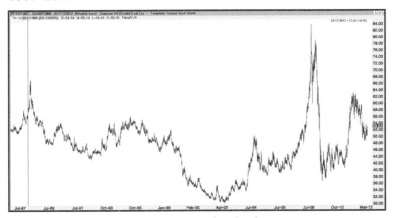

Source: Trade Navigator / Genesis Financial Technologies Inc.

Pricing

Soybean oil futures are traded on the Chicago Board of Trade (CBOT). Soybean oil futures are traded in cents per pound on a 60 000-pound contract. A 1 cent move in the price of soybean oil equates to $600 on the futures contract (60 000 pounds × $0.01 = $600.00). The minimum price move, or tick, is $0.0001 or $6.00 per contract (60 000 pounds × $0.0001 = $6.00).

Trading examples

Expecting the price of soybean oil to rise, a trader would BUY (go long) a futures contract. Let's say the long position is initiated at 52.68 cents per pound and the market rises to 54.87 cents per pound, a move of 2.19 cents per pound, or 219 ticks ($0.0219 ÷ $0.0001). The trader's profit (excluding brokerage and costs) would be $1314.00 (219 ticks × $6.00 per tick = $1314.00).

> 52.68 (sell price) − 54.87 (buy price) = 2.19 cents per pound × $600.00 per 1 cent = $1314.00

Expecting the price of soybean oil to fall, a trader would SELL (go short) a futures contract. Let's say the short position is initiated at 57.72 cents per pound and the market falls to 54.55 cents per pound, a move of 3.17 cents per pound, or 317 ticks ($0.0317 ÷ $0.0001). The trader's profit (excluding brokerage and costs) would be $1902.00 (317 ticks × $6.00 per tick = $1902.00).

> 57.72 (sell price) − 54.55 (buy price) = 3.17 cents per pound × $600.00 per 1 cent = $1902.00

Contract specifications

Full contract specifications for the CBOT soybean oil futures contract are shown in figure 6.12.

Trading hours

Soybean oil futures contracts are traded electronically 21 hours per day on CME's electronic Globex platform, from 5.00 pm each day until 2.00 pm (Chicago time) the following day, beginning at 5.00 pm on Sunday night. There is a three-hour gap in trading each day between 2.00 pm and 5.00 pm Monday to Thursday. Soybean oil futures are also traded on the CBOT in the traditional open outcry session between

9.30 am and 1.15 pm each weekday. The pit trading session occurs in conjunction with electronic trading during the pit session times.

Figure 6.12: CBOT soybean oil futures contract specifications

Contract Size	60,000 pounds (lbs) (~ 27 metric tons)	
Deliverable Grade	Crude soybean oil meeting exchange-approved grades and standards-see exchange Rules and Regulations for exact specifications.	
Pricing Unit	Cents per pound	
Tick Size (minimum fluctuation)	1/100 of a cent ($0.0001) per pound ($6.00 per contract)	
Contract Months/Symbols	January (F), March (H), May (K), July (N), August (Q), September (U), October (V) & December (Z)	
Trading Hours	CME Globex (Electronic Platform)	5:00 pm - 2:00 pm, Sunday - Friday Central Time
	Open Outcry (Trading Floor)	9:30 am - 1:15 pm, Central Time, Monday - Friday
Daily Price Limit	2.5 cents per pound expandable to 3.5 cents per pound and then to 5.5 cents per pound when the market closes at limit bid or limit offer. There shall be no price limits on the current month contract on or after the second business day preceding the first day of the delivery month.	
Settlement Procedure	Physical Delivery	
Last Trade Date	The business day prior to the 15th calendar day of the contract month.	
Last Delivery Date	Seventh business day following the last trading day of the delivery month.	
Product Ticker Symbols	CME Globex (Electronic Platform)	ZL 07=Clearing
	Open Outcry (Trading Floor)	BO
Exchange Rule	These contracts are listed with, and subject to, the rules and regulations of CBOT.	

Source: CME Group Inc.

Mini-sized corn, wheat and soybean futures contracts

In 2003 mini-sized (e-mini) futures contracts began trading on the CBOT for corn, soybeans and wheat. These mini-sized contracts are all one-fifth the size of the standard contracts, or 1000 bushels. The minimum price tick is ⅛ of 1 cent per bushel or $1.25 (1000 bushels × $0.00125 = $1.25) as opposed to $12.50 on the standard 5000-bushel contract. The mini-sized contracts have the same trading times and rules as the standard contracts. They were introduced to provide more flexibility for traders and hedgers in the grain markets and to give smaller traders the ability to participate in these markets. Liquidity in the mini-sized contracts is not as good as in the standard contracts, and price quotes and spreads can be wider at times as a result. Traders looking to use mini-sized contracts need to look at these two issues to ensure they can enter and exit positions readily and without too much slippage in price.

chapter 7

Food and fibre — the 'softs'

The term 'soft' was originally applied to any commodity that was not extracted or mined. These days it is used to describe those commodities that are grown on a plant but are not a grain or oilseed. The five major soft commodities are cocoa, coffee, cotton, orange juice and sugar.

Cocoa

Cocoa is produced from the cocoa or cacao tree, a tropical plant that produces large melon-like pods that contain cocoa beans. The cocoa beans are processed to produce cocoa, cocoa butter, cocoa powder and other sweetened chocolate products. Cocoa pods are harvested twice in a growing season, with the main harvest occurring in March and a secondary harvest occurring around August.

The chocolate market is the largest user of cocoa, which is also used in soaps, cosmetics and pharmaceutical products. Originally cultivated in Central and South America, cocoa trees are now grown in many African and Asian countries. Global cocoa production is around 3.5 million tons annually. The Ivory Coast (Côte d'Ivoire) in West Africa is the world's largest producer of cocoa beans, followed by Ghana, Indonesia, Cameroon, Nigeria and Brazil. According to figures from the World Cocoa Foundation, around two-thirds of global cocoa output comes from the four West African nations, with the Ivory Coast alone accounting for approximately 40 per cent.

Factors affecting price

Factors affecting the price of cocoa include the following:

⇒ Weather conditions in the major growing areas in West Africa will influence the supply of cocoa beans. Drought conditions will result in a smaller crop and may force prices up, while a 'normal' growing season may result in more stable prices. Excess production can lead to sharp and sudden declines in price. Cocoa futures prices tend to be heavily influenced by perceived changes in supply before and around harvest time, and volatility can increase around these times.

⇒ Political and economic conditions in the major producing nations, particularly the Ivory Coast, can cause sharp spikes in the price of cocoa futures. Political uncertainty, uprisings and civil wars have destabilised the Ivory Coast in recent times, leading to corruption and manipulation of the economy. Cocoa is the major industry, and production and export can be manipulated by government to achieve a desired political aim or result. Cocoa prices will often spike suddenly in response to unrest or political manoeuvring.

⇒ As such a large proportion of global production stems from only a few countries, export supplies can be hindered by political unrest and industrial action, particularly at the ports from which cocoa is shipped.

This can cause short-term price spikes, particularly if it occurs during a period of high production requirements.

⇒ Cocoa bean stocks are termed 'visible' or 'invisible', depending on where and by whom they are held. Visible stocks are those held in public warehouses, and these supply figures are readily available. Invisible stocks are those held in private warehouses, and they are much harder to estimate. More cocoa beans tend to be held in private warehouses than public warehouses. Fluctuations in estimates and spasmodic releases of cocoa bean stocks from these private warehouses can cause sharp price movements and lead to periods of increased volatility in the cocoa market.

⇒ Demand for chocolate, principally in the United States and Europe.

Figure 7.1 shows a weekly price chart of cocoa futures from 1987 to 2012.

Figure 7.1: weekly price chart of ICE cocoa futures, 1987–2012

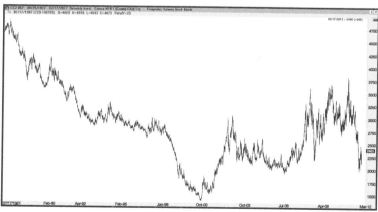

Source: Trade Navigator / Genesis Financial Technologies Inc.

Pricing

Cocoa futures trade electronically on the InterContinental Exchange (ICE), previously called the New York Board of Trade (NYBOT). Cocoa futures also trade on the NYSE Euronext exchange, previously the London International Financial and Futures Options Exchange (LIFFE) in London.

On the ICE exchange cocoa futures trade in dollars per tonne on a 10 metric tonne contract. A $1 move in the price of cocoa equates to $10 on the ICE contract (10 tonnes × $1 = $10.00), and the minimum price move, or tick value, is also $10.

On the NYSE Euronext exchange cocoa futures trade in British pounds per tonne on a 10 metric tonne contract. A £1 move in the price of cocoa equates to £10 on the Euronext contract (10 tonnes × £1 = £10), and the minimum price move, or tick value, is also £10.

Tip

The ICE-traded cocoa contract has the most liquidity and open interest of the two contracts.

Trading examples

Expecting the price of cocoa to rise, a trader would BUY (go long) a futures contract. Let's say the long position is initiated at $3191 per tonne and the market rises to $3639 per tonne due to drought conditions in West Africa, a move of $448 per tonne, or 448 ticks. The trader's profit (excluding brokerage and costs) would be $4480 (448 ticks × $10 per tick = $4480).

$3639 per tonne (sell price) − $3191 per tonne (buy price) = $448 per tonne × $10 per 1 tonne = $4480

Expecting the price of cocoa to fall, a trader would SELL (go short) a futures contract. Let's say the short position is initiated at $3146 per tonne and the market falls to $2923 per tonne, a move of $223 per tonne or 223 ticks. The trader's profit (excluding brokerage and costs) would be $2230 (223 ticks × $10 per tick = $2230).

$3639 per tonne (sell price) − $3191 per tonne (buy price) = $223 × $10 per 1 tonne = $2230

Contract specifications

Due to contractual restrictions, full contract specifications for the ICE-traded cocoa futures contract are unable to be reproduced in this book. Full contract specifications for the ICE-traded cocoa futures contract can be obtained at the Intercontinental Exchange website at www.theice.com.

An ICE-traded cocoa futures contract is for 10 metric tonnes of cocoa that calls for physical delivery. Cocoa trades in US dollars per metric tonne, with a minimum price move, or tick, of $1 per metric tonne, or $10 per contract. The available contract months are March, May, July, September and December.

Tip

The major differences between the ICE contract specifications and those of the NYSE Euronext are the currency (US dollars versus British pounds) and the accepted delivery points. The ICE contract calls for delivery to nominated US ports, while the NYSE Euronext contract calls for delivery to nominated European ports.

Trading hours

Trading hours for both contracts vary slightly, but they trade in unison for the majority of the trading session. The ICE opens at 4.00 am New York time (9.00 am London time) and closes at 2.00 pm New York time (7.00 pm London time). The NYSE Euronext opens at 9.30 am London time (4.30 am New York time) and closes at 4.50 pm London time (11.50 am New York time).

Coffee

The coffee bush is indigenous to Africa, having its origins in Ethiopia and Angola. In the 1600s coffee growing spread as the Dutch colonised parts of Asia and became the major suppliers of coffee to European markets. This trend continued as the Dutch brought coffee with them to their colonies in South America, where it was ideally suited to the tropical climate.

The coffee we drink is made from the roasted and ground beans of the coffee plant. Coffee is divided into two types—high-quality arabica and low-quality robusta. Arabica coffee has a mild taste, is more flavoursome, and accounts for the bulk of global production and consumption. This higher quality coffee is grown and produced in highland areas in Brazil, Colombia and other South American countries. Robusta coffee tends to be less mild and of lower quality, and is grown in the low, hot areas of Africa and Asia. Because of the geographical differences between where coffee is produced (tropical and subtropical climates) and where consumption is greatest (Europe and the United States), coffee is one of the most internationally traded of all commodities.

Tip

To help facilitate international trade, all coffee is packed in standardised 60-kilogram bags.

The International Trade Centre reports world coffee production in 2009–10 of around 126.2 million 60 kg bags, of which 93.4 million bags (around 74 per cent) were exported. Brazil is the largest producer and exporter of coffee, with combined exports of 43.4 million bags of both arabica (32.5 million bags) and robusta (10.9 million bags), followed by Vietnam (18 million bags of robusta), Colombia (9 million bags of arabica) and Indonesia (8 million bags of robusta).

Coffee is an extremely important crop for many of the world's least developed countries, providing them with a significant portion of their export and foreign exchange earnings, as well as being a huge employer through all stages of production, processing and transportation.

Tip

As coffee is a 'mature' market, demand tends to be relatively inelastic. As a result, changes in the price of coffee beans tend to be driven by changes in supply.

Factors affecting price

Factors affecting the price of coffee include the following:

⇒ Arabica coffee plants are very susceptible to frosts and insufficient rainfall. Weather conditions in the South American coffee-producing countries, particularly Brazil, are extremely important. Drought conditions during late summer and early autumn can impact heavily on production of quality arabica beans and cause prices to rise. Heavy frosts during the Brazilian winter, which can damage the plants and thus impact on the coming harvest, can cause sharp and unexpected price rallies. Coffee futures prices are capable of producing large and dramatic price moves as a result of these weather-driven events.

⇒ Industrial and political actions and events in some of the coffee-producing countries can affect the supply of coffee to export markets and have a short-term impact on price.

⇒ Long-term crop forecasts can cause changes in traders' expectations for the supply of coffee. If crop production forecasts are low or reduced, prices can rise in response. If crop production forecasts are 'normal' or improved, prices may decline.

⇒ High carryover stock levels can dampen price rises in response to weather-driven events, as consumption can make use of carryover stocks in lieu of new crop production.

⇒ Government policies in regard to production quotas or restrictions, any price support programs to encourage production, and other such incentives or restrictions in producing countries that impact on the supply of coffee can affect prices. The voluntary alliance of coffee exporting and importing nations, the International Coffee Organization (ICO), may also set import and export quotas at times in an attempt to achieve market price stability.

Tip

Coffee is the most volatile of all the agricultural commodities, and explosive price moves brought about by sudden changes in weather conditions are not uncommon. This extreme volatility can produce drastic price changes over a few days, and even within a day at times.

Figure 7.2 shows a weekly price chart of ICE coffee futures from 1987 to 2012.

Figure 7.2: weekly price chart of ICE coffee futures, 1987–2012

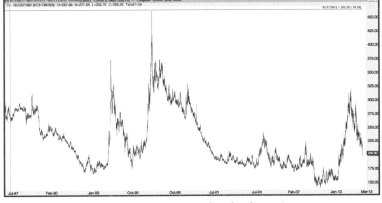

Source: Trade Navigator / Genesis Financial Technologies Inc.

Pricing

The two major markets for coffee futures are the InterContinental Exchange (ICE), previously called the New York Board of Trade (NYBOT) and the NYSE Euronext exchange, previously the London International Financial and Futures Options Exchange (LIFFE) in London. Coffee futures originated in 1882, trading on the Coffee Exchange of the City of New York. Coffee futures are now traded electronically.

Tip

The ICE coffee futures contract is for arabica coffee, while the NYSE Euronext contract is for robusta coffee. There are also smaller futures markets for coffee in Brazil and Japan.

On the ICE exchange coffee futures trade in cents per pound on a 37 500-pound contract. A 1-cent move in the price of coffee equates to $375.00 on the futures contract

(37 500 pounds × \$0.01 = \$375.00). The minimum price move or tick is \$0.0005 or \$18.75 per contract (37 500 pounds × \$0.0005 = \$18.75).

On the NYSE Euronext exchange coffee futures trade in US dollars per Imperial ton on a 10 Imperial ton contract. The minimum price move, or tick, is \$1.00 per Imperial ton.

Tip

The ICE-traded cocoa contract has the greater liquidity and open interest of the two contracts.

Trading examples

Expecting the price of coffee to rise, a trader would BUY (go long) a futures contract. Let's say the long position is initiated at 234.65 cents per pound and the market rises to 256.15 cents per pound, a move of 21.50 cents per pound, or 430 ticks (\$0.2150 ÷ \$0.0005). The trader's profit (excluding brokerage and costs) would be \$8062.50 (430 ticks × \$18.75 per tick = \$8062.50).

256.15 (sell price) − 234.65 (buy price) = 21.50 cents per pound × \$375.00 per 1 cent = \$8062.50

Expecting the price of coffee to fall, a trader would SELL (go short) a futures contract. Let's say the short position is initiated at 223.05 cents per pound and the market falls to 213.40 cents per pound, a move of 9.65 cents per pound, or 193 ticks (\$0.0965 ÷ \$0.0005). The trader's profit (excluding brokerage and costs) would be \$3618.75 (193 ticks × \$18.75 per tick = \$3618.75).

223.05 (sell price) − 213.40 (buy price) = 9.65 cents per pound × \$375.00 per 1 cent = \$3618.75

Contract specifications

Due to contractual restrictions, full contract specifications for the ICE-traded coffee futures contract are unable to be reproduced in this book. Full contract specifications for the ICE-traded coffee futures contract can be obtained at the Intercontinental Exchange website at www.theice.com.

An ICE-traded coffee futures contract is for 37,500 pounds of coffee that calls for physical delivery. Coffee trades in cents and hundredths of cents per pound, with a minimum price move or tick of 5 one-hundredths of 1 cent per pound, or $18.75 per contract. The available contract months are March, May, July, September and December.

Tip

The major differences between the ICE contract specifications and those of the NYSE Euronext are the type of coffee, the contract size and the accepted delivery points. The ICE contract is for 37 500 pounds of arabica coffee and the NYSE Euronext contract is for 10 Imperial tonnes of robusta coffee. The ICE contract calls for delivery to seven specified ports while the NYSE Euronext contract calls for delivery to 13 specified ports.

Trading hours

Trading hours for the two contracts vary slightly, but they trade in unison for the majority of the trading session. The ICE opens at 3.30 am New York time (8.30 am London time) and closes at 2.00 pm New York time (7.00 pm London time). The NYSE Euronext opens at 9.00 am London time (4.00 am New York time) and closes at 5.30 pm London time (12.30 pm New York time).

Cotton

Cotton is one of the oldest fibres used by humanity and is still the world's leading natural textile fibre. Archaeological findings have traced the cultivation and use of cotton in India and South America to more than 7000 years ago. It is produced in more than 75 countries throughout the world under a diverse range of growing conditions. Cotton is a soft fibre that grows in a capsule or 'boll' around the seed of a cotton plant. Once harvested from the plant, cotton is cleaned in a cotton gin, and the fibre, called 'lint', is removed from the seed, graded according to colour, staple length and fibre fineness, and pressed into standardised bales with a gross weight of 480 pounds. This lint, or raw cotton, is used to manufacture a huge range of cotton products, from clothing to linen.

Ideal growing conditions for cotton are a long frost-free period, long periods of sunshine, moderate rainfall and reasonably heavy soils. The use of irrigation to water cotton plants during the growing season means cotton can be grown in more arid areas provided water is available for irrigation. Irrigating cotton can put pressure on water supplies in drier regions, particularly in periods of drought and low natural rainfall, and has a heavy environmental impact. Cotton growing is very sensitive to weather and insects, and growers rely heavily on the use of insecticides, fertilisers and herbicides.

According to the Cotton Council of America, China is the world's largest producer of cotton (producing an estimated 33 million 480-pound bales, or 29 per cent of global production, in 2011), followed by India (27 million bales), the United States (18 million bales) and Pakistan (10 million bales). China is also the largest importer of cotton, while the United States is the largest exporter, followed by India and Australia. China's huge output of cotton is used in the manufacture of textiles and clothing, much of which is exported as finished goods to the United States and other Western nations. China uses around 43 per cent of the world's milled cotton.

Cotton faces continual competition from man-made synthetic fibres such as nylon, rayon and polyester.

Factors affecting price

Factors affecting the price of coffee include the following:

⇒ Cotton production is extremely sensitive to weather conditions and insects. Extremes in temperature and rainfall throughout the growing season will affect the quantity and quality of the cotton crop. Attacks by insects can also affect both the quality and quantity of cotton produced. While cotton production is spread throughout the world, any extreme weather conditions in any of the major growing countries can cause prices to spike suddenly and threaten supply.

⇒ Extreme drought conditions that severely impact on water availability for irrigated cotton growing can result in reduced production and supply and affect prices.

⇒ Carryover stock levels and stock-to-use ratios will influence the area planted to cotton, causing price fluctuations to occur. If carryover stock levels from previous years are high and the amount of cotton being used is stable, then demand can be maintained. Farmers may plant less cotton under such a scenario, preferring to plant alternate crops such as corn or soybeans if they offer a better price and return. This will result in reduced cotton production, lowering carryover stock levels and pushing prices higher. If potential returns improve, in the following season farmers may reallocate resources to growing cotton while reducing the acreages planted to other crops.

⇒ Higher prices for corn and soybeans and an increased demand for these crops for use in the biofuel and ethanol industry have displaced some of the acreages planted to cotton, particularly in the United States. Farmers will allocate their land, water and other resources to crops that allow them to maximise their returns, continually chasing the cropping opportunities that provide the greatest return for their time and capital investment. Reduced acreages of cotton leads to reduced production, and continued strong demand causes price to rise. This ongoing cycle and reallocation of cropping resources will always be a part of the agricultural industry.

Tip

Cotton is one of the more volatile agricultural commodities, and explosive price moves brought about by sudden changes in weather conditions and other supply concerns are not uncommon. This extreme volatility can produce drastic price changes over a few days, and sometimes even within a day.

Figure 7.3 shows a weekly price chart of cotton futures from 1987 to 2012.

Figure 7.3: weekly price chart of ICE cotton futures, 1987–2012

Source: Trade Navigator / Genesis Financial Technologies Inc.

Pricing

Cotton futures trade electronically on the InterContinental Exchange (ICE). Cotton futures contracts trade in cents per pound on a 50 000-pound contract. A 1-cent-per-pound move in the price of cotton equates to $500 on the futures contract (50 000 pounds × $0.01 = $500.00). The minimum price move, or tick, is $0.0001 or $5.00 per contract (50 000 pounds × 0.01 cents = $5.00).

Tip

Cotton quite often develops significant medium-term price trends interspersed with periods of short-term volatility.

Trading examples

Expecting the price of cotton to rise, a trader would BUY (go long) a futures contract. Let's say the long position is initiated at 97.49 cents per pound and the market rises to 99.85 cents per pound, a move of 2.36 cents per pound, or 236 ticks ($0.0236 ÷ $0.0001). The trader's profit (excluding brokerage and costs) would be $1180.00 (236 ticks × $5.00 per tick = $1180.00).

> 99.85 (sell price) − 97.49 (buy price) = 2.36 cents per pound × $500.00 per 1 cent = $1180.00

Expecting the price of cotton to fall, a trader would SELL (go short) a futures contract. Let's say the short position is initiated at 100.56 cents per pound and the market falls to 97.44 cents per pound, a move of 3.12 cents per pound, or 312 ticks ($0.0312 ÷ $0.0001). The trader's profit (excluding brokerage and costs) would be $1560.00 (312 ticks × $5.00 per tick = $1560.00).

> 100.56 (sell price) − 97.44 (buy price) = 3.12 cents per pound × $500.00 per 1 cent = $1560.00

Contract specifications

Due to contractual restrictions, full contract specifications for the ICE-traded cotton futures contract are unable to be reproduced in this book. Full contract specifications for the ICE-traded cotton futures contract can be obtained at the Intercontinental Exchange website at www.theice.com. An ICE-traded cotton futures contract is for 50,000 pounds of US-origin cotton that calls for physical delivery. Cotton trades in cents and hundredths of cents per pound, with a minimum price move or tick of 1 one-hundred of 1 cent per pound, or $5 per contract. The available contract months are March, May, July, October and December.

Trading hours

Cotton futures contracts are traded electronically on the ICE exchange between 9.00 pm and 2.30 pm the following day New York time.

Orange juice

The orange juice market changed considerably in 1944 with the invention in California of a process for freezing orange juice in a vacuum without destroying the flavour or vitamin content. This process allows the production of what is known as frozen concentrated orange juice (FCOJ). The harvested oranges are squeezed to remove the fresh juice, which is then pasteurised, concentrated by removing up to 85 per cent of the water content, and then frozen. This concentrate is approximately seven times stronger than the original orange juice. The purchaser then reconstitutes this frozen concentrate by adding back water. The demand for FCOJ in America after World War II saw a dramatic increase in the market as a result of the ease with which it could be transported and stored, and resulted in huge plantings of orange trees in Florida, Texas, California and Arizona.

Annual global production of oranges, according to the USDA, is now around 51 million metric tonnes. Brazil produces approximately 33 per cent or 17 million metric tonnes, followed by the United States, China and the Eurozone. It is estimated that almost all the Brazilian crop is exported (predominantly to the United States as FCOJ), with only around 1 per cent consumed in the domestic market. Together, Brazil and the United States account for over 85 per cent of global orange juice production. Up to 90 per cent of oranges grown in the United States are used for the production of orange juice. Oranges grown in Florida account for more than 50 per cent of the domestic US crop.

Frozen concentrates were the most popular form of orange juice in the United States until 1985, when reconstituted and Not from Concentrate (NFC) juices first outsold FCOJ. Both of these juice products can be transported and stored without refrigeration and have had a large impact on FCOJ market share.

Factors affecting price

Factors affecting the price of orange juice include the following:

⇒ Orange juice production is directly related to the overall yield of oranges from orange trees. Orange trees are grown in warm subtropical climates with long, sunny days during the growing season. Orange trees can be seriously affected by sudden cold snaps and frosts, extended periods of dry weather, extreme heat and strong winds. Any of these weather-related issues can stress the orange trees and impact negatively on production and thus on the supply of orange Juice. Weather-related events, particularly a sudden cold snap or frost, tend to impact immediately on price, often sending prices sharply higher in response to reduced supply.

⇒ Insects and disease can also affect the trees and orange production, but generally their impact is not as sudden and unexpected as a frost or wind-related event.

Tip

Orange juice prices can rally sharply as a result of weather-related events, and can often trade erratically.

Figure 7.4 shows a weekly price chart of orange juice futures from 1987 to 2011.

Figure 7.4: weekly price chart of ICE orange juice futures, 1987–2011

Source: Trade Navigator / Genesis Financial Technologies Inc.

Pricing

Orange juice futures trade electronically on the InterContinental Exchange (ICE). Orange juice futures trade in cents per pound on a 15 000-pound contract. A 1-cent-per-pound move in the price of orange juice equates to $150.00 on the futures contract (15 000 pounds × $0.01 = $150.00). The minimum price move, or tick, is ⁵⁄₁₀₀ of a cent ($0.0005) or $7.50 per contract (15 000 pounds × $0.0005 = $7.50).

Trading examples

Expecting the price of orange juice to rise, a trader would BUY (go long) a futures contract. Let's say the long position is initiated at 187.75 cents per pound and the market rises sharply on the back of frost damage to orange trees in Florida to 199.65 cents per pound, a move of 11.9 cents per pound, or 238 ticks ($0.119 ÷ $0.0005). The trader's profit (excluding brokerage and costs) would be $1785.00 (238 ticks × $7.50 per tick = $1785.00).

> 199.65 (sell price) − 187.75 (buy price) = 11.9 cents per pound × $150.00 per 1 cent = $1785.00

Expecting the price of orange juice to fall, a trader would SELL (go short) a futures contract. Let's say the short position is initiated at 160.65 cents per pound and the market falls to 158.45 cents per pound, a move of 2.2 cents per pound, or 44 ticks ($0.022 ÷ $0.0005). The trader's profit (excluding brokerage and costs) would be $330.00 (44 ticks × $7.50 per tick = $330.00).

> 160.65 (sell price) − 158.45 (buy price) = 2.2 cents per pound × $150.00 per 1 cent = $330.00

Contract specifications

Due to contractual restrictions, full contract specifications for the ICE-traded orange juice futures contract are unable to be reproduced in this book. Full contract specifications for the ICE-traded orange juice futures contract can be obtained at the Intercontinental Exchange website at www.theice.com.

An ICE-traded orange juice futures contract is for 15 000 pounds of orange juice solids that calls for physical delivery. Orange juice trades in cents and hundredths of cents per pound, with a minimum price move or tick of 5 one-hundredths of 1 cent per pound, or $7.50 per contract. The available contract months are March, May, July, September and November.

Trading hours

Orange juice futures contracts are traded electronically on the ICE exchange between 8.00 am and 2.00 pm New York time.

Sugar

Sugar is one of the world's oldest agricultural industries and is now produced in more than 100 countries worldwide. The sugar we consume is refined from sucrose, a crystalline carbohydrate that occurs naturally in sugar cane, where it is stored in the plant's stalk, and sugar beet, where it is stored in the fleshy root of the plant. Around 70 to 75 per cent of the sugar we consume comes from sugar cane grown in tropical and semitropical zones in the Southern Hemisphere. The remaining 25 to 30 per cent comes from sugar beet grown in temperate zones in the Northern Hemisphere. While the growing and processing techniques are completely different for sugar cane and sugar beet, the refined sugar produced from each is exactly the same.

Tip

Generally refined sugar can be produced from sugarcane significantly more cheaply than from sugar beet.

The USDA estimates global sugar production at around 170 million tonnes. Brazil is the largest producer, accounting for around 35 to 40 million tonnes, or between 20 and

25 per cent of global sugar production. Other important sugar-producing countries are India (25 million tonnes), the Eurozone (15 million tonnes—from sugar beet), China (12 million tonnes) and Thailand (10 million tonnes). The top 10 sugar-producing countries account for more than 75 per cent of global production.

The major global exporting countries are Brazil (26 million tonnes), Thailand (7 million tonnes) and Australia. Australia is the ninth-largest global sugar producer (around 4 million tonnes) but the third-largest exporter of sugar to world markets, exporting around 2.5 million tonnes, or more than 60 per cent of its total sugar production. The top five sugar-exporting countries account for more than 80 per cent of total world sugar exports.

It is currently estimated that around 70 to 75 per cent of sugar produced is consumed in its country of origin, or traded under a wide range of special agreements, such as US tariff-rate quotas and the European Union import quotas. As a result, only about 20 to 30 per cent of global sugar produced is available to trade on world markets at a free market price.

Tip

As sugar is a 'mature' market, demand tends to be relatively inelastic, growing by only about 1 per cent per year. As a result, changes in the price of sugar tend to be driven by changes in supply.

Factors affecting price

Factors affecting the price of sugar include the following:

⇒ Like all agricultural commodities, sugar cane and sugar beets can be affected by adverse weather conditions. Sugarcane can be affected by a lack of rain or, conversely, too much rain, particularly during harvest time. Hurricanes, cyclones and other tropical storms can severely damage the growing cane, thus reducing the production of sugar. Sugar producers and traders closely monitor the development of hurricanes in the Northern Hemisphere and cyclones in the Southern Hemisphere. Sugar beet can be impacted by periods of dry weather, excessively cold nights and wind.

⇒ Tariffs, quotas and export bans in some sugar-producing countries can affect the price of the freely traded global sugar price. Increases or decreases in the 'protected' price, or the quantities of sugar affected by the tariffs and quotas, will have an impact on the freely traded sugar price.

⇒ As only a small proportion of the sugar produced globally is freely traded, small changes in the availability of sugar can have a dramatic effect on price. A relatively small reduction, or anticipated reduction, in sugar available for export can cause sharp and sudden changes in price. Periods of stability in global production, or of increased production in exporting countries, can see global sugar prices stabilise or contract.

⇒ Carryover stock levels and reports of sugar stocks that measure the balance between global supply and demand will also influence current and future price levels. High stock holdings coupled with increased production levels can have a negative impact on prices, while low stock levels and a reduced production may well result in higher sugar prices.

⇒ The price of crude oil and the use of ethanol fuel substitutes also impact on the price of sugar. As prices for crude oil and other non-renewable energy sources increase, the demand, and price, for plant-based ethanol fuel sources also increases. Sugar cane is the most cost-efficient plant material for the production of ethanol fuel. As a result, when the demand and price for ethanol increases, sugar cane growers in Brazil, in particular, will supply sugar cane to the ethanol fuel plants. This results in less sugar cane available for refining for the production of sugar, which can cause prices to rise.

Tip

The correlation between the price of crude oil and the price of sugar should be closely monitored by sugar traders.

Figure 7.5 shows a weekly price chart of sugar futures from 1987 to the 2011.

Figure 7.5: weekly price chart of ICE sugar futures, 1987–2011

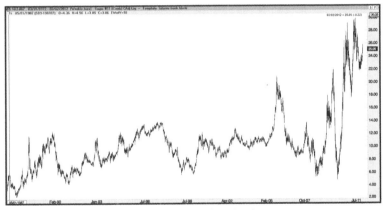

Source: Trade Navigator / Genesis Financial Technologies Inc.

Tip

The futures contract that reflects the freely traded sugar price is the ICE Sugar #11 contract. The ICE Sugar #16 contract reflects the price of domestically traded sugar in the United States. Sugar futures are also traded on the Euronext exchange and the Tokyo Grain Exchange, but at significantly lower volumes than on ICE.

Pricing

Sugar #11 futures trade electronically on the InterContinental Exchange (ICE). Sugar #11 futures trade in cents per pound on a 112 000-pound contract (50 metric tonnes). A 1-cent-per-pound move in the price of sugar equates to $1120.00 on the futures contract (112 000 pounds × $0.01 = $1120.00). The minimum price move, or tick, is $1/100$ of 1 cent ($0.0001) per contract or $11.20 (112 000 pounds × $0.0001 = $11.20).

Trading examples

Expecting the price of sugar to rise, a trader would BUY (go long) a futures contract. Let's say the long position is initiated at 21.56 cents per pound and the market rises to 24.23 cents per pound, a move of 2.67 cents per pound, or 267 ticks ($0.0267 ÷ $0.0001). The trader's profit (excluding brokerage and costs) would be $2990.40 (267 ticks × $11.20 per tick = $2990.40).

> 24.23 (sell price) − 21.56 (buy price) = 2.67 cents per pound × $1120.00 per 1 cent = $2990.40

Expecting the price of sugar to fall, a trader would SELL (go short) a futures contract. Let's say the short position is initiated at 25.02 cents per pound and the market falls to 23.10 cents per pound, a move of 1.92 cents per pound, or 192 ticks ($0.0192 ÷ $0.0001). The trader's profit (excluding brokerage and costs) would be $2150.40 (192 ticks × $11.20 per tick = $2150.40).

> 25.02 (sell price) − 23.10 (buy price) = 1.92 cents per pound × $1120.00 per 1 cent = $2150.40

Contract specifications

Due to contractual restrictions, full contract specifications for the ICE-traded sugar #11 futures contract are unable to be reproduced in this book. Full contract specifications for the ICE-traded sugar #11 futures contract can be obtained at the Intercontinental Exchange website at www.theice.com

An ICE-traded sugar #11 futures contract is for 112 000 pounds of sugar that calls for physical delivery. Sugar #11 trades in cents and hundredths of a cent per pound, with a minimum price move, or tick, of 1 one-hundredth of 1 cent per pound, or $11.20 per contract. The available contract months are March, May, July, and October.

Trading hours

Sugar #11 futures contracts are traded electronically on the ICE exchange between 1.30 am and 2.00 pm New York time.

chapter 8

Livestock — the meats

Meat is the major source of protein in the diets of Americans and people of other developed nations, and a growing source of protein in the diets of people in many developing nations, and the meat and livestock industry continues to grow throughout the world to meet this ever-increasing demand. The three main futures contracts associated with the meat industry are the live cattle, feeder cattle and lean hogs contracts. All three are traded on the CME in both the traditional open outcry or pit session and electronically on the Globex platform.

Feeder cattle

The beef cattle industry has three sectors or 'levels' of operation: cow and calf operations, feedlots, and meat packers. Cow and calf operators, often called ranchers or cattle producers, produce calves, which become feeder cattle. Feeder cattle are grain fed in feed lots, where they become known as live cattle, and are then slaughtered by meat packers for human consumption.

Feeder cattle are the weaned calves produced by cow and calf operators that have been raised to between 600 and 800 pounds before being sent to feedlots to be fattened. They are generally 8 to 10 months old and have been grass fed up until this point. Once in the feedlot, the cattle are fed a controlled diet of grains and other feeds designed to encourage rapid weight gain. They are fattened in the feedlot until they reach a desired finished weight of between 1000 and 1300 pounds. These feedlot operations vary in size from small, owner-operated feedlots of 100 head of cattle, to corporate operations of more than 50 000 head of cattle on feed.

The USDA estimates total global beef cattle numbers at around 1.3 billion head. The largest commercial beef producers are Brazil (187 million head), China (140 million head) and the United States (97 million head). According to the USDA *Cattle on Feed Report*, between 25 and 33 million head of cattle pass through US domestic feedlots annually.

Factors affecting price

Factors affecting the price of feeder cattle include the following:

⇒ Beef-cattle raising has a long lead-in time. From the time the cows are joined, through the nine-month gestation period, and the 8 to 10 months the calves remain with their mothers before being weaned and sent to the feedlot, is almost two years. As a result, adjustments to beef breeding and feeding operations are difficult to make and cannot happen quickly. Expansion and contraction cycles in terms of numbers of cows being bred to produce calves and, in turn, numbers of calves on feedlots, can take years.

⇒ When breeders decide to increase breeding stock in response to rising prices or expectations of rising prices, stock is held back for herd expansion, putting further pressure on prices by limiting supply. Rising prices also mean calves are kept on feed longer, allowing them to be sold at heavier weights for greater return. Eventually, the large number of calves from the expanding herds will mature, and the slaughter levels will increase. Prices will start to decline in response to oversupply. This decline in price causes breeders to reduce their numbers, and the whole cycle begins again.

⇒ Long periods of excessively hot, cold or wet weather can slow the rate of weight gain in feedlot cattle, increasing feeding costs and extending the feeding period, limiting supply in the short term and potentially pushing prices higher.

⇒ Consumer preferences and the price of alternative meats such as chicken and pork influence cattle prices. These are often driven by health statistics, marketing campaigns, dietary fads and other consumer-related decisions and perceptions.

Tip

Feeder cattle prices tend to maintain clearer and longer trends than live cattle prices, although with greater price swings.

Figure 8.1 (overleaf) shows a weekly price chart of feeder cattle futures from 1987 to 2012.

Pricing

Feeder cattle futures are traded on the Chicago Mercantile Exchange (CME). Feeder cattle futures trade in cents per pound on a 50000-pound contract. A 1-cent-per-pound move in the price of feeder cattle equates to $500.00 on the futures contract (50000 pounds × $0.01 = $500.00). The minimum price move, or tick, is $0.00025, or $12.50 per contract (50000 pounds × $0.00025 = $12.50).

Figure 8.1: weekly price chart of CME feeder cattle futures, 1987–2012

Source: Trade Navigator / Genesis Financial Technologies Inc.

Trading examples

Expecting the price of feeder cattle to rise, a trader would BUY (go long) a futures contract. Let's say the long position is initiated at 141.825 cents per pound and the market rises to 144.675 cents per pound, a move of 2.85 cents per pound, or 114 ticks ($0.0285 ÷ $0.00025). The trader's profit (excluding brokerage and costs) would be $1425.00 (114 ticks × $12.50 per tick = $1425.00).

144.675 (sell price) − 141.825 (buy price) = 2.85 cents per pound × $500.00 per 1 cent = $1425.00

Expecting the price of feeder cattle to fall, a trader would SELL (go short) a futures contract. Let's say the short position is initiated at 144.550 cents per pound and the market falls to 138.625 cents per pound, a move of 5.925 cents per pound or 237 ticks ($0.05925 ÷ $0.00025). The trader's profit (excluding brokerage and costs) would be $2962.50 (237 ticks × $12.50 per tick = $2962.50).

144.550 (sell price) − 138.625 (buy price) = 5.925 cents per pound × $500.00 per 1 cent = $2962.50

Contract specifications

Full contract specifications for the CME-traded feeder cattle futures contract are shown in figure 8.2.

Figure 8.2: CME feeder cattle futures contract specifications

Contract Size	50,000 pounds (~23 metric tons)	
Product Description	650-849 pound steers, medium-large #1 and medium-large #1-2	
Pricing Unit	Cents per pound	
Tick Size (minimum fluctuation)	$.00025 per pound ($12.50 per contract)	
Daily Price Limits	$.03 per pound above or below the previous day's settlement price	
Trading Hours (All times listed are Central Time)	CME Globex (Electronic Platform)	MON 9:05 a.m. - FRI 1:55 p.m. Central Time Daily trading halts 4:00 p.m. - 5:00 p.m. Central Time
	Open Outcry (Trading Floor)	MON-FRI: 9:05 a.m. -1:00 p.m. Central Time
Last Trade Date/Time View Calendar	Last Thursday of the contract month with exceptions for November and other months, 12:00 p.m. - See CME Rule 10202.H.	
Contract Months View Listings	Jan, Mar, Apr, May, Aug, Sep, Oct, Nov	
Settlement Procedure	Cash Settlement. See CME Rule 10203.	
Position Limits	Non-Spot: 1,950 contracts in any contract month Spot: 300 contracts All months combined: n/a See CME Rule: 10202.E	
Ticker Symbol	CME Globex (Electronic Platform)	GF 62=Clearing
	Open Outcry (Trading Floor)	FC
Rulebook Chapter	102	
Exchange Rule	These contracts are listed with, and subject to, the rules and regulations of CME.	

Source: CME Group Inc.

Trading hours

Feeder cattle futures are traded both electronically on the CME Globex platform and by traditional open outcry on the trading floor. The electronic market opens at 9.05 am Monday morning Chicago time and trades almost continuously through to 1.55 pm Friday afternoon Chicago time, with a daily break between 4.00 pm and 5.00 pm Chicago time. The pit session operates each weekday between 9.05 am and 1.00 pm Chicago time.

Live cattle

Live cattle are the end result of cattle feed-lotting operations. Having reached the desired weight of between 1000 and 1300 pounds, what were once 'feeder cattle' are now sold to meat-packing operators for slaughter and processing into the various cuts of meat and other meat products available to consumers in supermarkets and butcher shops.

Factors affecting price

Factors affecting the price of live cattle include the following:

⇒ The same factors that apply to feeder cattle and mentioned earlier also apply to live cattle.

⇒ The amount of beef produced in the US, or any other country, depends on a wide range of domestic demand factors. Meat consumption tends to rise as a result of greater affluence and higher disposable incomes. When economic conditions are tight and consumers are reducing spending, demand for more expensive meat products will often decrease.

⇒ If beef prices are high compared with alternative meat products such as pork and chicken, demand for beef will decrease and put downward pressure on prices.

⇒ Government quotas, tariffs, subsidies and other actions designed to control imports, exports and domestic demand for beef can also influence prices and, in turn, supply and demand levels.

⇒ Grain prices also affect the number of cattle in feedlots and thus the supply of live cattle to the meat packers. If grain prices are high and grain stocks are in short supply, cattle numbers in feedlots may be cut back, reducing supply and pushing prices of consumer beef products higher. If grain is relatively cheap and readily available, feedlot cattle numbers will increase and prices for consumer beef products may decline.

⇒ Livestock diseases such as BSE, or 'mad cow disease', influence consumer perceptions of meat products, reducing demand and suppressing prices until consumer confidence is restored.

Tip

Live cattle prices can trade erratically, within a trading band, for long periods of time as a result of one or more of the factors mentioned here, and volatility can occur very quickly.

Figure 8.3 shows a weekly price chart of live cattle futures from 1987 to 2012.

Figure 8.3: weekly price chart of CME live cattle futures, 1987–2012

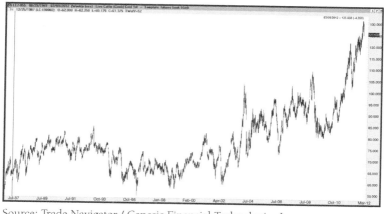

Source: Trade Navigator / Genesis Financial Technologies Inc.

Pricing

Live cattle futures are traded on the Chicago Mercantile Exchange (CME). Live cattle futures trade in cents per pound on a 40 000-pound contract. A 1-cent-per-pound move in the price of live cattle equates to $400.00 on the futures contract (40 000 pounds × $0.01 = $400.00). The minimum price move, or tick, is $0.00025 per contract or $10.00 (40 000 pounds × $0.00025 = $10.00).

Trading examples

Expecting the price of live cattle to rise, a trader would BUY (go long) a futures contract. Let's say the long position is initiated at 104.725 cents per pound and the market rises to 110.925 cents per pound, a move of 6.200 cents per pound, or 248 ticks, ($0.06200 ÷ $0.00025). The trader's profit (excluding brokerage and costs) would be $2480.00 (248 ticks × $10.00 per tick = $2480.00).

110.925 (sell price) − 104.725 (buy price) = 6.200 cents per pound × $400.00 per 1 cent = $2480.00

Expecting the price of live cattle to fall, a trader would SELL (go short) a futures contract. Let's say the short position is initiated at 115.125 cents per pound and the market falls to 109.750 cents per pound, a move of 5.375 cents per pound, or 215 ticks, ($0.05375 ÷ $0.00025). The trader's profit (excluding brokerage and costs) would be $2150.00 (215 ticks × $10.00 per tick = $2150.00).

115.125 (sell price) − 109.750 (buy price) = 5.375 cents per pound × $400.00 per 1 cent = $2150.00

Contract specifications

Full contract specifications for the CME-traded live cattle futures contract are shown in figure 8.4.

Figure 8.4: CME live cattle futures contract specifications

Contract Size	40,000 pounds (~18 metric tons)	
Product Description	55% Choice, 45% Select, Yield Grade 3 live steers	
Pricing Unit	Cents per pound	
Tick Size (minimum fluctuation)	$.00025 per pound (=$10 per contract)	
Daily Price Limits	$.03 per pound above or below the previous day's settlement price	
Trading Hours (All times listed are Central Time)	CME Globex (Electronic Platform)	MON 9:05 a.m. - FRI 1:55 p.m. Central Time Daily trading halts 4:00 p.m. - 5:00 p.m. Central Time
	Open Outcry (Trading Floor)	MON-FRI: 9:05 a.m. -1:00 p.m. Central Time
Last Trade Date/Time View Calendar	Last business day of the contract month, 12:00 p.m.	
Contract Months View Listings	Feb, Apr, Jun, Aug, Oct, Dec	
Settlement Procedure	Physical Delivery See CME Rule 10103.	
Position Limits	Non-Spot: 6,300 contracts in any contract month Spot: 450/300 contracts All months combined: n/a See CME Rule: 10102.E	
Ticker Symbol View Product Codes View Vendor Codes	CME Globex (Electronic Platform)	LE 48=Clearing
	Open Outcry (Trading Floor)	LC
Rulebook Chapter	101	
Exchange Rule	These contracts are listed with, and subject to, the rules and regulations of CME.	

Source: CME Group Inc.

Trading hours

Live cattle futures are traded both electronically on the CME Globex platform and by traditional open outcry on the trading floor. The electronic market opens at 9.05 am Monday morning Chicago time and trades almost continuously through to 1.55 pm Friday afternoon Chicago time, with a daily break between 4.00 pm and 5.00 pm Chicago time. The pit session operates each weekday between 9.05 am and 1.00 pm Chicago time.

Lean hogs

An emphasis on improved production efficiencies and the production of much leaner animals has helped changed the public perception of pork and boosted demand for pork products in recent years. Lean hogs are meat-type hogs that produce a higher proportion of lean meat to fat. They are raised in intensive lot-feeding operations, where they are fed controlled, grain-based diets, to a weight of between 220 and 260 pounds (100 to 115 kilograms). Intensive pig production facilities tend to be found close to grain-growing regions, reflecting the fact that feed costs are the primary cost in any livestock production operation. US pork production, for example, tends to be concentrated in the corn belt, providing easy access to this important feed source.

The relationship between lean hog and corn prices is so intertwined that lean hog producers monitor the hog–corn ratio to get a simple but sound indication of developments in hog production. This ratio divides the price of lean hog futures by the price of corn futures, and expresses the relationship of corn feed costs to the dollar value of lean hogs. It indicates the number of bushels of corn that are equal in value to 100 pounds (one hundredweight) of lean hogs. When corn prices are high relative to pork prices, it takes fewer units of corn to equal the dollar value of 100 pounds of pork. When corn prices are low relative to pork prices, it takes more units of corn to equal the dollar value of 100 pounds of pork. The higher the ratio, the more profitable it is to feed hogs. If, for example, the price of hogs is 87.80 cents per pound ($87.80 per hundredweight; 87.80 cents per pound × 100 pounds) and the price of corn is $6.43 per bushel, then the hog–corn ratio is 13.65

(87.80 ÷ 6.43 = 13.65). If the price of lean hogs is 87.80 cents per pound ($87.80 per hundredweight) and the price of corn is trading at $3.85 per bushel, then the hog–corn ratio is 22.81 (87.80 ÷ 3.85 = 22.81). It is obviously more profitable to feed hogs when the price of corn is lower.

By most estimates China has more than half of the global pig and hog population. Other major producers are the Eurozone, the United States, Brazil and Canada. Of these, the US is the largest net exporter of pork products.

Factors affecting price

Factors affecting the price of lean hogs include the following:

⇒ Access to feed grains, particularly corn, is one of the most important cost considerations in the production of pork. Feed costs account for more than half of all production costs and are the primary determinant of how much pork will be produced. They also influence producers' decisions as to when and at what weight to sell their hogs. If feed costs are high relative to the finished sales value of lean hogs, producers will tend to breed, feed and market fewer hogs and market hogs at lighter weights. This reduced supply can lead to increased prices if demand remains constant. When feed costs are relatively lower, making production more favourable, breeding, feeding and sales weights of lean hogs tend to increase. This increase in supply can put downward pressure on prices.

⇒ If pork prices are high compared with alternative meat products such as beef and chicken, demand for pork will decrease and put downward pressure on prices.

⇒ Lean hog prices tend to show a strong seasonal pattern in line with seasonal production factors. The largest number of pig farrowings, or births, tend to occur in March, April and May. It takes around six months for pigs to reach the desired market weight, which results in a peak in supply between August and December, causing prices to decline.

⇒ The use of corn and other feed grains for the production of ethanol has led to increased volatility in feed grain prices and adds price pressure to lean hog production costs. Increased demand for ethanol fuel products produced from corn leads to increased demand for feed grains as a fuel source, encouraging farmers to sell their grain products to ethanol producers at higher prices. Livestock producers need to pay higher prices for their feed requirements, adding significantly to their production costs. If pork prices are low it may become uneconomical to produce pork, resulting in a decrease in supply and eventually raising prices if demand remains constant or increases.

Tip

Lean hogs tend to trade quite erratically and in sideways bands for long periods of time. They tend to trade within a wide trading range, with volatile swings within that range.

Figure 8.5 shows a weekly price chart of lean hog futures from 1987 to 2012.

Pricing

Lean hog futures are traded on the Chicago Mercantile Exchange (CME). Lean hog futures trade in cents per pound on a 40000-pound contract. A 1-cent-per-pound move in the price of lean hogs equates to $400.00 on the futures contract (40000 pounds × $0.01 = $400.00). The minimum price move, or tick, is $0.00025, or $10.00 per contract (40000 pounds × $0.00025 = $10.00).

Figure 8.5: weekly price chart of CME lean hog futures, 1987–2012

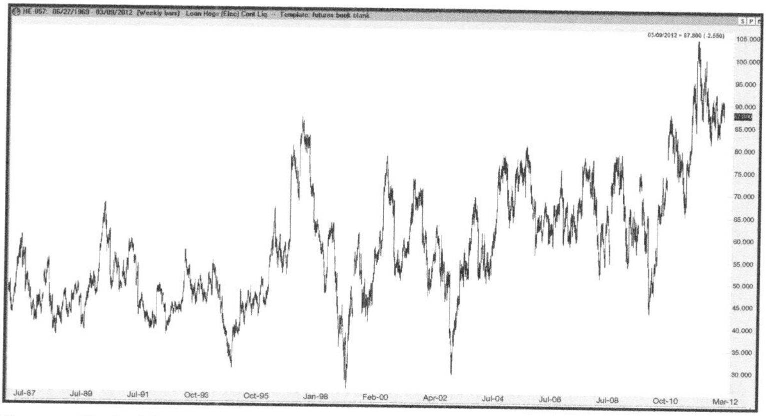

Source: Trade Navigator / Genesis Financial Technologies Inc.

Trading examples

Expecting the price of lean hogs to rise, a trader would BUY (go long) a futures contract. Let's say the long position is initiated at 84.275 cents per pound and the market rises to 92.400 cents per pound, a move of 8.125 cents per pound, or 325 ticks ($0.08125 ÷ $0.00025). The trader's profit (excluding brokerage and costs) would be $3250.00 (325 ticks × $10.00 per tick = $3250.00).

92.400 (sell price) − 84.275 (buy price) = 8.125 cents per pound × $400.00 per 1 cent = $3250.00

Expecting the price of lean hogs to fall, a trader would SELL (go short) a futures contract. Let's say the short position is initiated at 93.325 cents per pound and the market falls to 87.800 cents per pound, a move of 5.525 cents per pound, or 221 ticks ($0.05525 ÷ $0.00025). The trader's profit (excluding brokerage and costs) would be $2210.00 (221 ticks × $10.00 per tick = $2210.00).

93.325 (sell price) − 87.800 (buy price) = 5.525 cents per pound × $400.00 per 1 cent = $2210.00

Contract specifications

Full contract specifications for the CME-traded lean hog futures contract are shown in figure 8.6.

Figure 8.6: CME lean hog futures contract specifications

Contract Size	40,000 pounds (~18 metric tons)	
Product Description	Hog (barrow and gilt) carcasses	
Pricing Unit	Cents per pound	
Tick Size (minimum fluctuation)	$.00025 per pound ($10 per contract)	
Daily Price Limits	$.03 per pound above or below previous day's settlement price; none for expiring contract in last 2 trading days.	
Trading Hours (All times listed are Central Time)	CME Globex (Electronic Platform)	MON 9:05 a.m. - FRI 1:55 p.m. Central Time Daily trading halts 4:00 p.m. - 5:00 p.m. Central Time
	Open Outcry (Trading Floor)	MON-FRI: 9:05 a.m. -1:00 p.m. Central Time
Last Trade Date/Time View Calendar	10th business day of the contract month, 12:00 p.m.	
Contract Months View Listings	Feb, Apr, May, Jun, Jul, Aug, Oct, Dec	
Settlement Procedure	Cash Settlement. See CME Rule 15203.	
Position Limits	Non-Spot: 4,150 contracts in any contract month Spot: 950 contracts All months combined: n/a See CME Rule: 15202.E	
Product Ticker Symbols	CME Globex (Electronic Platform)	HE LN=Clearing
	Open Outcry (Trading Floor)	LH
Rulebook Chapter	152	
Exchange Rule	These contracts are listed with, and subject to, the rules and regulations of CME.	

Source: CME Group Inc.

Trading hours

Lean hog futures are traded both electronically on the CME Globex platform and by traditional open outcry on the trading floor. The electronic market opens at 9.05 am Monday morning Chicago time and trades almost continuously through to 1.55 pm Friday afternoon Chicago time, with a daily break between 4.00 pm and 5.00 pm Chicago time. The pit session operates each weekday between 9.05 am and 1.00 pm Chicago time.

chapter 9

Energy markets

Modern society is highly dependent on non-renewable energy sources as the principal source of power to drive automobiles, heat our houses, provide light and electricity, and provide power to industry. The four main futures contracts covering the energy sector are crude oil, RBOB gasoline, heating oil and natural gas. While there are others, once again space prevents us covering all of them.

Current annual global demand for energy is estimated at around 500 quadrillion British thermal units (Btu). One Btu is the amount of energy required to raise the temperature of one pound of water by one degree Fahrenheit and equates to 251.996 calories. One quadrillion Btu is equal to 251 996 000 000 000 000 calories. Of this total amount, 86 per cent comes from non-renewable fossil fuel sources, with oil alone accounting for 33 per cent. China is the world's largest energy consumer, accounting for more than 18 per cent of global energy consumption, but consumes only 2 kilowatts per person, compared with over 11 kilowatts per person in the United States. Global annual energy consumption is expected to rise to well over 700 quadrillion Btu by 2030.

Crude oil

Crude oil is a naturally occurring complex organic compound formed beneath the Earth's surface from decomposing marine and plant organisms put under extreme pressure and heat over millions of years. The first oil well drilled specifically to extract crude oil for commercial purposes was in Poland in 1853, following on from the earlier invention of the process to distil kerosene from crude oil. Crude oil exploration and extraction quickly spread around the globe, with the United States becoming the leading producer through to the 1960s. The discovery of crude oil in the Middle East saw the 'Arab 5' countries—Saudi Arabia, United Arab Emirates, Iraq, Qatar and Kuwait—quickly join the leading global oil-producing nations. The United States is still the third-largest producer of oil, behind Saudi Arabia and Russia, and is also the largest importer.

Tip

The Middle East has an estimated 80 per cent of the world's easily accessible crude oil reserves.

The Organization of Petroleum Exporting Countries (OPEC), a cartel comprising the 12 major oil-producing countries of Algeria, Angola, Ecuador, Iran, Iraq, Kuwait, Libya, Nigeria, Qatar, Saudi Arabia, United Arab Emirates and Venezuela, emerged as the major pricing power for crude oil during the 1970s. OPEC members meet regularly to discuss production quotas for the member nations designed to hold prices at favourable levels.

Tip

OPEC member countries collectively have access to in excess of 75 per cent of world crude oil reserves and are responsible for around 45 per cent of world crude oil production.

Often referred to as 'black gold', crude oil is perhaps the most politically and economically sensitive raw material in the world. Driven by an ever-increasing demand for oil for use in fuels, but also in plastics, fertilisers, insecticides, pharmaceuticals and a host of other products, and a limited and diminishing supply, crude oil prices are critical to all of the world's economies.

Tip

Crude oil production, consumption and price are quoted in barrels. A barrel is equivalent to 42 US gallons, or 159 litres; 1000 barrels is 42 000 US gallons.

Global consumption of oil is in excess of 88 million barrels per day. The United States, the world's largest consumer, uses more than 19 million barrels of crude oil per day, or around 23 per cent. China, the second-largest consuming nation, uses around 9 million barrels per day, or 10 per cent. Global oil production is estimated at around 90 million barrels per day. Consumption of crude oil is predicted to rise to more than 107 million barrels per day by 2030.

Tip

Crude oil futures contracts are the most actively traded futures contracts in the world.

Factors affecting price

Factors affecting the price of crude oil include the following:

⇒ The strength of the US and global economies is a key driver of crude oil prices. When the global economy is expanding, demand for crude oil increases and price rises in response. When the global economy is contracting, demand for crude oil slows down and the price falls or, at best, stabilises.

⇒ Geopolitical events, or the threat of events such as war, uprisings and political instability in oil-producing countries, can cause sudden spikes in the price of crude in response to fears of a contraction in supply.

⇒ Statements and announcements from OPEC concerning production levels, quotas and pricing policy can cause rapid changes in price.

⇒ The price of crude oil involves a complex interplay of several supply and demand factors. If demand is strong, prices are high and stored supplies low, the OPEC nations may consider a production increase. The resulting increase in supply may lower prices, or it may simply be absorbed by the market if demand remains strong. If demand is low, stored supplies are relatively high and prices low, they may decide to cut back production. This may cause the price to rise, particularly if it is perceived as an attempt to restrict supply or occurs during a period of political uncertainty.

⇒ Threats to the long-term supply of crude, whether perceived or real, can also cause sudden price fluctuations. These are often provoked by announcements concerning the demise of global crude oil production as this non-renewable energy source is eventually exhausted. The 'peak-oil' debate centres on whether or not global crude oil reserves are past the point where demand exceeds supply and no new oil deposits are being discovered, resulting in an ever-decreasing supply of 'black gold'.

Tip

Crude oil prices can be extremely volatile owing to the highly sensitive nature of the price of crude to a wide range of supply-related issues. Prices can spike sharply on the back of sudden announcements and perceived changes to supply. They can also decline rapidly in response to changes in demand, such as the rapid decline in price during and following the GFC.

Figure 9.1 shows a weekly price chart of crude oil futures from 1987 to 2012.

Figure 9.1: weekly price chart of NYMEX crude oil futures, 1987–2012

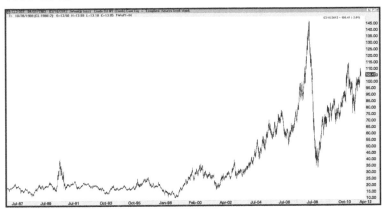

Source: Trade Navigator / Genesis Financial Technologies Inc.

Pricing

Light sweet crude oil futures are traded on the New York Mercantile Exchange (NYMEX). Crude oil futures trade in dollars and cents per barrel on a 1000-barrel contract. A $1-per-barrel move in the price of crude oil equates to $1000 on the futures contract (1000 barrels × $1.00 = $1000). The minimum price move, or tick, is 1 cent, or $10 per contract (1000 barrels × $0.01 = $10).

Trading examples

Expecting the price of crude oil to rise, a trader would BUY (go long) a futures contract. Let's say the long position is initiated at $95.77 per barrel and the market rises to $98.61 per barrel, a move of $2.84 per barrel or 284 ticks (2.84 ÷ 0.01). The trader's profit (excluding brokerage and costs) would be $2840.00 (284 ticks × $10.00 per tick = $2840.00).

> $98.61 (sell price) − $95.77 (buy price) =
> $2.84 per barrel × 1000 barrels = $2840.00

Expecting the price of crude oil to fall, a trader would SELL (go short) a futures contract. Let's say the short position is initiated at $97.41 per barrel and the market falls to $92.10 per barrel, a move of $5.31 per barrel, or 531 ticks (5.31 ÷ 0.01). The trader's profit (excluding brokerage and costs) would be $5310.00 (531 ticks × $10.00 per tick = $5310.00).

> $97.41 (sell price) − $92.10 (buy price) =
> $5.31 per barrel × 1000 barrels = $5310.00

Contract specifications

Full contract specifications for the NYMEX-traded crude oil futures contract are shown in figure 9.2.

Trading hours

Crude oil futures are traded both electronically on the CME Globex platform and by traditional open outcry on the trading floor of the New York Mercantile Exchange (now part of CME Group). The electronic market opens at 6.00 pm Sunday New York time and trades almost continuously through to 5.15 pm Friday afternoon New York time, with a daily break between 5.15 pm and 6.00 pm New York time. The pit session operates each weekday between 9.00 am and 2.30 pm New York time.

Figure 9.2: NYMEX crude oil futures contract specifications

NYMEX Crude Oil Futures

Crude Oil Futures

Product Symbol	CL	
Venue	CME Globex, CME ClearPort, Open Outcry (New York)	
Hours (All Times are New York Time/ET)	CME Globex	Sunday - Friday 6:00 p.m. - 5:15 p.m. New York time/ET (5:00 p.m. - 4:15 p.m. Chicago Time/CT) with a 45-minute break each day beginning at 5:15 p.m. (4:15 p.m. CT)
	CME ClearPort	Sunday – Friday 6:00 p.m. – 5:15 p.m. (5:00 p.m. – 4:15 p.m. Chicago Time/CT) with a 45-minute break each day beginning at 5:15 p.m. (4:15 p.m. CT)
	Open Outcry	Monday – Friday 9:00 AM to 2:30 PM (8:00 AM to 1:30 PM CT)
Contract Unit	1,000 barrels	
Price Quotation	U.S. Dollars and Cents per barrel	
Minimum Fluctuation	$0.01per barrel	
Termination of Trading	Trading in the current delivery month shall cease on the third business day prior to the twenty-fifth calendar day of the month preceding the delivery month. If the twenty-fifth calendar day of the month is a non-business day, trading shall cease on the third business day prior to the last business day preceding the twenty-fifth calendar day. In the event that the official Exchange holiday schedule changes subsequent to the listing of a Crude Oil futures, the originally listed expiration date shall remain in effect. In the event that the originally listed expiration day is declared a holiday, expiration will move to the business day immediately prior.	
Listed Contracts	Crude oil futures are listed nine years forward using the following listing schedule: consecutive months are listed for the current year and the next five years; in addition, the June and December contract months are listed beyond the sixth year. Additional months will be added on an annual basis after the December contract expires, so that an additional June and December contract would be added nine years forward, and the consecutive months in the sixth calendar year will be filled in.	
	Additionally, trading can be executed at an average differential to the previous day's settlement prices for periods of two to 30 consecutive months in a single transaction. These calendar strips are executed during open outcry trading hours.	
Settlement Type	Physical	

Source: CME Group Inc.

RBOB gasoline

Reformulated Blendstock for Oxygenate Blending (RBOB) gasoline futures replaced unleaded gasoline futures in 2006 as gasoline manufacturers began phasing out the use of methyl tertiary-butyl ether (MTBE) and producing unleaded gasoline with 10 per cent oxygenate content. It is the raw material for the manufacture of many different kinds of gasoline products and formulations, and is suitable for blending with ethanol.

Gasoline, or petrol, is the single largest product refined from crude oil, with almost half of each barrel of crude oil produced refined into gasoline. The US is both the largest producer and the largest consumer of refined unleaded gasoline, accounting for more than 40 per cent of global gasoline consumption.

Factors affecting price

Factors affecting the price of RBOB gasoline include the following:

⇒ The supply and geopolitical factors that affect the price of crude oil also impact on the price of RBOB gasoline. The price of RBOB gasoline is very sensitive to global political events, OPEC statements, and increases or decreases in the supply of crude oil.

⇒ The demand for gasoline is also influenced by the strength of the US and global economies. If economies are expanding there is a greater need for transportation of goods and people, and increased affluence and disposable incomes encourage people to travel more, increasing the use of and demand for gasoline. The reverse is true during periods of economic downturn or contraction.

⇒ Demand for RBOB gasoline in the US and Europe displays seasonal tendencies, with the peak demand for gasoline occurring during the summer 'driving months' and much lower demand during the winter months.

⇒ Refinery shutdowns and other disruptions to the supply of gasoline can cause sharp price spikes, particularly during the summer months.

Tip

RBOB gasoline prices can be extremely volatile. While generally trading in unison with the price of crude oil, the price of RBOB gasoline can move independently of crude particularly during the Northern Hemisphere summer months.

Figure 9.3 shows a weekly price chart of RBOB gasoline futures from 1987 to 2012.

Figure 9.3: weekly price chart of NYMEX RBOB gasoline futures, 1987–2012

Source: Trade Navigator / Genesis Financial Technologies Inc.

Tip

The price chart is the combined unleaded gas/RBOB gas contract, as the RBOB gas futures contract replaced the unleaded gas contract in 2006.

Pricing

RBOB gasoline futures are traded on the New York Mercantile Exchange (NYMEX). RBOB gasoline futures trade in dollars and cents per gallon on a 42 000-gallon (1000-barrel) contract. A 1-cent-per-gallon move in the price of RBOB gasoline equates to $420.00 on the futures contract (42 000 gallons × $0.01 = $420.00). The minimum price move, or tick, is $0.0001, or $4.20 per contract (42 000 gallons × $0.0001 = $4.20).

Trading examples

Expecting the price of RBOB gasoline to rise, a trader would BUY (go long) a futures contract. Let's say the long position is initiated at $3.1340 per gallon and the market rises to $3.2705 per gallon, a move of 13.65 cents per gallon, or 1365 ticks ($0.1365 ÷ $0.0001). The trader's profit (excluding brokerage and costs) would be $5733.00 (1365 ticks × $4.20 per tick = $5733.00).

> $3.2705 (sell price) − $3.1340 (buy price) =
> $0.1365 per gallon × 42 000 gallons = $5733.00

Expecting the price of RBOB gasoline to fall, a trader would SELL (go short) a futures contract. Let's say the short position is initiated at $3.3524 per gallon and the market falls to $3.2035 per gallon, a move of 14.89 cents per gallon, or 1489 ticks ($0.1489 ÷ $0.0001). The trader's profit (excluding brokerage and costs) would be $6253.80 (1489 ticks × $4.20 per tick = $6253.80).

> $3.3524 (sell price) − $3.2035 (buy price) =
> $0.1489 per gallon × 42 000 gallons = $6253.80

Contract specifications

Full contract specifications for the NYMEX-traded RBOB gasoline futures contract are shown in figure 9.4.

Trading hours

RBOB gasoline futures are traded both electronically on the CME Globex platform and by traditional open outcry on the trading floor of the New York Mercantile Exchange (now part of CME Group). The electronic market opens at 6.00 pm Sunday New York time and trades almost continuously through to 5.15 pm Friday afternoon New York time, with a daily break between 5.15 pm and 6.00 pm

New York time. The pit session operates each weekday between 9.00 am and 2.30 pm New York time.

Figure 9.4: NYMEX RBOB gasoline futures contract specifications

RBOB Gasoline Future		
Product Symbol	RB	
Venue	CME Globex, CME ClearPort, Open Outcry (New York)	
Hours (All Times are New York Time/ET)	CME Globex:	Sunday – Friday 6:00 p.m. – 5:15 p.m. (5:00 p.m. – 4:15 p.m. Chicago Time/CT) with a 45-minute break each day beginning at 5:15 p.m. (4:15 p.m. CT)
	CME ClearPort:	Sunday – Friday 6:00 p.m. – 5:15 p.m. (5:00 p.m. – 4:15 p.m. Chicago Time/CT) with a 45-minute break each day beginning at 5:15 p.m. (4:15 p.m. CT)
	Open Outcry:	Monday – Friday 9:00 AM to 2:30 PM (8:00 AM to 1:30 PM CT)
Contract Unit	42,000 gallons	
Price Quotation	U.S. dollars and cents per gallon.	
Minimum Fluctuation	$0.0001 per gallon	
Termination of Trading	Trading in a current delivery month shall cease on the last business day of the month preceding the delivery month.	
Listed Contracts	36 consecutive months	
Settlement Type	Physical	
Delivery		
Delivery Period	Please see rulebook chapter 191	
Grade and Quality Specifications		
Position Limits	NYMEX Position Limits	
Rulebook Chapter	191	
Exchange Rule	These contracts are listed with, and subject to, the rules and regulations of NYMEX.	

Source: CME Group Inc.

Heating oil

Heating oil is part of the family of refined petroleum products known as distillates. Distillates are refined from the middle to the bottom of a barrel of crude oil and are used primarily as fuels for heating in the Northern Hemisphere, and for powering diesel engines in automobiles, trains and farm machinery. Around 25 per cent of a barrel of crude oil is refined into distillate, compared with 44 per cent for unleaded gasoline. Heating oil, also referred to as No.2 fuel oil, accounts for around 20 per cent of total distillate fuel consumption. Heating oil competes with electricity and natural gas for use as an energy source in residential heating. The US is the largest consumer and producer of heating oil.

Factors affecting price

Factors affecting the price of heating oil include the following:

⇒ Demand for heating oil is highest during the Northern Hemisphere winter months, when its use as a source of energy for heating is at its highest.

⇒ The supply and geopolitical factors listed earlier that affect the price of crude oil also impact on the price of heating oil. The price of heating oil is sensitive to global political events, OPEC statements, and increases or decreases in the supply of crude oil.

⇒ While in the past demand for heating oil was relatively inelastic (buyers' responsiveness to changes in price was small), demand for heating oil now tends to be more elastic and to follow the price of crude oil much more closely. This can be attributed to the higher price of crude oil and hence for products such as heating oil that are derived from it.

⇒ There is typically a build-up of heating oil stocks by refiners during October and November, the months leading up to winter. Any disruptions to supply, or fears of events that may impact on production, can cause prices to rise sharply during this period.

⇒ Extremely cold, harsh winters can deplete stocks of heating oil faster than expected. This sudden increase in demand can lead to large price increases. Milder winters can lead to lower demand for heating oil and price declines.

⇒ Heating oil competes with electricity and natural gas as the main energy source for residential heating. Changes in the supply and price of these products can impact on the price of heating oil. If, for example, natural gas prices are much lower and appear as though they may stay lower than heating oil prices for an extended period, consumers may make changes to their heating arrangements to allow the switch to the cheaper heat source. This may eventually lead to reduced demand for heating oil, and prices may decline.

Tip

The price of heating oil tends to be very volatile and closely correlated to the price of crude oil.

Figure 9.5 shows a weekly price chart of heating oil futures from 1987 to 2012.

Figure 9.5: weekly price chart of NYMEX heating oil futures, 1987–2012

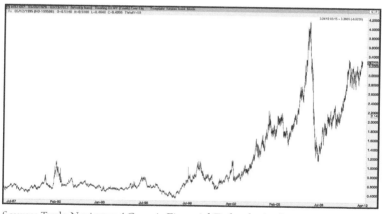

Source: Trade Navigator / Genesis Financial Technologies Inc.

Pricing

Heating oil futures are traded on the New York Mercantile Exchange (NYMEX). Heating oil futures trade in dollars and cents per gallon on a 42 000-gallon (1000-barrel) contract. A 1-cent-per-gallon move in the price of heating oil equates to

$420.00 on the futures contract (42 000 gallons × $0.01 = $420.00). The minimum price move, or tick, is $0.0001, or $4.20 per contract (42 000 gallons × $0.0001 = $4.20).

Trading examples

Expecting the price of heating oil to rise, a trader would BUY (go long) a futures contract. Let's say the long position is initiated at $3.1215 per gallon and the market rises to $3.2113 per gallon, a move of $0.089 (8.98 cents) per gallon, or 898 ticks ($0.0898 ÷ $0.0001). The trader's profit (excluding brokerage and costs) would be $3771.60 (898 ticks × $4.20 per tick = $3771.60).

$3.2113 (sell price) − $3.1215 (buy price) =
$0.0898 per gallon × 42 000 gallons = $3771.60

Expecting the price of heating oil to fall, a trader would SELL (go short) a futures contract. Let's say the short position is initiated at $3.0316 per gallon and the market falls to $2.8695 per gallon, a move of $0.1621 (16.21 cents) per gallon, or 1621 ticks ($0.1621 ÷ $0.0001). The trader's profit (excluding brokerage and costs) would be $6808.20 (1621 ticks × $4.20 per tick = $6808.20).

$3.0316 (sell price) − $2.8695 (buy price) =
$0.1621 per gallon × 42 000 gallons = $6808.20

Contract specifications

Full contract specifications for the NYMEX-traded heating oil futures contract are shown in figure 9.6.

Trading hours

Heating oil futures are traded both electronically on the CME Globex platform and by traditional open outcry on the trading floor of the New York Mercantile Exchange (now part of CME Group). The electronic market opens at 6.00 pm

Sunday New York time and trades almost continuously through to 5.15 pm Friday afternoon New York time, with a daily break between 5.15 pm and 6.00 pm New York time. The pit session operates each weekday between 9.00 am and 2.30 pm New York time.

Figure 9.6: NYMEX heating oil futures contract specifications

New York Harbor #2 Heating Oil Futures

Product Symbol	HO
Venue	CME Globex, CME ClearPort, Open Outcry (New York)
Hours (All Times are New York Time/ET)	**CME Globex:** Sunday - Friday 6:00 p.m. - 5:15 p.m. (5:00 p.m. - 4:15 p.m. Chicago Time/CT) with a 45-minute break each day beginning at 5:15 p.m. (4:15 p.m. CT)
	CME ClearPort: Sunday - Friday 6:00 p.m. - 5:15 p.m. (5:00 p.m. - 4:15 p.m. Chicago Time/CT) with a 45-minute break each day beginning at 5:15 p.m. (4:15 p.m. CT)
	Open Outcry: Monday - Friday 9:00 AM to 2:30 PM (8:00 AM to 1:30 PM CT)
Contract Unit	42,000 gallons
Price Quotation	U.S. dollars and cents per gallon.
Minimum Fluctuation	$0.0001 per gallon
Termination of Trading	Trading in a current delivery month shall cease on the last business day of the month preceding the delivery month.
Listed Contracts	36 consecutive months
Settlement Type	Physical
Delivery	
Delivery Period	Please see rulebook chapter 191
Grade and Quality Specifications	
Position Limits	NYMEX Position Limits
Rulebook Chapter	191
Exchange Rule	These contracts are listed with, and subject to, the rules and regulations of NYMEX.

Source: CME Group Inc.

Tip

CME Group has begun phasing out the heating oil contract, replacing it with a futures contract for ultra-low sulphur diesel with the product code LH. Pricing, minimum tick values, trading times and contract size are the same as for heating oil. Heating oil futures contracts will not be available after April 2013.

Natural gas

Natural gas was originally produced as a byproduct of crude oil extraction, as natural gas is often found in association with crude oil or dissolved in it. Unwanted natural gas was often burned off at the oil well, as it was difficult or too expensive to move it to where it could be used. In the second half of the 20th century, as other energy sources increased in price and advances in technology allowed for the extraction and transportation of natural gas via pipelines, it became economical to produce and use natural gas. Today natural gas accounts for around 25 per cent of all US energy consumption, with almost half of this amount being used by utility companies to produce electricity in power plants. Natural gas is considered the 'cleanest' fossil fuel, as burning natural gas produces around 30 per cent less carbon dioxide than burning petroleum products, and around 44 per cent less than burning coal.

Further advances in drilling and extraction technologies have allowed easy access to large quantities of natural gas in shale deposits and other sources, resulting in a huge increase in production without a corresponding increase in demand. Because of the difficulties involved in transporting natural gas over long distances, other than by pipeline, markets tend to be confined domestically. Natural gas produced in the US is consumed in the US; natural gas produced in Europe is consumed in Europe. Some natural gas is converted back into liquid for transport to other markets. As technologies improve, and demand increases, transporting natural gas over long distances may become more economically viable. Major natural gas reserves are found in Qatar, Russia, the US, Canada, Mexico, the North Sea and the North West Shelf off the northern Australian coast.

Tip

The price of natural gas is quoted for delivery to the Henry Hub in Louisiana. This is a central point of 16 intra- and inter-state pipeline systems that draw natural gas from gas producers and then distribute it throughout the US East Coast and Midwest and as far north as the Canadian border.

Factors affecting price

Factors affecting the price of natural gas include the following:

⇒ The major factor affecting the price of natural gas in the past five years has been the huge increase in stored supplies as a result of production increases brought about by improvements in technology for natural gas extraction.

⇒ The price of competing energy sources such as heating oil, coal and electricity can affect the price of natural gas in the short term.

⇒ Severe weather can increase demand for natural gas and cause short-term price spikes. This can occur as a result of cold snaps in winter increasing the demand for heat and power, and also heat waves in the summer months increasing the demand for power to run air-conditioning units. The threat of hurricanes and other extreme weather events in the Gulf of Mexico, where the majority of US natural gas operations are located, that may disrupt production and supply, can also cause short-term price spikes.

⇒ Changes to governmental standards and laws for carbon emissions and other pollution controls may impact on the demand and thus the price for natural gas in the future.

⇒ The long-term price of crude oil will also impact on the price of natural gas in the future. While the natural gas price is now at a historical low, continued upward price pressure on crude oil, coupled with any laws to encourage the increased use of natural gas, may well lead to increased demand and a significant shift in price.

Tip

Natural gas is the most independent and least correlated to crude oil of the energy markets. It is also the most volatile and is capable of making large moves very quickly.

Figure 9.7 shows a weekly price chart of natural gas futures from 1989 to 2012.

Figure 9.7: weekly price chart of NYMEX natural gas futures, 1989–2012

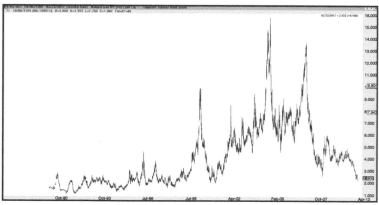

Source: Trade Navigator / Genesis Financial Technologies Inc.

Pricing

Natural gas futures are traded on the New York Mercantile Exchange (NYMEX). Natural gas futures trade in dollars and cents per million British thermal units (mmBtu) on a 10000 mmBtu contract. A $1.00-per-mmBtu move in the price of natural gas equates to $10 000.00 on the futures contract (10 000 mmBtu × $1.00 = $10 000.00). The minimum price move, or tick, is 0.1 cents, or $10.00 per contract (10 000mmBtu × $0.001 = $10.00).

Trading examples

Expecting the price of natural gas to rise, a trader would BUY (go long) a futures contract. Let's say the long position is initiated at $4.274 per mmBtu and the market rises to $4.876 per mmBtu, a move of $0.602 (60.2 cents) per mmBtu or 602 ticks ($0.602 ÷ $0.001). The trader's profit (excluding brokerage and costs) would be $6020.00 (602 ticks × $10.00 per tick = $6020.00).

$4.876 (sell price) − $4.274 (buy price) =
$0.602 per mmBtu × 10 000mmBtu = $6020.00

Expecting the price of natural gas to fall, a trader would SELL (go short) a futures contract. Let's say the short position is initiated at $4.353 per mmBtu and the market falls to $3.840 per mmBtu, a move of $0.513 (51.3 cents) per mmBtu or 513 ticks ($0.513 ÷ $0.001). The trader's profit (excluding brokerage and costs) would be $5130.00 (513 ticks × $10.00 per tick = $5130.00).

$4.353 (sell price) − $3.840 (buy price) =
$0.513 per mmBtu × 10 000mmBtu = $5130.00

Contract specifications

Full contract specifications for the NYMEX-traded natural gas futures contract are shown in figure 9.8 (overleaf).

Trading hours

Natural gas futures are traded both electronically on the CME Globex platform and by traditional open outcry on the trading floor of the New York Mercantile Exchange (now part of CME Group). The electronic market opens at 6.00 pm

Sunday New York time and trades almost continuously through to 5.15 pm Friday afternoon New York time, with a daily break between 5.15 pm and 6.00 pm New York time. The pit session operates each weekday between 9.00 am and 2.30 pm New York time.

Figure 9.8: NYMEX natural gas futures contract specifications

Henry Hub Natural Gas Futures

Code	NG
Venue	CME ClearPort, CME Globex, Open Outcry (New York)
Hours (All Times are New York Time/ET)	CME Globex: Sunday - Friday 6:00 p.m. - 5:15 p.m. New York time/ET (5:00 p.m. - 4:15 p.m. Chicago Time/CT) with a 45-minute break each day beginning at 5:15 p.m. (4:15 p.m. CT)
	CME ClearPort: Sunday - Friday 6:00 p.m. - 5:15 p.m. New York time/ET (5:00 p.m. - 4:15 p.m. Chicago Time/CT) with a 45-minute break each day beginning at 5:15 p.m. (4:15 p.m. CT)
	Open Outcry: Monday - Friday 9:00 a.m. - 2:30 p.m. ET (8:00 a.m. - 1:30 p.m. CT)
Contract Unit	10,000 million British thermal units (mmBtu).
Pricing Quotation	U.S. dollars and cents per mmBtu.
Minimum Price Increment	$0.001 (0.1¢) per mmBtu ($10.00 per contract).
Maximum Daily Price Fluctuation	$3.00 per mmBtu ($30,000 per contract) for all months. If any contract is traded, bid, or offered at the limit for five minutes, trading is halted for five minutes. When trading resumes, the limit is expanded by $3.00 per mmBtu in either direction. If another halt were triggered, the market would continue to be expanded by $3.00 per mmBtu in either direction after each successive five-minute trading halt. There will be no maximum price fluctuation limits during any one trading session.
Termination of Trading	Trading of any delivery month shall cease three (3) business days prior to the first day of the delivery month. In the event that the official Exchange holiday schedule changes subsequent to the listing of a Natural Gas futures, the originally listed expiration date shall remain in effect. In the event that the originally listed expiration day is declared a holiday, expiration will move to the business day immediately prior.
Listed Contracts	The current year plus the next twelve years. A new calendar year will be added following the termination of trading in the December contract of the current year. On CME Globex: The current year plus the next eight years.
Settlement Type	Physical
Grade and Quality Specifications	Natural Gas meeting the specifications set forth in the FERC-approved tariff of Sabine Pipe Line Company as then in effect at the time of delivery shall be deliverable in satisfaction of futures contract delivery obligations.
Position Limits	NYMEX Position Limits
Rulebook Chapter	220
Exchange Rule	These contracts are listed with, and subject to, the rules and regulations of NYMEX.

Source: CME Group Inc.

Mini-sized energy contracts

Mini-sized (e-mini) futures contracts are also available for crude oil, RBOB gasoline, heating oil and natural gas. These mini-sized contracts are half the size of the standard contracts for crude oil, RBOB gasoline and heating oil, and one-quarter the size for natural gas. The minimum price ticks are also less, as shown in table 9.1.

Table 9.1: e-mini contract specifications

Contract name	Code	Size	Price quote	Minimum price move	Tick value
E-mini crude oil	QM	500 barrels	US $ & cents/ barrel	0.0250	$12.50
E-mini RBOB gasoline	QU	21 000 gallons	US $ & cents/ gallon	0.0001	$2.10
E-mini heating oil	QH	21 000 gallons	US $ & cents/ gallon	0.0001	$2.10
E-mini natural gas	QG	2500 mmBtu	US $ & cents/ mmBtu	0.0050	$12.50

The mini-sized contracts have the same trading times and rules as the standard contracts. They were introduced to provide more flexibility for traders and hedgers in the energy markets and to give smaller traders the opportunity to participate in these markets. Liquidity in the mini-sized contracts is not as good as in the standard contracts, and price quotes and spreads can be wider at times as a result. Liquidity issues are now rarely a problem in the e-mini crude oil and e-mini natural gas contracts, but liquidity in the e-mini RBOB gasoline and e-mini heating oil contracts is very low. Traders looking to use mini-sized contracts need to check these two issues to ensure they can enter and exit positions readily and without too much slippage in price.

chapter 10

Metals

A metal is defined as an elementary substance that is crystalline when solid, ductile, opaque, conductive of heat and electricity, malleable, and lustrous when fractured. People have extracted and worked metals for thousands of years. The use of gold, silver, copper, mercury, tin, iron and lead can be traced back to antiquity. Metals are used in jewellery and coins and have a wide range of commercial and industrial applications. Many metals futures contracts are available on a number of exchanges throughout the world. Once again, though, we will look at just three of the most liquid and actively traded contracts—gold, silver and copper.

Gold

Because of its relative scarcity, its malleable and non-corrosive nature, and its colour, gold has been used since ancient times in jewellery and as a medium of exchange or money. Gold was first discovered and used ornamentally in the Stone Age and it is still highly prized and valued in jewellery. Much of gold's appeal stems from its scarcity and perceived value.

Tip

The World Gold Council estimates that only 166 000 tonnes of gold have been mined since the beginning of civilisation.

Gold has been used as a medium of exchange and store of value throughout history, its value recognised by traders and merchants across the globe. In the 19th century many European countries implemented 'gold standards' linking their currencies to the value of gold. The use of gold as a store of value was further enhanced following World War II when, under the Bretton Woods Accord, the value of the US dollar was linked or 'pegged' to gold at a rate of US$35 per troy ounce. This system was terminated in 1971 when currencies began a free-floating mechanism of exchange and were no longer directly convertible to gold. They are now referred to as *fiat* currencies, deriving their value from government regulation and laws.

Tip

For more information on trading currencies, refer to my book Forex Made Simple, *also published by Wrightbooks.*

As a result, many investors, 'gold bugs' and theorists still believe in the use of gold as an absolute store of value, arguing it is the only commodity that allows wealth to be stored 'safely'. Gold bars can be purchased and held in ultra-secure storage vaults, giving the owner a tangible asset that will always have a value driven by supply and demand, unlike paper 'fiat' money, which can be mass-produced whenever authorities choose to print more and is still regarded by many as an abstract idea. The relative scarcity of gold, according to this theory, means it will work as a hedge against inflation. The reality is actually quite different!

Tip

The gold price in 2010, adjusted for inflation, was the same as its price in 1265. A person who invested all their wealth in gold in 1265 would have seen their investment decrease by more than 500 per cent up to this point in time. If the price of gold reaches US$2300 per troy ounce, it will be the equivalent of its inflation-adjusted January 1980 price — not much of a 'hedge' or long-term store of value!

Investors are also attracted to gold during times of political, economic and social unrest, drawn by the fact that it is a tangible asset that will hold value while fiat currencies and other measures of wealth, including property, may decline in value. The rising price of gold compared with the falling value of the US dollar and US property values since the GFC support this approach, as can be seen in figure 10.1.

Figure 10.1: value of gold versus the US dollar

Source: Trade Navigator / Genesis Financial Technologies Inc.

Gold is found in two main types of deposits in the Earth's crust — lode deposits found in solid rock, and placer deposits found in gravelly stream beds that are eroding lode deposits. Gold deposits are found on every continent on Earth. This geographical diversity means geopolitical issues in one country or region are less likely to have a significant impact on supply. Compare this with a commodity such as cocoa, which has only a few major growing areas, where supply can be influenced by local political issues and events.

The major producers of gold in 2011, according to the Mineral Commodity Summaries conducted by the US Department of the Interior, were China (360 tonnes), Australia (274 tonnes), the United States (241 tonnes), Russia (203 tonnes), South Africa (193 tonnes) and Canada (112 tonnes). These six countries account for just over 50 per cent of global gold mine production.

Tip

The current annual global supply of gold is just under 4400 tonnes, of which 2800 tonnes is 'new' mined gold and 1600 tonnes is recycled.

According to the World Gold Council, total annual global demand for gold is just over 4000 tonnes. Of this, 1960 tonnes is used in jewellery, 1600 tonnes is 'investment gold' such as gold bullion and gold coins, and around 460 tonnes is consumed in technology, electronics, dentistry and industrial applications and uses. India is the world's largest gold-consuming nation at 933 tonnes in 2011, of which more than 500 tonnes was used in jewellery and 366 tonnes was purchased as investment gold by private investors. It is estimated that Indian households hold more than 18000 tonnes of gold, mainly in jewellery, representing around 11 per cent of total global gold holdings. China is the second-largest gold consumer, at 770 tonnes annually, with around 270 tonnes purchased by private investors in 2011.

Tip

India and China account for more than 49 per cent of global demand for gold.

Factors affecting price

Factors affecting the price of gold include the following:

⇒ The key driver of the gold price is fear. When the global economy is experiencing periods of economic, political and social instability, investors will seek to hold their wealth in gold as a safe and secure store of value. The increase in demand causes price to rise as supply is relatively static or inelastic, meaning gold miners and producers cannot adjust or react quickly to increase production in response to growing demand.

⇒ Periods of high inflation, or fears of impending inflation, will also push the price of gold higher as investors seek to maintain their wealth in real terms and not in a depreciating asset such as currency. Note the inverse relationship between the value of the US dollar and the price of gold in figure 10.1 (see p. 223).

⇒ During periods of economic stability and low inflation, the gold price can remain unchanged for prolonged periods.

⇒ Selling down of gold reserves by central banks and other large investors can cause the price of gold to drop suddenly.

⇒ The price of gold displays some seasonal tendencies related to jewellery demand in the Indian market.

Tip

The gold price can maintain significant trends for prolonged periods of time. It is capable of spectacular rallies that can be explosive at times in reaction to war, and in periods of political and economic unrest.

Figure 10.2 shows a weekly price chart of gold futures from 1975 to 2012. The rapid and prolonged increase in the price of gold since the GFC and its after-effects on the global economy can be clearly seen.

Figure 10.2: monthly price chart of COMEX gold futures, 1975–2012

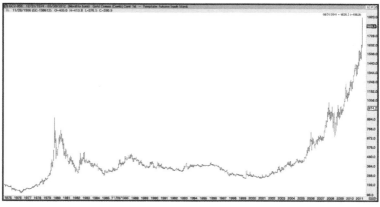

Source: Trade Navigator / Genesis Financial Technologies Inc.

Pricing

Gold futures are traded on the New York Commodity Exchange (COMEX) division of the New York Mercantile Exchange (NYMEX), owned and operated by CME Group; and electronically on the CME Globex platform. Gold futures trade in dollars and cents per troy ounce on a 100-troy-ounce contract. A $1-per-troy-ounce move in the price of gold equates to $100 on the futures contract

(100 troy ounces × \$1 = \$100). The minimum price move, or tick, is 10 cents or \$10 per contract (100 troy ounces × \$0.10 per troy ounce = \$10).

Tip

A troy ounce equals 31.103 grams; 100 troy ounces equals 3.1103 kilograms.

Trading examples

Expecting the price of gold to rise, a trader would BUY (go long) a futures contract. Let's say the long position is initiated at \$1685.80 per troy ounce and the market rises to \$1755.90 per troy ounce, a move of \$70.10 per troy ounce or 701 ticks (70.10 ÷ 0.10). The trader's profit (excluding brokerage and costs) would be \$7010.00 (701 ticks × \$10.00 per tick = \$7010.00).

> \$1755.90 (sell price) − \$1685.80 (buy price) = \$70.10 per troy ounce × 100 troy ounces = \$7010.00

Expecting the price of gold to fall, a trader would SELL (go short) a futures contract. Let's say the short position is initiated at \$1706.70 per troy ounce and the market falls to \$1650.10 per troy ounce, a move of \$56.60 per troy ounce or 566 ticks (56.60 ÷ 0.10). The trader's profit (excluding brokerage and costs) would be \$5660.00 (566 ticks × \$10.00 per tick = \$5660.00).

> \$1706.70 (sell price) − \$1650.10 (buy price) = \$56.60 per troy ounce × 100 troy ounces = \$5660.00

Contract specifications

Full contract specifications for the COMEX-traded gold futures contract are shown in figure 10.3 (overleaf).

Figure 10.3: COMEX gold futures contract specifications

Product Symbol	GC	
Venue	CME Globex, CME ClearPort, Open Outcry (New York)	
Hours (All Times are New York Time/ET)	CME Globex:	Sunday – Friday 6:00 p.m. – 5:15 p.m. (5:00 p.m. – 4:15 p.m. Chicago Time/CT) with a 45-minute break each day beginning at 5:15 p.m. (4:15 p.m. CT)
	CME ClearPort:	Sunday – Friday 6:00 p.m. – 5:15 p.m. (5:00 p.m. – 4:15 p.m. Chicago Time/CT) with a 45-minute break each day beginning at 5:15 p.m. (4:15 p.m. CT)
	Open Outcry:	Monday – Friday 8:20 a.m. - 1:30 p.m. (7:20 a.m. - 12:30 p.m. CT)
Contract Size	100 troy ounces	
Price Quotation	U.S. Dollars and Cents per troy ounce	
Minimum Fluctuation	$0.10 per troy ounce	
Termination of Trading	Trading terminates on the third last business day of the delivery month.	
Listed Contracts	Trading is conducted for delivery during the current calendar month; the next two calendar months; any February, April, August, and October falling within a 23-month period; and any June and December falling within a 72-month period beginning with the current month.	
Settlement Type	Physical	
Delivery Period	Delivery may take place on any business day beginning on the first business day of the delivery month or any subsequent business day of the delivery month, but not later than the last business day of the current delivery month.	
Trading at Settlement (TAS)	Trading at Settlement is allowed in the active contract month. The active contract months will be February, April, June, August and December. On any given date, TAS transactions will be allowed only in a single contract month. TAS transactions may be executed at the current day's settlement price or at any valid price increment ten ticks higher or lower than the settlement price.	
Grade and Quality Specifications	Gold delivered under this contract shall assay to a minimum of 995 fineness.	
Position Limits	NYMEX Position Limits	
Rulebook Chapter	113	
Exchange Rule	These contracts are listed with, and subject to, the rules and regulations of COMEX.	

Source: CME Group Inc.

Trading hours

Gold futures are traded both electronically on the CME Globex platform and by traditional open outcry on the trading floor of the New York Commodity Exchange (COMEX) division of NYMEX (now part of CME Group). The electronic market opens at 6.00 pm Sunday New York time and trades almost continuously through to 5.15 pm Friday afternoon New York time, with a daily break between 5.15 pm and 6.00 pm New York time. The pit session operates each weekday between 8.20 am and 1.30 pm New York time.

Smaller size gold contracts

In addition to the full-size gold contract outlined earlier, traders and investors can also gain access to gold futures contracts through a number of smaller sized contracts. These contracts provide the opportunity for traders with smaller accounts to actively participate in the gold futures markets. Details of these contracts are shown in table 10.1.

Table 10.1: smaller size gold contract details

Contract name	Exchange	Contract size	Price quote	Min. tick	Tick value
Mini-sized gold	NYSE Euronext	33.2 troy ounces	$1 = $33.20	$0.10/troy ounce	$3.32
miNY gold	COMEX	50.0 troy ounces	$1 = $50.00	$0.25/troy ounce	$12.50
E-micro gold	COMEX	10.0 troy ounces	$1 = $10.00	$0.10/troy ounce	$1.00

Tip

Open interest and liquidity levels in the small-sized contracts are significantly lower than in the standard gold contract. Open interest in the standard gold contract is currently in excess of 250 000 contracts, compared with around 2500 contracts in both the NYSE Euronext mini-sized gold contract and the COMEX miNY gold contract. As a result, price spreads are often wider and price slippage can be an issue when entering or exiting trades

(continued)

during volatile periods when prices are moving quickly. Those interested in trading these contracts should check liquidity levels to ensure they meet their requirements before placing trades.

Silver

Like gold, silver is also considered a precious metal. It is a soft, ductile, malleable and highly conductive metal. It has been used for jewellery and money since around 3000 BC. Many nations used silver as the basis for currency standards, such as the British pound, which is thought to have acquired its name when payments were made in 'pounds of sterling' — coins minted from silver.

Tip

Sterling silver is an alloy that contains 92.5 per cent silver by mass and 7.5 per cent by mass of another metal, usually copper. Pure silver is too soft on its own for practical use; the addition of copper gives it strength while maintaining its other qualities.

In 1792 the US Congress based the currency on the 'silver dollar', with its value fixed to that of gold. Silver was used for producing coins in the US and many other countries until the late 1960s, and was phased out as free-floating fiat currencies were removed from the gold standard.

Silver is now used mainly for industrial purposes and jewellery. Silver conducts heat and electricity better than any other metal and is highly resistant to corrosion. It is used extensively for circuits, contacts, switches and wiring, and screens in the electronics, computer and telecommunications industries, and also in the production of photographic film. According to the World Silver Institute, 487.4 million ounces of silver were used in industrial applications in 2010, 167 million ounces in jewellery and 72.7 million ounces in photography.

Silver is mined in association with other metals including gold, lead, copper and zinc. The World Silver Institute puts global silver supply at 1056.8 million ounces in 2010, with 215 million ounces from recycled sources. The top-producing silver countries in 2010 were Mexico (128.6 million ounces), Peru (116.1 million ounces), China (99.2 million ounces), Australia (59.9 million ounces) and Chile (41 million ounces). Like gold, silver is found throughout the world. This geographical diversity means geopolitical issues in one country or region are less likely to have a significant impact on supply.

Tip

The largest silver-producing company in 2010 was BHP Billiton, from the Carrington mine in Queensland, Australia.

Factors affecting price

Factors affecting the price of silver include the following:

⇒ Increasing demand for computers, electronic equipment, mobile telephones, and a wide range of other electronics consumables, has led to an increase in the use of silver in these industries, causing demand to increase significantly. Global economic conditions can cause short-term fluctuations in consumer spending patterns on these items, impacting on the demand for silver.

⇒ The economic, political and social instability experienced since the GFC has seen investors seeking to hold their wealth in precious metals, including silver, as a safe and secure store of value. The increase in demand causes price to rise as supply is relatively static or inelastic, meaning silver miners and producers cannot adjust or react quickly to increase production in response to growing demand.

⇒ Periods of high inflation, or fears of impending inflation, will also push the price of silver higher as investors seek to maintain their wealth in real terms and not in a depreciating asset such as currency.

⇒ During periods of economic stability and low inflation, the silver price can remain unchanged for prolonged periods.

⇒ The silver price correlates closely to the price of gold, with the two prices generally following the same price movements.

Tip

Although the price of silver and gold are closely correlated over the long term, short-term prices for silver can be more erratic and volatile, reflecting the different demand influences impacting on the silver price.

Figure 10.4 shows a monthly price chart of silver futures from 1975 to 2012. The rapid and prolonged increase in the price of silver since the GFC and its after-effects on the global economy can be clearly seen. This chart also shows the close correlation of the prices of silver and gold over the same period of time.

Pricing

Silver futures are traded on the New York Commodity Exchange (COMEX) division of the New York Mercantile Exchange (NYMEX), owned and operated by CME Group; and electronically on the CME Globex platform. Silver futures trade in cents per troy ounce on a 5000-troy-ounce contract. A 1-cent-per-troy-ounce move in the price of silver equates to $50.00 on the futures contract (5000 troy ounces × 1 cent = $50.00). The minimum price move, or tick, is ½ cent ($0.005) or $25.00 per contract (5000 troy ounces × $0.005 per troy ounce = $25.00).

Figure 10.4: COMEX monthly silver and gold futures chart, 1975–2012

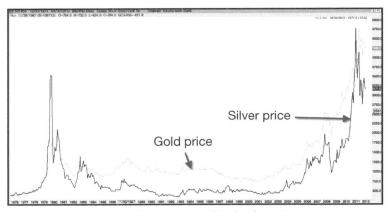

Source: Trade Navigator / Genesis Financial Technologies Inc.

Tip

A troy ounce equals 31.103 grams; 100 troy ounces equals 3.1103 kilograms. A 5000-troy-ounce contract equals 155.515 kilograms.

Trading examples

Expecting the price of silver to rise, a trader would BUY (go long) a futures contract. Let's say the long position is initiated at 3137.50 cents per troy ounce ($31.375) and the market rises to 3296.00 cents per troy ounce ($32.960), a move of 158.50 cents per troy ounce ($1.585), or 317 ticks (158.50 ÷ 0.5). The trader's profit (excluding brokerage and costs) would be $7925.00 (317 ticks × $25.00 per tick = $7925.00).

> 3296.00 cents per troy ounce (sell price) − 3137.50 cents per troy ounce (buy price) = 158.50 cents per troy ounce × 5000 troy ounces = $7925.00

Expecting the price of silver to fall, a trader would SELL (go short) a futures contract. Let's say the short position is initiated at 3433.50 cents per troy ounce ($34.335) and the market falls to 3313.00 cents per troy ounce ($33.130), a move of 120.50 cents per troy ounce ($1.205), or 241 ticks (120.50 ÷ 0.5). The trader's profit (excluding brokerage and costs) would be $6025.00 (241 ticks × $25.00 per tick = $6025.00).

> 3433.50 cents per troy ounce (sell price) − 3313.00 cents per troy ounce (buy price) = 120.50 cents per troy ounce × 5000 troy ounces = $6025.00

Contract specifications

Full contract specifications for the COMEX-traded silver futures contract are shown in figure 10.5.

Trading hours

Silver futures are traded both electronically on the CME Globex platform and by traditional open outcry on the trading floor of the New York Commodity Exchange (COMEX) division of NYMEX (now part of CME Group). The electronic market opens at 6.00 pm Sunday New York time and trades almost continuously through to 5.15 pm Friday afternoon New York time, with a daily break between 5.15 pm and 6.00 pm New York time. The pit session operates each weekday between 8.25 am and 1.25 pm New York time.

Figure 10.5: COMEX silver futures contract specifications

Product Symbol	SI	
Venue	CME Globex, CME ClearPort, Open Outcry (New York)	
Hours (All Times are New York Time/ET)	CME Globex:	Sunday – Friday 6:00 p.m. – 5:15 p.m. (5:00 p.m. – 4:15 p.m. Chicago Time/CT) with a 45-minute break each day beginning at 5:15 p.m. (4:15 p.m. CT)
	CME ClearPort:	Sunday – Friday 6:00 p.m. – 5:15 p.m. (5:00 p.m. – 4:15 p.m. Chicago Time/CT) with a 45-minute break each day beginning at 5:15 p.m. (4:15 p.m. CT)
	Open Outcry:	Monday – Friday 8:25 AM to 1:25 PM (7:25 AM to 12:25 PM CT)
Contract Size	5,000 troy ounces	
Price Quotation	U.S. Cents per troy ounce *Please note: Prices are disseminated in U.S. Dollars and Cents*	
Minimum Fluctuation	Outright transactions including EFP: $0.005 per troy ounce. Straddle or spread transactions and settlement prices: $0.001 per troy ounce.	
Termination of Trading	Trading terminates on the third last business day of the delivery month.	
Listed Contracts	Trading is conducted for delivery during the current calendar month; the next two calendar months; any January, March, May, and September falling within a 23-month period; and any July and December falling within a 60-month period beginning with the current month.	
Settlement Type	Physical	
Delivery Period	Delivery may take place on any business day beginning on the first business day of the delivery month or any subsequent business day of the delivery month, but not later than the last business day of the current delivery month.	
Trading at Settlement (TAS)	Trading at Settlement is allowed in the active contract month. The active contract months will be March, May, July, September and December. On any given date, TAS transactions will be allowed only in a single contract month. TAS transactions may be executed at the current day's settlement price or at any valid price increment ten ticks higher or lower than the settlement price.	
Grade and Quality Specifications	Silver delivered under this contract shall assay to a minimum of 999 fineness.	
Position Limits	NYMEX Position Limits	
Rulebook Chapter	112	
Exchange Rule	These contracts are listed with, and subject to, the rules and regulations of COMEX.	

Source: CME Group Inc.

Smaller size silver contracts

In addition to the full-size silver contract outlined here, traders and investors can also gain access to silver futures through a number of smaller sized contracts. These contracts provide the opportunity for traders with smaller accounts to actively participate in the silver futures markets. Details of these contracts are shown in table 10.2.

Table 10.2: smaller size silver contract details

Contract name	Exchange	Contract size	Price quote	Min. tick	Tick value
Mini-sized silver	NYSE Euronext	1000 troy ounces	1 cent = $10	$0.001/ troy ounce	$1.00
miNY silver	COMEX	2500 troy ounces	1 cent = $25	$0.0125/ troy ounce	$31.35

Tip

Open interest and liquidity levels in the small-sized contracts are significantly lower than in the standard silver contract. Open interest in the standard silver contract is currently in excess of 46 000 contracts, compared with around 2800 contracts in the NYSE Euronext mini-sized silver contract and around 300 in the COMEX miNY silver contract. As a result, price spreads are often wider and price slippage can be an issue when entering or exiting trades during volatile periods when prices are moving quickly. Those interested in trading these contracts should check liquidity levels to ensure they meet their requirements before placing trades. Traders should be particularly aware of the extremely low levels of open interest and daily trading volume in the COMEX miNY silver contract and note that although the contract size is only half that of the standard 5000 troy ounce contract, at 2500 troy ounces, the tick size is actually larger.

Copper

Copper was the first metal used by humans, with archaeological evidence dating copper objects and coins discovered in northern Iraq to 8700 BC. Copper is the world's third most widely used metal after iron and aluminium. Copper is a highly versatile base metal that is valued for its excellent conductivity, malleability, ductility and resistance to heat and corrosion. It has a wide range of uses in the building and plumbing, electrical and electronics, and telecommunications industries. Major uses include pipes, cables, wiring and electrical circuits, and communication lines. Copper can also be alloyed (combined) with other metals, such as zinc to form brass and aluminium, and tin to form bronze. Copper is still used in the coins of many currencies, including in the US and the Eurozone.

According to the International Copper Association, China is the largest user of copper, consuming in excess of 7.8 million tonnes annually. This figure is expected to continue to increase as China's economy continues to modernise and expand, increasing the use of copper in electronics, televisions, electrical wiring and vehicles. Other major users are Europe (3.1 million tonnes), the United States (2.5 million tonnes) and Japan (1.2 million tonnes). Total global copper consumption is estimated at around 22 million tonnes annually.

Most copper is mined as copper sulphide from open-pit mines that contain between 0.4 and 1.0 per cent copper along with varying amounts of other metals including gold, silver, lead and zinc. A very complex process involving milling (crushing the ore and using chemicals and water to concentrate and isolate the copper), smelting (roasting the copper concentrate and then melting and re-treating) and refining (melting in a furnace and then using electrolysis to further purify the copper) is needed to obtain pure copper. The copper ingots produced from this process are then rolled to produce sheets, or melted and further extruded to produce wire products. It is a costly, complex and environmentally 'heavy' process that requires a huge amount of power, water and chemical resources.

Total annual global mined copper production is around 16 million tonnes. The major producing countries are Chile (5.4 million tonnes), Peru (1.3 million tonnes), China (1.2 million tonnes), the United States (1.1 million tonnes) and Australia (900 million tonnes).

Tip

Approximately 25 per cent (5 million tonnes) of all copper consumed is from recycled copper sources.

Factors affecting price

Factors affecting the price of copper include the following:

⇒ Demand for copper is heavily associated with the strength of the global economy. When economies are expanding, disposable incomes are high and jobs are 'safe', spending on items that contain copper such as houses, electronics and appliances increases. A slow economy and tighter economic times result in reduced demand for these items and less demand for copper as a result. The price of copper will follow the business cycle.

⇒ The complex nature of the refining process can result in supply constraints during periods of high demand, causing prices to rise.

⇒ The capital- and infrastructure-intense nature of copper refining restricts the process to a few major refining operators. Any major breakdowns, industrial disputes, or other social or political issues that impact on these operators will also have an impact on the supply of copper, and hence the price if these events disrupt the refining operations for an extended period.

⇒ Increased demand for copper by China and other Asian countries as they continue to expand and Westernise is having an impact on the copper price. The increased demand for electrical goods that contain copper wiring and Western-style housing that uses copper pipes and copper electrical wiring are key drivers in these markets. China's consumption of copper is predicted to increase more than threefold in the next 20 years.

Figure 10.6 shows a weekly price chart of copper futures from 1987 to 2012.

Figure 10.6: weekly price chart of COMEX copper futures, 1987–2012

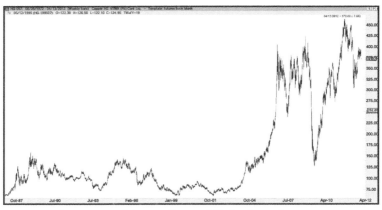

Source: Trade Navigator / Genesis Financial Technologies Inc.

Pricing

Copper futures are traded on the New York Commodity Exchange (COMEX) division of the New York Mercantile Exchange (NYMEX), owned and operated by CME Group; and electronically on the CME Globex platform. Copper futures trade in cents per pound on a 25 000-pound contract. A 1-cent-per-pound move in the price of copper equates to $250.00 on the futures contract (25 000 pounds × $0.01 = $250.00). The minimum price move, or tick, is $0.0005 or $12.50 per contract (25 000 pounds × $0.0005 = $12.50).

Trading examples

Expecting the price of copper to rise, a trader would BUY (go long) a futures contract. Let's say the long position is initiated at 341.40 cents per pound ($3.4140) and the market rises to 368.70 cents per pound ($3.6870), a move of 27.30 cents per pound ($0.2730), or 546 ticks ($0.273 ÷ $0.0005). The trader's profit (excluding brokerage and costs) would be $6825.00 (546 ticks × $12.50 per tick = $6825.00).

> 368.70 cents per pound (sell price) − 341.40 cents per pound (buy price) = 27.30 cents per pound × 25 000 pounds = $6825.00

Expecting the price of copper to fall, a trader would SELL (go short) a futures contract. Let's say the short position is initiated at 393.55 cents per pound ($3.9355) and the market falls to 376.10 cents per pound ($3.7610), a move of 17.45 cents per pound ($0.1745), or 349 ticks ($0.1745 ÷ $0.0005). The trader's profit (excluding brokerage and costs) would be $4362.50 (349 ticks × $12.50 per tick = $4362.50).

> 393.55 cents per pound (sell price) − 376.10 cents per pound (buy price) = 17.45 cents per pound × 25 000 pounds = $4362.50

Contract specifications

Full contract specifications for the COMEX-traded copper futures contract are shown in figure 10.7.

Trading hours

Copper futures are traded both electronically on the CME Globex platform and by traditional open outcry on the trading floor of the New York Commodity Exchange (COMEX) division of NYMEX (now part of CME Group). The electronic market opens at 6.00 pm Sunday New York time and trades almost continuously through to 5.15 pm Friday afternoon

New York time, with a daily break between 5.15 pm and 6.00 pm New York time. The pit session operates each weekday between 8.10 am and 1.00 pm New York time.

Figure 10.7: COMEX copper futures contract specifications

Product Symbol	HG	
Venue	CME Globex, CME ClearPort, Open Outcry (New York)	
Hours (All Times are New York Time/ET)	CME Globex:	Sunday – Friday 6:00 p.m. – 5:15 p.m. (5:00 p.m. – 4:15 p.m. Chicago Time/CT) with a 45-minute break each day beginning at 5:15 p.m. (4:15 p.m. CT)
	CME ClearPort:	Sunday – Friday 6:00 p.m. – 5:15 p.m. (5:00 p.m. – 4:15 p.m. Chicago Time/CT) with a 45-minute break each day beginning at 5:15 p.m. (4:15 p.m. CT)
	Open Outcry:	Monday – Friday 8:10 a.m. – 1:00 p.m. (7:10 a.m. – 12:00 p.m. CT)
Contract Size	25,000 pounds	
Price Quotation	U.S. Cents per pound *Please note: Prices are disseminated in U.S. Dollars and Cents*	
Minimum Fluctuation	$0.0005 per pound	
Termination of Trading	Trading terminates on the third last business day of the delivery month.	
Listed Contracts	Trading is conducted for delivery during the current calendar month, the next 23 calendar months, and any March, May, July, September, and December falling within a 60-month period beginning with the current month.	
Settlement Type	Physical	
Delivery Period	Delivery may take place on any business day beginning on the first business day of the delivery month or any subsequent business day of the delivery month, but not later than the last business day of the current delivery month.	
Trading at Settlement (TAS)	Trading at Settlement is allowed in the active contract month. The active contract months will be March, May, July, September and December. On any given date, TAS transactions will be allowed only in a single contract month. TAS transactions may be executed at the current day's settlement price or at any valid price increment ten ticks higher or lower than the settlement price.	
Grade and Quality Specifications	The contract (basis) grade for the Grade 1 copper contract shall be Grade 1 Electrolytic Copper Cathodes (full plate or cut) and shall conform to the specifications (as to chemical and physical requirements) for Grade 1 Electrolytic Copper Cathode as adopted by the American Society for Testing and Materials (B115-00), or its latest revision.	
Position Limits	NYMEX Position Limits	
Rulebook Chapter	111	
Exchange Rule	These contracts are listed with, and subject to, the rules and regulations of COMEX.	

Source: CME Group Inc.

Smaller size copper contract

In addition to the full-size copper contract outlined here, traders and investors can also gain access to copper futures through a smaller e-mini copper contract offered by COMEX. This e-mini contract is for 12 500 pounds of copper with a minimum tick move of 0.2 cents per pound or $25.00. At the time of writing the open interest in this e-mini contract was less than 100 contracts, compared with more than 50 000 for the standard copper contract. This extremely low level of open interest should discourage anyone from attempting to trade this contract.

Part III

Financial markets futures contracts

Financial futures, which today account for around 80 per cent of global futures trading volume, began trading in 1972 with the release by the Chicago Mercantile Exchange (CME) of futures contracts on eight major currencies. These were followed by US Treasury bill futures in 1976, Eurodollar futures in 1981 and the Standard and Poor's S&P 500 index futures contract in 1982.

chapter 11

Interest rates futures

Financial instruments are either *debt instruments* or *equity instruments*. Debt instruments are loans with an agreement to repay the borrowed funds plus interest at either a fixed or a variable rate. The term of the loan may vary from overnight to 30 years or more. Equity instruments are shares of a company's stock that represent ownership of the company. As part owners, shareholders can receive a share in the company's profits through the payment of dividends.

Debt instruments are loans that state the terms agreed by the borrower and the lender, including the loan amount, the repayment date, the interest rate, and how and when the interest is to be paid. There is a huge range of interest rate futures contracts spanning a variety of time periods across many different markets throughout the world. We will take a look at three of the most actively traded interest rate futures products—Eurodollars, US 30-year Treasury bonds, and US 10-year Treasury notes.

Tip

When trading interest rate products it is important to remember that the price or value of the interest rate product is inverse to the quoted interest rate. An interest rate product priced at, say, 95.00 equates to an interest rate of 5 per cent (100 − 95 = 5%). If interest rates rise to, say, 5.25 per cent, then the price of the debt instrument DECREASES in price to 94.75 (100 − 5.25 = 94.75). If interest rates fall to 4.75 per cent, then the price of the debt instrument INCREASES to 95.25 (100 − 4.75 = 95.25).

Eurodollars

Eurodollars are time, or term, deposits denominated in US dollars held in banks outside the US, and are not under the jurisdiction of the US Federal Reserve banking system. Eurodollars originally referred to US dollars held in European banks but these days refers to all US dollar deposits held in any country other than the United States. During the Cold War, the Soviet Union and its Eastern Bloc allies feared the US might freeze their accounts and confiscate any cash assets held in US banks. To prevent this occurring, they transferred their US dollar balances to London and other European financial centres, via the Soviet bank in Paris, Banque Commerciale pour l'Europe du Nord, also referred to as Eurobank, giving rise to the term *Eurodollar*.

Tip

Eurodollars are NOT euro currency. Eurodollars are a debt or interest rate instrument. The euro is the currency of the Eurozone traded in the foreign exchange markets and as a currency futures contract.

Eurodollar deposits are fixed-rate, non-negotiable US dollar-denominated deposits. They are generally less regulated than similar deposits held within the United States and as such tend to return a higher interest rate. The interest rate paid by banks on Eurodollar deposits is the London Interbank Offer Rate (LIBOR) minus a margin taken by the issuing bank, paid using the *simple add-on method*: if $100 000 is deposited for one year at 4 per cent interest, then the bank *adds on* $4000 to the account balance at the end of a 360-day period (a year for money market calculations), and the depositor can withdraw $104 000.

The Eurodollar market also benefits from regulatory controls in the US that limit the interest rates banks can pay on deposits and the Federal Reserve requirement that banks hold specified levels of cash reserves. These restrictions make it attractive for banks to compete for funds and to provide higher interest rates on deposits in the Eurodollar market. The Eurodollar market is enormous. Exact figures are hard to determine, as transactions take place on an ongoing basis between banks and their clients. Eurodollar deposits are direct obligations between the commercial banks and their clients and are not guaranteed by any government rules or regulations. They are considered low risk but, like everything since the GFC, not risk free. Eurodollar deposits play a major role in international capital markets and act as the benchmark interest rate for commercial and corporate funding.

Tip

Eurodollar futures are the most actively traded futures contract in the world, with average daily volumes in excess of 3 million contracts with a notional value of over $3 trillion.

Factors affecting price

Factors affecting the price of Eurodollars include the following:

⇒ US Federal Reserve monetary policy announcements and actions frequently affect interest rates.

⇒ Key economic indicator announcements and/or changes, including GDP, employment, balance of trade, retail sales, consumer confidence and others, can affect short-term interest rates either directly or indirectly.

⇒ Inflation and/or expected changes to the rate of inflation can lead to changes in short-term interest rates.

⇒ Economic conditions in both the US and the global economy as a whole will impact on interest rates.

Figure 11.1 shows a weekly price chart of Eurodollar futures from 1987 to 2012. The inverse relationship between interest rates and the price of a debt instrument such as the Eurodollar can be clearly seen. When interest rates are rising the price of Eurodollars will decline; a fall in interest rates means the price of Eurodollars will rise. The fact that interest rates have been held in a tight band by the US Federal Reserve since the GFC is clearly evident in the extended period of flat prices for Eurodollars since the middle of 2009.

Figure 11.1: weekly price chart of CME Eurodollar futures, 1987–2012

Source: Trade Navigator / Genesis Financial Technologies Inc.

Pricing

Eurodollar futures are traded on the Chicago Mercantile Exchange (CME) and electronically on the CME Globex platform. Over 85 per cent of Eurodollar futures are traded electronically on Globex. Eurodollar futures are priced as 100 minus the current interest rate. For example, a rate of

2.75 per cent is quoted as 97.25 (100 − 2.75 = 97.25) on a $1 000 000 contract; 1 basis point (1 one-hundredth of 1 per cent, or 0.01%) equates to $25.00. A 1 per cent interest rate move equals $2500.00 (100 basis points × $25.00 = $2500.00). The minimum price move or tick is one-quarter of 1 basis point (0.0025) or $6.25 in the nearest expiring month (0.0025 × $2500.00 = $6.25); and half of 1 basis point (0.005) or $12.50 in all other months (0.005 × $2500.00 = $12.50).

Trading examples

Expecting the price of Eurodollars to rise (interest rates to fall), a trader would BUY (go long) a futures contract. Let's say the long position is initiated when the interest rate is 4.8475 per cent, pricing Eurodollars at 95.1525 (100 − 4.8475 = 95.1525). A cut in interest rates by 0.5 per cent (half of 1 per cent) or 50 basis points to 4.3475 per cent (4.8475% − 0.500% = 4.3475%) means the price of Eurodollars will rise by 0.500 to 95.6525 (95.1525 + 0.500 = 95.6525), or 200 ticks (50 ÷ 0.25). The trader's profit (excluding brokerage and costs) would be $1250.00 (200 ticks × $6.25 per tick = $1250.00).

> 95.6525 (sell price) − 95.1525 (buy price) =
> 0.500 × $2500.00 = $1250.00, or 50 basis points ×
> $25.00 per basis point = $1250.00

Expecting the price of Eurodollars to fall (interest rates to rise), a trader would SELL (go short) a futures contract. Let's say the short position is initiated when the interest rate is 3.7550 per cent, pricing Eurodollars at 96.2450 (100 − 3.7550 = 96.2450). An increase in interest rates by 0.25 per cent (one-quarter of 1 per cent) or 25 basis points to 4.0100 per cent (3.7550% + 0.25% = 4.0100%) means the price of Eurodollars will fall by 0.2500 to 95.9950 (96.2450 − 0.2500 = 95.9950), or 100 ticks (25 ÷ 0.25). The trader's profit (excluding brokerage and costs) would be $625.00 (100 ticks × $6.25 per tick = $625.00).

> 96.2450 (sell price) − 95.9950 (buy price) =
> 0.25 × $2500.00 = $625.00, or 25 basis points ×
> $25.00 per basis point = $625.00

Contract specifications

Full contract specifications for the GLOBEX-traded Eurodollar futures contract are shown in figure 11.2.

Figure 11.2: GLOBEX Eurodollar futures contract specifications

Underlying Instrument	Eurodollar Time Deposit having a principal value of USD $1,000,000 with a three -month maturity.
Price Quote	Quoted in IMM Three-Month LIBOR index points or 100 minus the rate on an annual basis over a 360 day year (e.g., a rate of 2.5% shall be quoted as 97.50). 1 basis point = .01 = $25.
Tick Size (minimum fluctuation)	One-quarter of one basis point (0.0025 = $6.25 per contract) in the nearest expiring contract month; One-half of one basis point (0.005 = $12.50 per contract) in all other contract months. The "new" front-month contract begins trading in 0.0025 increments on the same Trade Date as the Last Trading Day of the expiring "old" front-month contract.
Contract Months	Mar, Jun, Sep, Dec, extending out 10 years (total of 40 contracts) plus the four nearest serial expirations (months that are not in the March quarterly cycle). The new contract month terminating 10 years in the future is listed on the Tuesday following expiration of the front quarterly contract month.
Last Trading Day	The second London bank business day prior to the third Wednesday of the contract expiry month. Trading in the expiring contract closes at 11:00 a.m. London Time on the last trading day.
Settlement Procedure	Final Eurodollar Futures Settlement Procedure (PDF)
Position Limits	None
Block Minimum	Block Trading Minimums
All or None Minimum	All or None Minimums
Rulebook Chapter	CME Chapter 452
Trading Hours (All times listed are Central Time)	OPEN OUTCRY — MON-FRI: 7:20 a.m. - 2:00 p.m. CME GLOBEX — SUN - FRI: 5:00 p.m. - 4:00 p.m. CT
Ticker Symbol	OPEN OUTCRY — ED CME GLOBEX — GE
Exchange Rule	These contracts are listed with, and subject to, the rules and regulations of CME.

Source: CME Group Inc.

Trading hours

Eurodollar futures are traded both electronically on the CME Globex platform and by traditional open outcry on the trading floor of the Chicago Mercantile Exchange (CME). The electronic market opens at 5.00 pm Sunday Chicago time and trades continuously through to 4.00 pm Friday afternoon Chicago time. The pit session operates each weekday between 7.20 am and 2.00 pm Chicago time.

US 30-year Treasury bonds

Governments throughout the world issue long-term debt instruments to the investing public to help finance their borrowing requirements for the purposes of long-term government expenditure. They are a long-term, fixed-interest debt instrument with a specified maturity date. The US Federal Government issues 30-year Treasury bonds with a face value or par value of $100 000 and a maturity date of up to 30 years. Interest is paid twice each year until the maturity date. At the maturity date the face value ($100 000) is repaid to the holder of the bond. Bonds are effectively a 'low risk' loan to the government. Because of the long-term nature of bonds and the volume of bonds on issue, the secondary market is very active. Investors can buy and sell bonds depending on their view on the interest rate market. There is currently in excess of US$1 trillion worth of US Treasury bonds on issue.

Tip

The annualised interest rate on bonds is quoted as a coupon rate paid in semi-annual instalments. A coupon rate is the amount of interest paid on the par value of the bond.

(continued)

Tip (cont'd)

Neither the par value of the bond nor the coupon interest rate change over the life of the bond, giving rise to the term 'fixed-income security'. A $100 000 bond with a coupon rate of 5 per cent per annum returns the investor $5000 per annum ($100 000 × 5%), paid in two instalments of $2500 each.

The current level of interest rates will determine the price of the bond in the secondary market. The relationship between the price of the bond and the interest rate is inverted. If interest rates increase, the price of the bond will decrease; if interest rates decrease, the price of the bond will rise. For example, a $100 000 bond issued with a coupon rate of 5 per cent ($5000) will fall in value if interest rates rise to 5.5 per cent, as new bonds issued will now return $5500 per annum. The original owner of the bond paying a 5 per cent coupon rate will have to sell it at a lower price to reflect the current yield or interest rate of 5.5 per cent on the new bond issuance. The original bond will fall in value to around $99 950 in order for a new purchaser to achieve the same effective return ($99 950 × 5.5% = $5500).

Falling interest rates will produce the reverse situation. If rates fall from 5 per cent to 4.5 per cent, then the $100 000 bond yielding 5 per cent has a better yield than currently issued bonds yielding 4.5 per cent. It can now be offered at a premium to the par value and will increase in value to around $100 050 to achieve the same effective return ($100 050 × 4.5% = $4500).

Tip

Thirty-year Treasury bonds are referred to as T-Bonds, 30-year bonds or simply '30 years'.

Factors affecting price

Factors affecting the price of 30-year Treasury bonds include the following:

⇒ US Federal Reserve monetary policy announcements and actions frequently affect interest rates.

⇒ Key economic indicator announcements and/or changes, including GDP, employment, balance of trade, retail sales, consumer confidence and others, can affect short-term interest rates either directly or indirectly.

⇒ Inflation and/or expected changes to the rate of inflation can lead to changes in short-term interest rates.

⇒ Economic conditions in both the US and global economy as a whole will impact on interest rates.

⇒ International geopolitical and economic instability can lead to a 'flight to quality', leading overseas investors to purchase US Treasury bonds as a 'low risk' investment backed by the US Federal Government. This can have the effect of increasing prices for bonds and decreasing the yield as investors seek perceived safety rather than higher returns.

⇒ The level and volume of future bond issues by the US Government can affect price. The exact effect will be determined by prevailing and anticipated economic conditions, inflation, interest rates and returns for other investment types.

Figure 11.3 (overleaf) shows a weekly price chart of US 30-year Treasury bond futures from 1987 to 2012. The inverse relationship between interest rates and the price of

30-year bonds can be clearly seen. When interest rates are rising, the price of 30-year bonds will decline; a fall in interest rates means the price of 30-year bonds will rise.

Figure 11.3: weekly price chart of CBOT 30-year Treasury bond futures 1987–2012

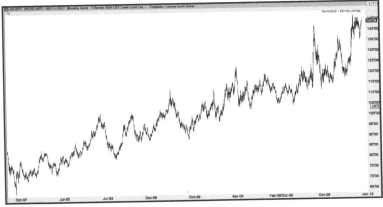

Source: Trade Navigator / Genesis Financial Technologies Inc.

Pricing

Thirty-year Treasury bond futures are traded on the Chicago Board of Trade (CBOT) and electronically on the CME Globex platform. They are priced in dollars per basis point on a $100 000.00 contract size, where 1 basis point = $1000.00. The par or face value is based on 100 basis points (100 points × $1000.00 per basis point = $100 000.00). The minimum tick value is 1 thirty-second or $31.25 ($1000.00 × 1/32 = $31.25). Each basis point is 32 thirty-seconds. One basis point equals 1 one-hundredth of 1 per cent or 0.01.

Unlike Eurodollars that are quoted on a yield basis (100–the current interest rate), 30-year bonds as a coupon-bearing security are quoted in per cent of par or face value to the nearest 1 thirty-second of 1 per cent of par. For example, a 30-year bond quoted at 110^12 equates to a value of 110 per cent of par plus 12 thirty-seconds.

The decimal equivalent is 110.375. A $100 000.00 face value bond would therefore be priced at $110 375.00. If the price moves by 1 thirty-second from 110^12 to 110^13, this equates to a move of 1 tick ($31.25), pricing the bond at $110 406.25 (110% of par + ¹³⁄₃₂). The decimal equivalent is 110.40625.

Tip

The pricing of 30-year bond futures is a complex calculation involving the issue price (a constant 6 per cent coupon rate for the first 20 years of the bond), the price at which the bond is originally purchased (subject to the prevailing interest rate), the amount of any outstanding coupon interest, time to maturity, the current interest rate, economic and geopolitical conditions, current inflation rates, and anticipated interest and inflation rates.

Trading examples

Expecting the price of 30-year bond futures to rise, a trader would BUY (go long) a futures contract. Let's say the long position is initiated at 128^10 (128% of par value + ¹⁰⁄₃₂) and the market rises to 134^23 (134% of par value + ²³⁄₃₂), a move of 6^13 (6% of par value + ²³⁄₃₂) or 205 ticks (6 basis points of ³²⁄₃₂ + ²³⁄₃₂ = ²⁰⁵⁄₃₂). This represents a fall in interest rates on 30-year bond futures of 6^13 basis points or 0.0640625 per cent. The trader's profit (excluding brokerage and costs) would be $6406.25 (205 ticks × $31.25 per tick = $6406.25).

Alternatively, the total dollar value of the contract at each price quote can be calculated and the profit or loss determined.

134^23 (sell price) = 1.34 + ²³⁄₃₂ of 1 per cent = 1.3471875 × $100 000.00 = $134 718.75 − 128^10 (buy price) = 1.28 + ¹⁰⁄₃₂ of 1 per cent = 1.2831250 × $100 000.00 = $128 312.50

The increase in the dollar value of the 30-year bond futures contract is $6406.25 ($134718.75 − $128312.50 = $6406.25).

Expecting the price of 30-year bond futures to fall, a trader would SELL (go short) a futures contract. Let's say the short position is initiated at 140^22 (144% of par value + $^{22}/_{32}$) and the market falls to 136^04 (136% of par value + $^4/_{32}$), a move of 4^18 (4% of par value + $^{18}/_{32}$) or 146 ticks (4 basis points of $^{32}/_{32}$ + $^{18}/_{32}$ = $^{146}/_{32}$). This represents a rise in interest rates on 30-year bond futures of 4^18 basis points or 0.0456250 per cent. The trader's profit (excluding brokerage and costs) would be $4562.50 (146 ticks × $31.25 per tick = $4562.50).

Alternatively, the total dollar value of the contract at each price quote can be calculated and the profit or loss determined.

140^22 (sell price) = 1.40 + $^{22}/_{32}$ of 1 per cent = 1.4068750 × $100000.00 = $140687.50 − 136^04 (buy price) = 1.36 + $^4/_{32}$ of 1 per cent = 1.3612500 × $100000.00 = $136125.00

The decrease in the dollar value of the 30-year bond futures contract is $462.50 ($140687.50 − $136125.00 = $4562.50).

Contract specifications

Full contract specifications for the CBOT-traded 30-year bond futures contract are shown in figure 11.4.

Trading hours

US 30-year bond futures are traded both electronically on the CME Globex platform and by traditional open outcry on the trading floor of the Chicago Board of Trade. The electronic market opens at 5.00 pm Sunday Chicago time and trades continuously through to 4.00 pm Friday afternoon Chicago time. The pit session operates each weekday between 7.20 am and 2.00 pm Chicago time.

Figure 11.4: CBOT 30-year bond futures contract specifications

Underlying Unit	One U.S. Treasury bond having a face value at maturity of $100,000.
Deliverable Grades	U.S. Treasury bonds that, if callable, are not callable for at least 15 years from the first day of the delivery month or, if not callable, have a remaining term to maturity of at least 15 years from the first day of the delivery month. **Note: Beginning with the March 2011 expiry, the deliverable grade for T-Bond futures will be bonds with remaining maturity of at least 15 years, but less than 25 years, from the first day of the delivery month.** The invoice price equals the futures settlement price times a conversion factor, plus accrued interest. The conversion factor is the price of the delivered bond ($1 par value) to yield 6 percent.
Price Quote	Points ($1,000) and 1/32 of a point. For example, 134-16 represents 134 16/32. Par is on the basis of 100 points.
Tick Size (minimum fluctuation)	One thirty-second (1/32) of one point ($31.25), except for intermonth spreads, where the minimum price fluctuation shall be one-quarter of one thirty-second of one point ($7.8125 per contract).
Contract Months	The first three consecutive contracts in the March, June, September, and December quarterly cycle.
Last Trading Day	Seventh business day preceding the last business day of the delivery month. Trading in expiring contracts closes at 12:01 p.m. on the last trading day.
Last Delivery Day	Last business day of the delivery month.
Delivery Method	Federal Reserve book-entry wire-transfer system.
Settlement Procedure	Daily Treasury Settlement Procedures (PDF) Final Treasury Settlement Procedures (PDF)
Position Limits	Current Position Limits
Block Minimum	Block Trade Minimums
All or None Minimum	All or None Minimums
Rulebook Chapter	CBOT Chapter 18
Trading Hours (All times listed are Central Time)	OPEN OUTCRY	MON - FRI: 7:20 a.m. - 2:00 p.m.
	CME GLOBEX	SUN - FRI: 5:00 p.m. - 4:00 p.m.
Ticker Symbol	OPEN OUTCRY	US
	CME GLOBEX	ZB
Exchange Rule	These contracts are listed with, and subject to, the rules and regulations of CBOT.

Source: CME Group Inc.

Treasury notes

Like Treasury bonds, Treasury notes are fixed-interest paying debt instruments that are issued by governments for short

(2-year) and intermediate (5- and 10-year) periods. They pay a fixed rate of interest twice a year until maturity. At maturity the face value (or par value) of the note is repaid to the lender. Like bonds, they can be resold and traded in the secondary market, which is actively traded. The prevailing level of interest rates will determine the price of the notes in the secondary market and in the futures market. As with all debt securities, the relationship between the price of notes and interest rates is inverse. A rise in interest rates will cause a fall in the price of Treasury notes, while a fall in interest rates will cause the price of Treasury notes to rise.

Tip

At the time of writing there is in excess of $6.7 trillion worth of US Treasury notes on issue — that is $6.7 trillion that the US Government has borrowed from buyers of US Treasury notes.

Factors affecting price

Factors affecting the price of Treasury notes include the following:

⇒ US Federal Reserve monetary policy announcements and actions frequently affect interest rates.

⇒ Key economic indicator announcements and/or changes, including GDP, employment, Balance of Trade, retail sales, consumer confidence and others, can affect short-term interest rates either directly or indirectly.

⇒ Inflation and/or expected changes to the rate of inflation can lead to changes in short-term interest rates.

⇒ Economic conditions in both the US and global economy as a whole will impact on interest rates.

⇒ International geopolitical and economic instability can lead to a 'flight to quality', leading overseas investors to purchase US Treasury notes as a 'low risk' investment backed by the US Federal Government. This can have the effect of increasing prices for notes and decreasing the yield as investors seek perceived safety rather than higher returns.

⇒ The level and volume of future note issues by the US Government can affect price. The exact effect will be determined by prevailing and anticipated economic conditions, inflation, interest rates and returns for other investment types.

Tip

Of the three time periods for which Treasury notes are issued, the 10-year notes are the most actively traded in the secondary cash market and the futures market. We look here at the 10-year Treasury notes.

Figure 11.5 shows a weekly price chart of US 10-year Treasury note futures from 1987 to 2012. The inverse relationship between interest rates and the price of 10-year notes can be clearly seen. When interest rates are rising, the price of 10-year notes will decline; a fall in interest rates means the price of 10-year notes will rise.

Figure 11.5: weekly price chart of CBOT 10-year Treasury note futures, 1987–2012

Source: Trade Navigator / Genesis Financial Technologies Inc.

Pricing

Ten-year Treasury note futures are traded on the Chicago Board of Trade (CBOT) and electronically on the CME Globex platform. Ten-year Treasury note futures are priced in dollars per basis point on a $100 000.00 contract size where 1 basis point = $1000.00. The par or face value is based on 100 basis points (100 points × $1000.00 per basis point = $100 000.00). The minimum tick value is 1 sixty-fourth or $15.625 ($1000.00 × ⅟₆₄ = $15.625). Each basis point is 64 sixty-fourths. One basis point equals 1 one-hundredth of 1 per cent or 0.01.

Tip

The quoting of Treasury notes in sixty-fourths of a basis point can be confusing; 1 sixty-fourth is often referred to as one-half of 1 thirty-second (⅟₃₂ × ½ = ⅟₆₄). When first trading Treasury notes it is advisable to double-check your calculations to ensure you have the correct figures. Then, to be sure, check them again!

Ten-year Treasury notes as a coupon-bearing security (the same as 30-year Treasury bonds) are quoted in per cent of par or face value to the nearest 1 sixty-fourth of 1 per cent of par (1 sixty-fourth is often referred to as one-half of 1 thirty-second). For example, a 10-year note quoted at 110^12.5 equates to a value of 110 per cent of par plus 12 thirty-seconds plus 1 sixty-fourth (effectively 25 sixty-fourths). The decimal equivalent is 110.390625. A $100 000.00 face value 10-year note would therefore be priced at $110 390.625. If the price moves by 1 sixty-fourth from 110^12.5 to 110^13, this equates to a move of 1 tick ($15.625), pricing the note at $110 406.25 (110% of par + ²⁶⁄₆₄). The decimal equivalent is 110.406250.

Tip

The pricing of 10-year Treasury notes is a complex calculation involving the issue price (a constant 6 per cent coupon rate for the life of the Treasury note), the price at which the note is originally purchased (subject to the prevailing interest rate), the amount of any outstanding coupon interest, time to maturity, the current interest rate, economic and geopolitical conditions, current inflation rates, and anticipated interest and inflation rates.

Trading examples

Expecting the price of 10-year Treasury note futures to rise, a trader would BUY (go long) a futures contract. Let's say the long position is initiated at 126^25.5 (126% of par value + $^{25}/_{32}$ + $^1/_{64}$, or 126% of par value + $^{51}/_{64}$) and the market rises to 129^05 (129% of par value + $^5/_{32}$ or 129% of par value + $^{10}/_{64}$), a move of 2^23 (2% of par value + $^{23}/_{64}$) or 151 ticks (2 basis points of $^{64}/_{64}$ + $^{23}/_{64}$ = $^{151}/_{64}$). This represents a fall in interest rates on 10-year Treasury note futures of 2^23 basis points or 0.02359375 per cent. The trader's profit (excluding brokerage and costs) would be $2359.38 (151 ticks × $15.625 per tick = $2359.38).

Alternatively, the total dollar value of the contract at each price quote can be calculated and the profit or loss determined.

129^05 (sell price) = 1.29 + $^5/_{32}$ of 1 per cent = 1.2915625 × $100 000 = $129 156.25 − 126^25.5 (buy price) = 1.28 + $^{51}/_{64}$ of 1 per cent = 1.26796875 × $100 000 = $126 796.87

The increase in the dollar value of the 10-year Treasury note futures contract is $129 156.25 − $126 796.87 = $2359.38.

Expecting the price of 10-year Treasury note futures to fall, a trader would SELL (go short) a futures contract. Let's say the short position is initiated at 133^22 (133% of par value + $^{22}\!/_{32}$, or 133% of par value + $^{44}\!/_{64}$) and the market falls to 129^04.5 (129% of par value + $^{4}\!/_{32}$ + $^{1}\!/_{64}$, or 129% of par value + $^{9}\!/_{64}$), a move of 4^35 (4% of par value + $^{35}\!/_{64}$) or 291 ticks (4 basis points of $^{64}\!/_{64}$ + $^{35}\!/_{64}$ = $^{291}\!/_{64}$). This represents a rise in interest rates on 10-year Treasury note futures of 4^35 basis points or 0.04546875 per cent. The trader's profit (excluding brokerage and costs) would be $4546.88 (291 ticks × $15.62 per tick = $4546.88).

Alternatively, the total dollar value of the contract at each price quote can be calculated and the profit or loss determined.

133^22 (sell price) = 1.33 + $^{22}\!/_{32}$ of 1 per cent = 1.336875 × $100 000 = $133 687.50 − 129^04.5 (buy price) = 1.29 + $^{9}\!/_{64}$ of 1 per cent = 1.29140625 × $100 000 = $129 140.63

The decrease in the dollar value of the 10-year Treasury note futures contract is $4546.88 ($133 687.50 − $129 140.62 = $4546.88).

Contract specifications

Full contract specifications for the CBOT-traded 10-year Treasury note futures contract are shown in figure 11.6.

Trading hours

Ten-year Treasury note futures are traded both electronically on the CME Globex platform and by traditional open outcry on the trading floor of the Chicago Board of Trade. The electronic market opens at 5.00 pm Sunday Chicago time and trades continuously through to 4.00 pm Friday afternoon Chicago time. The pit session operates each weekday between 7.20 am and 2.00 pm Chicago time.

Figure 11.6: CBOT 10-year Treasury note futures contract specifications

Underlying Unit	One U.S. Treasury note having a face value at maturity of $100,000.
Deliverable Grades	U.S. Treasury notes with a remaining term to maturity of at least six and a half years, but not more than 10 years, from the first day of the delivery month. The invoice price equals the futures settlement price times a conversion factor, plus accrued interest. The conversion factor is the price of the delivered note ($1 par value) to yield 6 percent.
Price Quote	Points ($1,000) and halves of 1/32 of a point. For example, 126-16 represents 126 16/32 and 126-165 represents 126 16.5/32. Par is on the basis of 100 points.
Tick Size (minimum fluctuation)	One-half of one thirty-second (1/32) of one point ($15.625, rounded up to the nearest cent per contract), except for intermonth spreads, where the minimum price fluctuation shall be one-quarter of one thirty-second of one point ($7.8125 per contract).
Contract Months	The first five consecutive contracts in the March, June, September, and December quarterly cycle.
Last Trading Day	Seventh business day preceding the last business day of the delivery month. Trading in expiring contracts closes at 12:01 p.m. on the last trading day.
Last Delivery Day	Last business day of the delivery month.
Delivery Method	Federal Reserve book-entry wire-transfer system.
Settlement Procedure	Daily Treasury Settlement Procedures (PDF) Final Treasury Settlement Procedures (PDF)
Position Limits	Current Position Limits
Block Minimum	Block Trade Minimums
All or None Minimum	All or None Minimums
Rulebook Chapter	CBOT Chapter 19
Trading Hours (All times listed are Central Time)	OPEN OUTCRY	MON - FRI: 7:20 a.m. - 2:00 p.m.
	CME GLOBEX	SUN - FRI: 5:00 p.m. - 4:00 p.m.
Ticker Symbol	OPEN OUTCRY	TY
	CME GLOBEX	ZN
Exchange Rule	These contracts are listed with, and subject to, the rules and regulations of CBOT.

Source: CME Group Inc.

chapter 12

Equity index futures

Equity or share/stock price indices are based on the current market price of a group of shares trading on a stock exchange such as the Australian Securities Exchange (ASX), the New York Stock Exchange (NYSE) or the Tokyo Stock Exchange (TSE). The index represents the prices of a 'basket' of shares that are listed and trading on the exchange and that meet the specified criteria for inclusion in the index. The S&P/ASX200 Index, for example, is an index of the top 200 shares by market capitalisation trading on the ASX and covers approximately 78 per cent of Australian equity market capitalisation. Equity index futures are based on the actual share price index, just as wheat futures are based on the actual price of wheat. Equity index futures provide traders and investors with a flexible and efficient way to participate in the equity market in a number of ways, the main ones being:

⇒ *speculation.* Traders can speculate on the value of the index in the future. If they are bullish, they will buy the index and sell for a profit if they are correct and prices rise. If they are bearish and expect share prices to decline, they can short sell the index and buy it back at a lower price.

⇒ *hedging and portfolio management*. Investors with long-term share portfolios can 'protect' the value of the portfolio and manage their exposure to declining share prices by short selling the relevant index during bear markets and periods of declining share prices. By selling stock index futures during these periods they are able to keep their long-term share portfolio intact while using the short sale of the Index to offset the losses experienced in the share portfolio. In this case, the plan is that the profit from short selling the index will offset the losses experienced in the actual share portfolio.

Tip

Trading index futures provides a great deal of flexibility for those interested in sharemarket trading. Rather than attempting to pick the moves of individual share prices, the trader is essentially trading the basket of shares that make up the index. Given the high degree of correlation that exists between individual shares trading on an index, trading the index itself encapsulates the overall market direction and sentiment in one transaction, rather than continually buying and selling a basket of shares.

Equity or share/stock index futures are available on almost every global share index. Space prevents us from reviewing them all, so we will look at six of the most actively traded and monitored stock index futures contracts—the S&P 500 and the E-mini S&P 500, the European Euro Stoxx 50, the Japanese Nikkei, England's FTSE and the Australian Share Price Index.

Tip

Equity securities are generally considered a riskier investment than debt securities, so higher returns are expected from equity investments.

Shareholders, as co-owners, are last in line to receive any assets if a company goes out of business or is declared bankrupt. Purchasers of debt securities, on the other hand, are lenders, and their claims to both principal and interest payments have a higher priority.

S&P 500

The Standard and Poor's 500 Index (S&P 500) is an index of the prices of 500 of the largest actively traded stocks listed on the NYSE, the American Stock Exchange (ASE) and the NASDAQ Exchange in the United States. Standard and Poor's is a credit rating agency that issues credit ratings for the debt of both private and public companies. The companies included in the index have an S&P credit rating. The actual composition of the index is decided by a committee rather than being based on strict guidelines or inclusion conditions, so selection can be influenced by personal bias.

The S&P 500 Index began in March 1957 and is the largest of the stock market indices in terms of both market capitalisation and volumes traded. The S&P 500 companies account for approximately 75 per cent of the market capitalisation of all publicly listed companies in the US. The index is widely used by traders and investors the world over as a general indicator of stock prices in the US and the general outlook of US business sentiment and economic conditions.

Tip

The S&P 500 is a much better barometer of the condition of the US equity market than the Dow Jones Industrial Average (DJIA), which is an index of only 30 of the largest US stocks.

Factors affecting price

Factors affecting the price of the S&P 500 include the following:

⇒ The price of the index is directly affected by the prices of the stocks that are included in the index. A 'bull market' in equities equates to a rising equity index value, while a 'bear market' in equities will see the value of the index decline.

⇒ The current and perceived level of economic activity and general economic conditions being experienced by businesses and the overall economy will impact on share prices and hence the value of the index. During periods of sustained economic growth and stability, share prices will rise as investor confidence grows and traders and investors accept risk in anticipation of greater rewards. During periods of economic slowdown and uncertainty, share prices will decline as nervous investors retreat from the stock market to invest in cash, bonds and other 'less risky' investments with lower rates of return.

⇒ Current interest rates and expectations of future interest rate moves can impact on equity prices and thus the index.

⇒ Current and anticipated inflation rates and the impact of inflation on economic growth will impact on share prices.

⇒ Political uncertainty and instability will influence share prices.

⇒ External influences including geopolitical factors, uprisings, terrorist activities, unexpected announcements around crude oil reserves, global growth considerations (both positive and negative) and a huge range of other factors can directly impact on the economic outlook for the US economy and the level of business activity. This has a direct impact on listed share prices, which in turn impacts on the value of the S&P 500 and all other US and global equity indices.

Tip

Investor sentiment has a huge influence on stock prices and hence equity index values. Positive investor sentiment and complacency that the 'good times will keep rolling on' almost always leads to overpriced equity markets during times of economic growth and prosperity, pushing individual stock prices and equity indices to inflated and overvalued levels. Inevitably economic events flip to the downside, market sentiment turns negative and share prices tumble to lower than expected values, and 'the market' and its participants overcorrect to the downside. These gyrations give rise to the never-ending ups and downs of the equity markets.

Figure 12.1 (overleaf) shows a weekly chart of the S&P 500 Index futures contract from 1987 to 2012. Some of the more pronounced price moves to both the upside and the downside have been highlighted.

Pricing

S&P 500 stock price index futures are traded on the Chicago Mercantile Exchange (CME) and electronically on the CME Globex platform. S&P 500 futures trade in US dollars per index point, with 1 index point worth $250. The contract size varies with the value of the index and is calculated at $250 × index value. If, for example, the S&P 500 index is trading at 1302.20, the contract value is $325 550.00 (1302.20 × $250 per index point = $325 550). The minimum price move or tick is 0.10 points or $25 ($250 × 0.1 = $25.00).

Figure 12.1: weekly chart of S&P 500 Index futures contract, 1987–2012

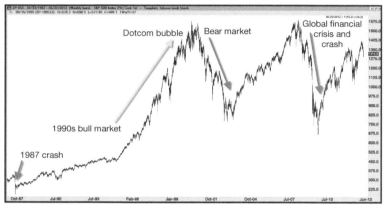

Source: Trade Navigator / Genesis Financial Technologies Inc.

Tip

The S&P 500 Index can be volatile, with sudden, large moves not uncommon as traders and investors react to global economic, geopolitical and other factors that impact directly or indirectly on economic conditions and share prices.

Trading examples

Expecting the S&P 500 Index to rise, a trader would BUY (go long) a futures contract. Let's say the long position is initiated with the S&P 500 Index at 1278.70 and the market rises to 1302.40, a move of 23.70 index points, or 237 ticks (23.70 ÷ 0.1 = 237). The trader's profit (excluding brokerage and costs) would be $5925 (237 ticks × $25 per tick = $5925).

1302.4 index value (sell price) – 1278.7 index value
(buy price) = 23.7 index points × $250 per index
point = $5925

Expecting the S&P 500 Index to fall, a trader would SELL
(go short) a futures contract. Let's say the short position
is initiated with the S&P 500 Index at 1382.9 and the
market falls to 1375.3, a move of 7.6 index points, or
76 ticks (7.60 ÷ 0.1 = 76). The trader's profit (excluding
brokerage and costs) would be $1900 (76 ticks × $25 per
tick = $1900).

1382.9 index value (sell price) – 1375.3 index value
(buy price) = 7.6 index points × $250 per index
point = $1900

Contract specifications

Full contract specifications for the CME-traded S&P 500
Stock Price Index futures contract are shown in figure 12.2
(overleaf).

Trading hours

S&P 500 Stock Price Index futures are traded both
electronically on the CME Globex platform and by traditional
open outcry on the trading floor of the Chicago Mercantile
Exchange. The pit session operates each weekday between
8.30 am and 3.15 pm Chicago time. Electronic trading on
Globex opens at 5.00 pm Sunday evening Chicago time and
trades through to 8.15 am Monday morning Chicago time,
closing 15 minutes before the opening of the pit session at
8.30 am. After the pit trading session closes at 3.15 pm,
electronic trading reopens at 3.30 pm and continues through
to 8.15 am each weekday. Trading ceases at 3.15 pm Friday
afternoon at the close of the pit trading session. To make
the trading times even more confusing, there is a 'daily
maintenance shutdown' of the electronic trading platform

each weekday between 4.30 pm and 5.00 pm Chicago time! Trading times and opening and closing times of the various sessions are shown in figure 12.3.

Figure 12.2: CME-traded S&P 500 Stock Price Index futures contract specifications

Opening Date	4/21/1982	
Ticker Symbol	SP SP= Clearing View product and vendor codes	
Contract Size	$250 x S&P 500 futures price	
Tick Size (minimum fluctuation)	OUTRIGHT	0.10 index points=$25
	CALENDAR SPREAD	0.05 index points=$12.50
Trading Hours All time listed are Central Time	Open Outcry	MON-FRI: 8:30 a.m.-3:15 p.m.
	CME Globex (Electronic Platform)	MON-THURS: 3:30 p.m.-8:15 a.m. (daily maintenance shutdown from 4:30 p.m.-5:00 p.m.) SUN: 5:00 p.m.-8:15 a.m
Contract Months	Open Outcry	Eight months in the March Quarterly Cycle (Mar, Jun, Sep, Dec)
	CME Globex	One month in the March Quarterly Cycle (Mar, Jun, Sep, Dec)
Last Trade Date/Time View Calendar	Open Outcry	3:15 p.m. on Thursday prior to 3rd Friday of the contract month
	CME Globex	On the rollover date (typcially eight days prior to last trade date for open outcry) when the lead month goes off the screen and the deferred month becomes the new lead month. View Rollover Dates
Settlement Procedure	Daily S&P Settlement Procedure (PDF) Final S&P Settlement Procedure (PDF)	
Daily Price Limits	RTH: Successive 10%, 20%, 30% limits (downside only) ETH (overnight): 5% up or down View price limits details	
Position Limits	20,000 net long or short in all contract months combined.	
Block Trade Eligibility	No. View more on block-trade eligibile contracts.	
Block Minimum	N/A	
Rulebook Chapter	351	
Exchange Rule	These contracts are listed with, and subject to, the rules and regulations of CME.	

Source: CME Group Inc.

Figure 12.3: S&P 500 Index futures trading times

Electronic Trading (Sunday)	15 minute gap	Open Outcry Mon - Fri	15 minute gap	Electronic Trading Mon -Thurs	30 minute gap	Electronic Trading
5.00pm - 8.15am		8.30am - 3.15pm		3.30pm - 4.30pm		5.00pm - 8.15am

E-mini S&P 500

Although it is arguably the most important and most actively monitored of all the global share price indices, the S&P 500 Index (often referred to as the Big S&P) can be difficult to trade for smaller traders because of the $250 per index point value. In recognition of this, the CME introduced the E-mini S&P contract (referred to simply as the E-mini) with a notional value of $50 per index point, or one-fifth the size of the Big S&P. First introduced in September 1997, the E-mini became the most actively traded stock index futures contract in the world. As well as providing access for smaller traders, the E-mini is also preferred by many large traders and investors. The electronic market provides instant price quotes and order fills compared with the delays and other issues associated with trading during the pit session, especially for large orders.

Tip

According to CME Group, average daily turnover in E-mini futures contracts in 2011 was in excess of 2.4 million, compared with just under 29000 contracts for the Big S&P—almost 80 times the volume!

Pricing

E-mini S&P 500 futures are traded electronically on the CME Globex platform. E-mini S&P 500 futures trade in US dollars per index point, with 1 index point worth $50.00. The contract size varies with the value of the index and is calculated at $50 × index value. If, for example, the E-mini S&P 500 index is trading at 1302.25, the contract value is $65 112.50 (1302.25 × $50.00 per index point = $65 112.50). The minimum price move, or tick, is 0.25 points or $12.50, per contract ($50.00 × 0.25 = $12.50).

Tip

The E-mini virtually mirrors the Big S&P, although some slight price variations can occur owing to the difference in the minimum price move, or tick value. The E-mini has a tick value of 0.25 points, compared with 0.1 for the Big S&P. The Big S&P can therefore move up or down in 0.1 point increments whereas the E-mini can move only in 0.25 point increments.

Trading examples

Expecting the E-mini S&P 500 Index to rise, a trader would BUY (go long) a futures contract. Let's say the long position is initiated with the S&P 500 Index at 1278.75, and the market rises to 1302.50, a move of 23.75 index points, or 95 ticks (23.75 ÷ 0.25 = 95). The trader's profit (excluding brokerage and costs) would be $1187.50 (95 ticks × $12.50 per tick = $1187.50).

1302.50 index value (sell price) − 1278.75 index value (buy price) = 23.75 index points × $50 per index point = $1187.50

Expecting the E-mini S&P 500 Index to fall, a trader would SELL (go short) a futures contract. Let's say the short position is initiated with the S&P 500 Index at 1382.75, and the market falls to 1375.50, a move of 7.25 index points, or 29 ticks (7.25 ÷ 0.25 = 29). The trader's profit (excluding brokerage and costs) would be $362.50 (29 ticks × $12.50 per tick = $362.50).

1382.75 index value (sell price) – 1375.50 index value (buy price) = 7.25 index points × $50 per index point = $362.50

Contract specifications

Full contract specifications for the CME Globex–traded E-mini S&P 500 futures contract are shown in figure 12.4.

Figure 12.4: CME Globex–traded E-mini S&P 500 futures contract specifications

Opening Date	9/9/1997	
Ticker Symbol	ES ES= Clearing View product and vendor codes	
Contract Size	$50 x E-mini S&P 500 futures price	
Tick Size (minimum fluctuation)	OUTRIGHT	0.25 index points=$12.50
	CALENDAR SPREAD	0.05 index points=$2.50
Trading Hours All time listed are Central Time	CME Globex (ETH)	MON-THURS: 5:00 p.m.-3:15 p.m. & 3:30 p.m.-4:30 p.m. (Daily maintenance shutdown 4:30 p.m.-5:00 p.m.) SUN: 5:00 p.m.-3:15 p.m.
Contract Months	Five months in the March Quarterly Cycle (Mar, Jun, Sep, Dec)	
Last Trade Date/Time View Calendar	CME Globex	Trading can occur up to 8:30 a.m. on the 3rd Friday of the contract month
Settlement Procedure	Daily E-mini S&P 500 Settlement Procedure (PDF) Final E-mini S&P 500 Settlement Procedure (PDF)	
Daily Price Limits	RTH: Successive 10%, 20%, 30% limits (downside only) ETH (overnight): 5% up or down View price limits details	
Position Limits	Work in conjunction with existing S&P 500 position limits	
Block Trade Eligibility	No. View more on block-trade eligibile contracts	
Block Minimum	N/A	
Rulebook Chapter	358	
Exchange Rule	These contracts are listed with, and subject to, the rules and regulations of CME	

Source: CME Group Inc.

Trading hours

E-mini S&P 500 futures contracts trade solely on the CME Globex electronic trading platform. There is no open outcry or 'pit' session for E-mini S&P 500 futures. Electronic trading occurs for 23 hours and 15 minutes per day, beginning at 5.00 pm Sunday evening Chicago time and closing at 3.15 pm Friday afternoon Chicago time. There is a daily break of 15 minutes from 3.15 pm until 3.30 pm, in line with the close of the Big S&P floor trading session and the resumption of electronic trading in both the Big S&P and the E-mini S&P. There is also a daily 'maintenance shutdown' between 4.30 pm and 5.00 pm Chicago time.

Euro Stoxx 50

The Euro Stoxx 50 Index futures contract is based on the Euro Stoxx 50 stock index of 50 major European companies from 12 European countries: Austria, Belgium, Finland, France, Germany, Greece, Ireland, Italy, Luxembourg, the Netherlands, Portugal and Spain. The index aims to provide a representation of leading Eurozone stocks, and includes such household names as BNP Paribas, BMW, L'Oreal, Nokia and Volkswagen. The Euro Stoxx 50 Index was designed by STOXX Limited, a joint venture of Deutsche Boerse AG, Dow Jones & Company and SWX Group.

Tip

With average daily trading volumes of over 1.5 million contracts, the Euro Stoxx 50 Index futures contract is the second most actively traded stock index futures contract in the world, after the E-mini S&P.

Factors affecting price

Factors affecting the price of the E-mini S&P 500 include the following:

⟹ The same factors noted earlier for the S&P 500 affect the Euro Stoxx 50.

⟹ Interest rate and inflation rate expectations specific to the Eurozone may have a particular impact on the Euro Stoxx 50.

⟹ Economic conditions specific to the Eurozone will directly impact the Euro Stoxx 50.

⟹ Price moves in overseas equity markets, particularly in the US, will affect the Euro Stoxx 50.

Figure 12.5 shows a weekly chart of the Euro Stoxx 50 Index futures contract from its inception in May 2001 to June 2012.

Figure 12.5: weekly chart of Euro Stoxx 50 Index futures contract, May 2001–June 2012

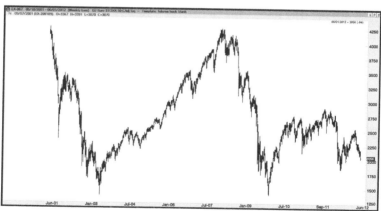

Source: Trade Navigator / Genesis Financial Technologies Inc.

Pricing

Euro Stoxx 50 futures are traded electronically on the Eurex exchange. Euro Stoxx 50 futures trade in euros per index point, with 1 index point worth €10. The contract size varies with the value of the index and is calculated at €10 × index value. If, for example, the Euro Stoxx 50 index is trading at 2257, the contract value is €22570 (2257 × €10 per index point = €22570). The minimum price move, or tick, is 1 point or €10.

Trading examples

Expecting the Euro Stoxx 50 Index to rise, a trader would BUY (go long) a futures contract. Let's say the long position is initiated with the Euro Stoxx 50 Index at 2252 and the market rises to 2381, a move of 129 index points, or 129 ticks (129 ÷ 1 = 129). The trader's profit (excluding brokerage and costs) would be €1290 (129 ticks × €10 per tick = €1290).

> 2381 index value (sell price) – 2252 index value (buy price) = 129 index points × €10 per index point = €1290

Expecting the Euro Stoxx 50 Index to fall, a trader would SELL (go short) a futures contract. Let's say the short position is initiated with the Euro Stoxx 50 Index at 2385, and the market falls to 2121, a move of 264 index points, or 264 ticks (264 ÷ 1 = 264). The trader's profit (excluding brokerage and costs) would be €2640 (264 ticks × €10 per tick = €2640).

> 2385 index value (sell price) – 2121 index value (buy price) = 264 index points × €10 per index point = €2640

Contract specifications

Full contract specifications for the Eurex-traded Euro Stoxx 50 futures contract are shown in figure 12.6.

Trading hours

Euro Stoxx 50 futures contracts trade solely on the Eurex electronic trading platform. There is no open outcry or 'pit' session for Euro Stoxx 50 futures. Electronic trading occurs from 7.50 am Central European Time until 10.00 pm Central

European time (3.50 pm to 6.00 am the following morning Sydney time), Monday to Friday.

Figure 12.6: Eurex-traded Euro Stoxx 50 futures contract specifications

EURO STOXX 50 futures		
Exchange	Eurex	
Settlement	Cash settled	
Trade Unit	€10 multiplied by the value of the index	
Point Value	€10	
Tick Value	€10	
Contract Months	Up to 9 months. The three nearest quarterly months of the March, June, September and December cycle.	
Last Trading Day	Last Trading Day is the Final Settlement Day, which is the third Friday of each maturity month if this is an exchange day; otherwise the exchange day immediately preceding that day. Close of trading in the maturing futures on the Last Trading Day is at the Beginning of the Xetra® intraday auction starting at 12:00 CET.	
Note: This contract is electronic ONLY -- no open outcry		
	No Open Outcry	Electronic
Trading Hours	N/A	7:50 am CET to 22:00 (10:00 pm) CET, except on last trading day, when trading ends at 12:30 pm CET (Eurex operates in three trading phases: pre-trading, trading and post-trading. The post-trading phase is further split in several periods where different functions are available. Pre-trading begins at 7:30 am CET, and post-trading ends at 22:30 (10.30 pm) CET, except on the last trading day, when trading ends at 12:00 CET)
Ticker Symbol	N/A	FESX
Price Limits	N/A	N/A

Source: MarketsWiki / Creative Commons (GNU Free Documentation License) / Eurex.

FTSE 100

The FTSE 100 futures contract is based on the FTSE 100 stock index. It represents the top 100 stocks by market capitalisation in the United Kingdom trading on the London Stock Exchange. Referred to as the 'footsie', the FTSE 100 Index is owned and maintained by the FTSE Group—a joint venture of the *Financial Times* and the London Stock Exchange. Like the S&P 500, the FTSE is weighted by market capitalisation, meaning the larger companies make up a proportionately larger share of the index.

Factors affecting price

Factors affecting the price of the FTSE 100 include the following:

⇒ The same factors noted earlier for the S&P 500 affect the FTSE 100.

⇒ Interest rate and inflation rate expectations specific to Britain and the UK may have a particular impact on the FTSE 100.

⇒ Economic conditions specific to Britain and the UK will have a direct impact on the FTSE 100.

⇒ Price moves in overseas equity markets, particularly in the US, will affect the FTSE 100.

Figure 12.7 shows a weekly chart of the FTSE 100 Index futures contract from 1987 to 2012.

Figure 12.7: weekly chart of the FTSE 100 Index futures contract, 1987 to 2012

Source: Trade Navigator / Genesis Financial Technologies Inc.

Pricing

FTSE 100 futures are traded electronically on the LIIFE Connect platform of the NYSE Euronext exchange. FTSE 100 futures trade in British pounds per index point, with 1 index point worth £10. The contract size varies with the value of the index and is calculated at £10 × index value. If, for example, the FTSE 100 index is trading at 5425.5, the contract value is £54255 (5425.5 × £10 per index point = £54255). The minimum price move, or tick, is 0.5 points or £5 (£10 × 0.5 = £5).

Trading examples

Expecting the FTSE 100 Index to rise, a trader would BUY (go long) a futures contract. Let's say the long position is initiated with the FTSE 100 Index at 5148.5 and the market rises to 5496, a move of 347.5 index points, or 695 ticks (347.5 ÷ 0.5 = 695). The trader's profit (excluding brokerage and costs) would be £3475 (695 ticks × £5 per tick = £3475).

> 5496 index value (sell price) − 5148.5 index value (buy price) = 347.5 index points × £10 per index point = £3475

Expecting the FTSE 100 Index to fall, a trader would SELL (go short) a futures contract. Let's say the short position is initiated with the FTSE 100 Index at 5753 and the market falls to 5527.5, a move of 225.5 index points, or 451 ticks (225.5 ÷ 0.5 = 451). The trader's profit (excluding brokerage and costs) would be £2255 (451 ticks × £5 per tick = £2255).

> 5753 index value (sell price) − 5527.5 index value (buy price) = 225.5 index points × £10 per index point = £2255

Contract specifications

Full contract specifications for the NYSE Euronext–traded FTSE 100 futures contract are shown in figure 12.8 (overleaf).

Trading hours

FTSE 100 index futures contracts trade solely on the LIFFE Connect electronic trading platform of the NYSE Euronext exchange. There is no open outcry session for FTSE 100 futures. Electronic trading occurs from 1.00 am London time until 7.50 am London time, in line with Asian market trading times, Monday to Friday. There is a 10-minute trading halt between 7.50 am and 8.00 am London time. Trading then resumes and continues until 9.00 pm London time Monday to Friday.

Figure 12.8: NYSE Euronext FTSE 100 futures contract specifications

FTSE 100 Index Futures (No. 29)	
Unit of trading	Contract Valued at £10 per index point (e.g. value £65,000 at 6500.0)
Delivery day	First business day after the Last Trading Day
Delivery months	March, June, September, December (nearest four available for trading)
Quotation	Index points (eg 6500.0)
Minimum price movement (tick size and value)	0.5 (£5.00)
Last trading day	Trading shall cease as soon as reasonably practicable after 10:15 (London time) once the Expiry Value of the Index has been determined. Please refer to London Notice LON2693 for more information. Third Friday in delivery month¹
Exchange delivery Settlement Price (EDSP)	The value of the FTSE 100 Index is calculated by FTSE International with reference to the outcome of the EDSP intra-day auction at the London Stock Exchange carried out on the Last Trading Day.
Last update	Tue, 10/12/2010
Trading Hours	01:00 - 21:00²
Legal Delivery/Expiry Month	Sep 2007 Onwards
Trading platform	LIFFE CONNECT® Trading Host for Futures and Options
Full contract specification and related documents	📄 FTSE 100 Index Futures Contract (No. 29)
Algorithm	Central order book applies a price-time trading algorithm with priority given to the first order at the best price.
Wholesale service	Asset Allocation, Block Trading, Basis Trading
Clearing	NYSE Liffe Clearing.
Exchange contract	10 - No. 29

Nikkei 225

The Nikkei 225 futures contract is based on the Nikkei 225 stock index. It represents the top 225 companies trading on the Tokyo Stock Exchange in Japan. Commonly referred to as 'the Nikkei', it has been calculated by the *Nihon Keizai Shimbun* (Nikkei) newspaper since 1950 and is recognised as the international benchmark for Japanese equities. Stocks on the Nikkei index are given an equal weighting based on a par value of ¥50 per share. The index is reviewed annually and any changes to the stocks included are made at the beginning of October each year.

Factors affecting price

Factors affecting the price of the Nikkei 225 include the following:

⇒ The same factors noted earlier for all the other global equity indices affect the Nikkei 225.

⇒ Interest rate and inflation rate expectations specific to Japan may have a particular impact on the Nikkei 225.

⇒ Economic conditions specific to Japan will directly impact the Nikkei 225.

⇒ Price moves in overseas equity markets, particularly in the US, will affect the Nikkei 225.

⇒ Because of Japan's heavy dependence on exports, economic activity in the economies of Japan's major trading partners, such as the US, Europe and other Asian countries, will have a direct influence on the earnings and share prices that constitute the Nikkei index.

Figure 12.9 (overleaf) shows a weekly chart of the Singapore Exchange–traded Nikkei 225 Index futures contract from its inception in 1989 to 2012.

Pricing

Nikkei 225 Index futures are traded electronically on three different exchanges—the Singapore Exchange (SGX), the Osaka Securities Exchange (OSE) and the Chicago Mercantile Exchange (CME), where both a US dollar–denominated contract and a yen-denominated contract are traded. We will look at the Nikkei 225 Index futures contract traded on the SGX, as it is the most actively traded of the four contracts, and it is fungible with the CME yen-denominated contract through a mutual offset system between the SGX and the CME.

Figure 12.9: weekly chart of the Nikkei 225 Index futures contract, 1989–2012

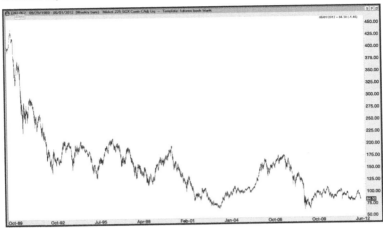

Source: Trade Navigator / Genesis Financial Technologies Inc.

Tip

The mutual offset system between the SGX and the CME allows round-the-clock trade, and exposure management.

The SGX Nikkei 225 Index futures contract trades in Japanese yen per index point, with 1 index point worth ¥500. The contract size varies with the value of the index and is calculated at ¥500 × index value. If, for example, the Nikkei 225 index is trading at 9430, the contract value is ¥4 715 000 (9430 × ¥500 per index point = ¥4 715 000). The minimum price move or tick is 5 points or ¥2500 (¥500 × 5 = ¥2500).

Trading examples

Expecting the SGX Nikkei 225 Index to rise, a trader would BUY (go long) a futures contract. Let's say the long position is initiated with the SGX Nikkei 225 Index at 8975 and the market rises to 9390, a move of 415 index points, or 83 ticks (415 ÷ 5 = 83). The trader's profit (excluding brokerage and costs) would be ¥207 500 (83 ticks × ¥2500 per tick = ¥207 500).

> 9390 index value (sell price) − 8975 index value (buy price) = 415 index points × ¥500 per index point = ¥207 500

Expecting the SGX Nikkei 225 Index to fall, a trader would SELL (go short) a futures contract. Let's say the short position is initiated with the SGX Nikkei 225 Index at 9305 and the market falls to 8660, a move of 645 index points, or 129 ticks (645 ÷ 5 = 129). The trader's profit (excluding brokerage and costs) would be ¥322 500 (129 ticks × ¥2500 per tick = ¥322 500).

> 9305 index value (sell price) − 8660 index value (buy price) = 645 index points × ¥500 per index point = ¥322 500

Contract specifications

Full contract specifications for the SGX-traded Nikkei 225 Index futures contract are shown in figure 12.10 (overleaf).

Trading hours

SGX Nikkei 225 Index futures contracts trade solely on the electronic trading platform of the Singapore Exchange. There is no open outcry or 'pit' session for Nikkei 225 Index futures. Electronic trading occurs from 7.45 am Singapore time until 2.30 pm Singapore time. There is a 45-minute trading halt between 2.30 pm and 3.15 pm Singapore time. Trading then continues until 2.00 am, in line with European and London market closing times, Monday to Friday.

Figure 12.10: SGX Nikkei 225 Index futures contract specifications

Contract Size	¥500 x Nikkei 225 Index Futures Price	
Ticker Symbol	NK	
Contract Months	3 nearest serial months & 12 nearest quarterly months.	
Minimum Price Fluctuation	Outright: 5 index points (¥2500) Strategy Trades : 1 index point (¥500)	
Trading Hours	Singapore Time T Session:	
	Pre -Opening	7.30am -7.43 am
	Non -Cancel Period	7.43am -7.45 am
	Opening	7.45 am - 2.25 pm
	Pre-Closing	2.25 pm- 2.29 pm
	Non-Cancel Period	2. 29 pm - 2.30 pm
	T+1 Session:	
	Pre -Opening	3.00 pm - 3.13 pm
	Non -Cancel Period	3.13 pm - 3.15 pm
	Opening	3.15 pm - 2.00 am
Last Trading Day	The day before the second Friday of the contract month.	
Settlement Basis	Cash settlement	
Final Settlement Price	The final settlement price shall be the Special Nikkei 225 Index Quotation based on the opening prices of each component issue in the Nikkei 225 Index on the business day following the last trading day.	
Position Limit	A person shall not own or control more than 10,000 futures or futures equivalent contracts net long or net short in all contract months combined.	
Additional Trading Facilities	Negotiated Large Trade : Minimum 50 lots EFP Trade : Eligible for EFP transaction	

Source: Singapore Exchange Limited.

Share Price Index (SPI)

The ASX SPI 200 futures contract is based on the S&P/ASX 200 stock index. It represents the top 200 companies listed on the Australian Securities Exchange (ASX) and covers approximately 87 per cent of the market capitalisation of listed securities on the ASX. Although small by global standards, with an average daily turnover of less than 40 000 contracts, the SPI is an important instrument for Australian traders and those with exposure to the Australian economy.

Tip

The SPI can be a volatile trading instrument and the lower liquidity levels can lead to slippage.

Factors affecting price

Factors affecting the price of the Share Price Index include the following:

⇒ The same factors noted earlier for all the other global equity indices also affect the SPI.

⇒ Interest rate and inflation rate expectations specific to Australia may have a particular impact on the SPI.

⇒ Economic conditions specific to Australia will have a direct impact on the SPI.

⇒ Price moves in overseas equity markets, particularly in the US, will affect the SPI.

⇒ Because of Australia's heavy dependence on raw material exports, economic activity in the economies of Australia's major trading partners, such as the US, Europe and other Asian countries, will have a direct influence on the earnings and share prices that constitute the S&P/ASX 200 Index and hence the SPI.

Figure 12.11 (overleaf) shows a weekly chart of the ASX-traded SPI 200 Index futures contract from its inception in 1991 to 2012.

Pricing

SPI 200 futures are traded electronically on the ASX Trade 24 platform of the Australian Securities Exchange (ASX). SPI 200 futures trade in Australian dollars per index point, with 1 index point worth A$25. The contract size varies with the value of the index and is calculated at A$25 × index value. If, for example, the SPI 200 index is trading at 4384, the contract value is A$109600 (4384 × A$25 per index point = A$109600). The minimum price move, or tick, is 1 index point or A$25.

Figure 12.11: weekly chart of the ASX SPI 200 futures contract, 1991–2012

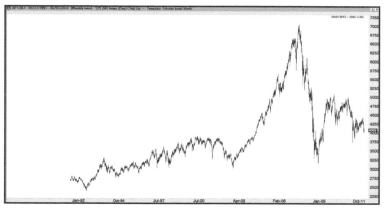

Source: Trade Navigator / Genesis Financial Technologies Inc.

Trading examples

Expecting the SPI 200 Index to rise, a trader would BUY (go long) a futures contract. Let's say the long position is initiated with the SPI 200 Index at 4582 and the market rises to 4711, a move of 129 index points, or 129 ticks (1 index point = 1 tick). The trader's profit (excluding brokerage and costs) would be A$3225 (129 ticks × A$25 per tick = A$3225).

> 4711 index value (sell price) − 4582 index value (buy price) = 129 index points × A$25 per index point = A$3225

Expecting the SPI 200 Index to fall, a trader would SELL (go short) a futures contract. Let's say the short position is initiated with the SPI 200 Index at 4270 and the market falls to 4055, a move of 215 index points, or 215 ticks (1 index point = 1 tick). The trader's profit (excluding brokerage and costs) would be A$5375 (215 ticks × A$25 per tick = A$5375).

4270 index value (sell price) − 4055 index value (buy price) = 215 index points × A$25 per index point = A$5375

Contract specifications

Full contract specifications for the ASX-traded SPI 200 Index futures contract are shown in figure 12.12.

Figure 12.12: ASX SPI 200 Index futures contract specifications

CONTRACT	ASX SPI 200™ FUTURES
Commodity	Code AP
Contract Unit	Valued at A$25 per index point (e.g. A$117,500 at 4,700 index points).
Contract Months	March/June/September/December up to six quarter months ahead and the nearest two non-quarterly expiry months
Minimum Price Movement	One index point (A$25)
Exercise Prices	Set at intervals of 25 index points
Last Trading Day[2]	All trading in expiring contracts ceases at 12.00pm on the third Thursday of the settlement month. Non-expiring contracts underlying futures contract will continue to trade as per the trading hours.
Cash Settlement Price[2]	The Special Opening Quotation of the underlying S&P/ASX 200 Index on the Last Trading Day. The Special Opening Quotation is calculated using the first traded price of each component stock in the S&P/ASX 200 Index on the Last Trading Day, irrespective of when those stocks first trade in the ASX trading day. This means that the first traded price of each component stock may occur at any time between ASX market open and ASX market close (including the Closing Single Price Auction) on the Last Trading Day. Should any component stock not have traded by ASX market close on the Last Trading Day, the last traded price of that stock will be used to calculate the Special Opening Quotation.
Trading Hours[2]	5.10pm to 7.00am and 9.50am to 4.30pm (during US daylight saving time) 5.10pm to 8.00am and 9.50am to 4.30pm (during US non daylight saving time)
Settlement Day	The first business day after expiry, ASX Clear (Futures) publishes the final settlement price of the contract. On the second business day after expiry, ASX Clear (Futures) settles cash flows as a result of the settlement price.

2 Unless otherwise indicated, all times are Sydney times. US daylight saving begins first Sunday in April and ends last Sunday in October.

Trading hours

ASX SPI 200 Index futures contracts trade solely on the ASX Trade 24 electronic trading platform of the Australian Securities Exchange. There is no open outcry session for ASX SPI 200 futures. Electronic trading occurs from 9.50 am until 4.30 pm Sydney time Monday to Friday, in line with local sharemarket hours of operation. There is a 40-minute trading halt between 4.30 pm and 5.10 pm Sydney time. Trading then resumes for the 'overnight session', continuing until 7.00 am (8.00 am during Australian daylight savings time), in line with trading on the US markets. There is another trading halt between the close of the overnight session and the open of the day session at 9.50 am Sydney time.

Glossary

calendar spread A futures position established by simultaneously entering a long and a short position on the same underlying asset but with different delivery months — for example, buying March and selling December.

carryover stocks Grains not consumed during the year that remain in storage at the commencement of the new season harvest. They are 'carried-over' and added to the new crop production.

clearing house An agency of a futures exchange (or a separate company) responsible for settling trading accounts, clearing trades, collecting and maintaining margin monies, regulating delivery and reporting trading data. Clearing houses act as third parties to all futures contracts, acting as a buyer to every clearing member seller and as a seller to every clearing member buyer.

close a position/close out Exit an open trade at either a profit or a loss.

counterparty The 'other' party to your trade or transaction. Every transaction has a counterparty, as every buyer needs a seller, and every seller a buyer.

day trader A trader who opens and closes positions within a short space of time, and closes all positions at the end of each trading day.

first notice day (FND) The first day on which a notice of intent to deliver a commodity in fulfilment of a given month's futures contract can be made to a buyer.

forward contract A cash contract privately negotiated between a buyer and a seller to deliver a specified commodity at a given price at some future time. Forward contracts are not standardised, as futures contracts are.

fundamental analysis The use of economic data, news announcements and other research to arrive at trading and investing decisions.

fungible Any commodity or instrument that is capable of mutual substitution and is freely exchangeable or replaceable.

good all markets (GAM) order Order that works in both the pit or floor trading session and the electronic trading session.

good till cancelled (GTC) order Order used in conjunction with stop and limit orders that remains valid and working until it is cancelled or filled.

hedging Offsetting the price risk in a cash market by taking an equal but opposite position in the futures market.

hedge fund An aggressively managed portfolio of investments that uses advanced investment strategies such as leveraged, long, short and derivative positions in both domestic and international markets with the goal of generating high returns.

iceberg order   A large order to buy or sell that is divided into smaller parcels so only a small portion of the total can be seen at any one time.

initial margin   The amount of money that futures traders must have available in their trading accounts at the time they place an order to open either a long or short futures position.

last trading day (LTD)   The final day on which trading can occur for the month specified in the futures contract. Outstanding futures contracts on the last trading day must be settled either by delivery of the underlying commodity or by cash transfer.

leverage/leverage up   The use of margin to increase the size of trades you are able to make.

limit order   An entry order to buy a futures contract below the prevailing market price or to sell a futures contract above the prevailing market price. Also used as 'take profit' orders once a trade has been entered either above the prevailing market price for a long position or below the prevailing market price for a short position.

liquidity   The volume of transactions. The more liquid a futures contract is the more buyers and sellers there are participating in the market, and the easier it is to enter and exit trades.

long position/going long   Buying a currency pair in anticipation of a further increase in the price of the base currency.

lock-limit   The limit, determined by the relevant exchange, to which the price of a futures contract can move either up or down during a trading session. Once the lock-limit price is reached, prices can't move any further in that direction during the trading session and trading comes to a halt. If prices begin to move in the opposite direction, then trade will resume and the market will no longer be locked.

long hedge   Buying futures contracts to protect against a possible price increase in a cash commodity that will need to be purchased at a future date. When the cash commodity is purchased the open futures position is closed out.

maintenance margin   A set minimum amount of money per futures contract that must be maintained in a client's trading account.

margin call   Issued by an exchange when the mark-to-market loss on a trade exceeds the amount of money in your trading account, requiring you to increase the margin deposited or close out the position.

market order   Any order to buy or sell at the prevailing market price.

mark-to-market   Recording the value of open positions and total account value on a daily basis to calculate profits and losses and margin requirements.

market maker   A company, or individual, that quotes both a buy and a sell price in a financial instrument or commodity held in inventory, hoping to make a profit on the bid/offer spread.

novation   Operation of the clearing house in the futures markets whereby the clearing house assumes the role of buyer against the seller and seller against the buyer, to ensure that the counterparties to a trade are never exposed to default risk by the other party.

offsetting   Closing an open futures position by taking the opposite trade to the initial open position.

open long position   A position bought in anticipation of future price increases.

open outcry   Verbal bids and offers in the auction process in the trading pits of futures exchanges.

open position   Any current trade in which the trader is either long or short.

open short position   A position sold in anticipation of future price falls.

order cancels order/one cancels other (OCO) order   When one order is executed, the other is automatically cancelled.

over-the-counter (OTC) transaction   The trading of any financial instrument or security directly between two parties rather than through the use of a regulated exchange.

pit trading   The open outcry auction system for futures contracts that occurs on the trading floors, or pits, of futures exchanges.

position trader   A trader who holds open positions for any period of time longer than one day.

price discovery   The generation of future cash market prices through the auction system of the futures markets.

price gap   A significant move in the price of a contract between the close of one trading session and the open of the next. The move appears as a gap on a price chart.

prop trader   Proprietary trading firm that supplies its traders with the capital they need to execute trades according to a specified system or strategy. By using the capital provided by the firm, the traders are able to trade larger positions than if they were trading their own account.

ring trading   *See* pit trading.

rollover/rolling   Closing out an open futures position as first notice day approaches and simultaneously reopening the same position in another delivery month.

scalper   Any trader who trades for small, short-term profits throughout the course of a trading session.

short hedge   Selling futures contracts to protect against a possible price decline in a cash commodity that will need to be sold at a future date. When the cash commodity is sold the open futures position is then closed out.

short selling/position   Selling a futures contract to open a position in anticipation of a further fall in the price of the contract. Profit is made when the position is bought back at a lower price.

slippage   The difference between the price at which you expect to enter or exit a trade and the actual fill price.

spot month   The futures contract month closest to expiration; also called the nearby month or delivery month.

stop order   An entry order to buy above the prevailing market price or sell below the prevailing market price; also used as stop-loss orders once a trade is entered either below the prevailing market price in a long trade or above the prevailing market price in a short trade.

stop-loss   A predefined price point at which a trade will be exited if it moves in the opposite direction to the one anticipated.

technical analysis   The use of price charts, indicators, patterns and algorithms to arrive at trading decisions.

tick value   The minimum price move of a futures contract.

trading pit   *See* pit trading.

trailing stop   The price at which you will exit a profitable trade that eventually reverses. The trailing stop price moves in line with the prevailing price trend.

Useful websites

Australian Securities Exchange	www.asx.com.au
CME Group	www.cmegroup.com
Eurex	www.eurexchange.com
Intercontinental Exchange	www.theice.com
London Metal Exchange	www.lme.com
National Futures Association	www.nfa.futures.org
NYSE Euronext	www.euronext.com

Index

FREE 30-DAY
TRADE NAVIGATOR
TRIAL

Let Trade Navigator give you the trading edge!

Simply type the following address into your browser and follow the instructions for your free 30-day trial of Trade Navigator software:

http://www.tradenavigator.com/trial/index.php?V=webwisdom

Your trial period gives you access to Trade Navigator software and all the market data you require to trial the program for 30 days.

Trade Navigator's training department provides you with one-on-one training and technical advice to help you get the most out of this gift—at no cost to you. Tradenavigator.com also has a large collection of online training videos and webinars for you to use at your leisure.

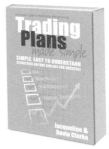

Printed and bound by CPI Group (UK) Ltd, Croydon, CR0 4YY
10/05/2022

03123347-0001